Jihad, Radicalism, and the New Atheism

Is Islam fundamentally violent? For influential New Atheists such as Sam Harris, Ayaan Hirsi Ali, and Richard Dawkins, the answer is an emphatic yes, largely because of the Islamic doctrine of jihad. According to this view, when al-Qaeda plotted 9/11 or ISIS planned any one of its recent terrorist attacks, they were acting in accord with Islamic scripture. *Jihad, Radicalism, and the New Atheism* scrutinizes this claim by comparing the conflicting interpretations of jihad offered by mainstream Muslim scholars, violent Muslim radicals, and New Atheists. Mohammad Hassan Khalil considers contemporary Muslim terrorism to be a grave problem that we must now confront. He shows, however, that the explanations offered for this phenomenon by the New Atheists are highly problematic and that their own interpretations of the role of violence in Islam exceed those of even radicals such as Osama bin Laden. In showing all this, Khalil offers critical insights on a most pressing issue.

Mohammad Hassan Khalil is Associate Professor of Religious Studies, Adjunct Professor of Law, and Director of the Muslim Studies Program at his hometown institution, Michigan State University. He is the author of *Islam and the Fate of Others: The Salvation Question* (2012) and editor of *Between Heaven and Hell: Islam, Salvation, and the Fate of Others* (2013). He serves on multiple editorial boards and on the board of directors of the Society for the Study of Muslim Ethics. In 2015, he received the Michigan State University Teacher-Scholar Award.

D1452732

Jihad, Radicalism, and the New Atheism

MOHAMMAD HASSAN KHALIL

Michigan State University

CAMBRIDGE
UNIVERSITY PRESS

CAMBRIDGE
UNIVERSITY PRESS

University Printing House, Cambridge CB2 8BS, United Kingdom

One Liberty Plaza, 20th Floor, New York, NY 10006, USA

477 Williamstown Road, Port Melbourne, VIC 3207, Australia

314–321, 3rd Floor, Plot 3, Splendor Forum, Jasola District Centre, New Delhi – 110025, India

79 Anson Road, #06–04/06, Singapore 079906

Cambridge University Press is part of the University of Cambridge.

It furthers the University's mission by disseminating knowledge in the pursuit of education, learning, and research at the highest international levels of excellence.

www.cambridge.org
Information on this title: www.cambridge.org/9781108432757
DOI: 10.1017/9781108377263

First published 2018

Printed in the United States of America by Sheridan Books, Inc.

A catalogue record for this publication is available from the British Library.

ISBN 978-1-108-42154-6 Hardback
ISBN 978-1-108-43275-7 Paperback

To my teachers

Contents

Acknowledgments

I was fortunate to have studied under two of the authorities I cite in this book, my former doctoral advisor and mentor Sherman A. Jackson and my former master's advisor Michael Bonner. It is with these and other exceptional educators in mind that I have chosen to dedicate this book to my teachers.

All mistakes in this book are my own. That said, I am grateful to Valerie Turner, Mairaj Syed, my father Hassan Khalil, and the anonymous reviewers for their insightful feedback on earlier drafts of this book. For their helpful suggestions – and, in many cases, for providing me with useful resources – I must thank and recognize the following scholars: Ahmed Al-Dawoody, Asma Afsaruddin, Muhammad Afifi al-Akiti, Mohammed Ayoob, Jonathan A. C. Brown, Amy DeRogatis, Mohammed Fadel, Chris Frilingos, Ramon Harvey, Sohail Hashmi, Jon Hoover, Deborah Margolis, Younus Mirza, Yasir Qadhi, Linda Racioppi, Mohammed Rustom, Omid Safi, Michael Sayegh, Laury Silvers, Jessica Stern, Arthur Versluis, and Corri Zoli. I must also express my heartfelt appreciation for my wonderful colleagues, coworkers, and students in the Michigan State University Department of Religious Studies, Muslim Studies Program, and College of Law. For obvious reasons, I am greatly indebted to Beatrice Rehl of Cambridge University Press and her outstanding staff and production team.

For their indefatigable support, I am especially grateful to my loving family. Here I must single out my awe-inspiring parents Amina and Hassan, my brilliant siblings Omar and Yousuf, and my better half, my wife Suzanne, and our incredible daughters Maryam and Aya. (In response to one of your favorite questions, Aya, I am *now* done with the book.)

Introduction

In the midst of a lively televised exchange between journalist Fareed Zakaria and author Sam Harris on the topic of jihad, Zakaria declared, "The problem is you and Osama bin Laden agree ... after all, you're saying ... his interpretation of Islam is correct."

"Well," Harris responded, "his interpretation ... this is the problem. His interpretation of Islam is very straightforward and honest and you really have to split hairs and do some interpretive acrobatics in order to get it ... to look non-canonical."[1]

This exchange took place a little more than thirteen years after bin Laden and his associates masterminded the deadliest terrorist operation on American soil. In the immediate aftermath of the September 11, 2001, tragedy, the notion that such violence was representative of the world's second-largest religion was widespread enough to prompt then American president George W. Bush to counter that Islam "is a religion of peace." Numerous skeptics have since dismissed this claim, some viewing it as nothing more than a politically correct token. Among the skeptics are individuals known as "New Atheists," a label given to popular figures such as Harris who have produced influential anti-theistic and anti-religious works in the years following the September 11 attacks and who focus much of their attention on "the problem with Islam."[2]

---

[1] CNN, "Zakaria, Harris Debate Extremism in Islam." See the widely viewed video clip, "Sam Harris: Islam Is Not a Religion of Peace," in which Harris is shown at a 2010 event in Berkeley, California, making a nearly identical statement.

[2] See, for example, chapter 4 of Sam Harris's *The End of Faith*. The term "New Atheists," as used in the present book, was coined by journalist Gary Wolf in a 2006 *Wired* article entitled "The Church of the Non-Believers" (see "New Atheism").

Some New Atheist writers were themselves profoundly transformed by 9/11. In the case of the prominent ex-Muslim writer Ayaan Hirsi Ali, for instance, her doubts about Islam were supplanted by nonbelief when she found it "impossible" to discount bin Laden's "claims that the murderous destruction of innocent (if infidel) lives is consistent with the Quran."[3] As for Harris, he reportedly began writing his landmark book *The End of Faith* on September 12, 2001.[4] In this best seller, Harris writes that the feature of Islam "most troubling to non-Muslims" is the very principle bin Laden invoked to justify 9/11: jihad.[5]

As Islamic studies scholar Michael Bonner observes, in contemporary debates on Islam, "no principle is invoked more often than jihad."[6] Muslims generally understand *jihad* to be a noble "struggle" or "striving" for the sake of God. It comprises various actions, from fighting on the battlefield to endeavoring to attain inner peace in the prayer hall. It is, therefore, simplistic to define it – as many writers do – as "holy war." It is also problematic to insist – as many apologists do – that it has nothing to do with warfare. In fact, in the specific context of Islamic law, *jihad* typically denotes an armed struggle against outsiders.

The purpose of this book is to offer a succinct, accessible examination of the ways in which bellicose Muslim radicals such as bin Laden and New Atheists such as Harris and Ali have conceptualized the purpose and boundaries of *armed* jihad. As one might deduce, here I use the term "radicals" to denote those seeking extreme changes, and my focus is strictly *violent* radicals, specifically those who sponsor or engage in terrorism in the name of Islam. My intention is not to offer an exhaustive analysis of jihad, violent radicalism, or the New Atheism; rather, I am interested in the intersection of the three. Nor is it my intention to explore (at least not thoroughly) other contentious aspects of Islamic law that often appear in the writings of radicals and New Atheists, including gender norms and punishments for adultery, apostasy, blasphemy, and treason – topics nonetheless worthy of scholarly consideration and engagement.

I have chosen to focus on the New Atheists largely because of their unique and ostensibly significant influence on Western – and to some

---

[3] Ali, *Nomad*, xii.
[4] Segal, "Atheist Evangelist."
[5] Harris, *The End of Faith*, 111.
[6] Bonner, *Jihad in Islamic History*, 1.

extent non-Western – intellectual discourse. Notwithstanding their numerous detractors,[7] what they say about jihad and Islam more broadly has ramifications within academia, to say nothing of the political and cultural spheres. Having taught in the humanities at two public research universities in the American Midwest, I have found that many of my own colleagues and students have been more profoundly impacted by the writings of New Atheists than, say, polemical works by far-right religiously affiliated critics of Islam (whose impact is more obvious in other contexts).[8] And for those working to combat the very real problem of Muslim terrorism, it is critical to scrutinize influential discourses on the root causes of and potential solutions to this problem.

In Part I of this book, I introduce the themes of war and peace in the foundational texts of Islam (Chapter 1) and discuss pertinent medieval and modern Muslim scholarly rules of armed jihad (Chapter 2). In Part II, I examine the phenomenon of contemporary Muslim radicalism, specifically the discourse of the man behind 9/11, bin Laden, and his justifications for the attacks (Chapter 3); interrogate these justifications and survey the reactions and responses of prominent Muslim scholars, clerics, and leaders (Chapter 4); and proffer some observations on the contemporary radical organization ISIS and its conceptions of armed jihad (Chapter 5). In Part III, I discuss and evaluate the portrayals of jihad and radicalism that appear in the popular works of notable New Atheists, particularly Harris (Chapter 6) and Ali (Chapter 7), and offer additional reflections on the writings of other well-known New Atheists, namely Richard Dawkins, Christopher Hitchens, and Daniel Dennett (Chapter 8). Readers will notice that I quote extensively from the individuals I examine, be they Muslim radicals or New Atheists. These extensive quotations are not intended to privilege their particular claims but rather to convey each individual's manner of thinking and tone (in some cases, through the filter of translation).

As we shall see, although many of the concerns expressed by the New Atheists regarding terrorism are shared by many Muslims, the

---

[7] Some examples include writer Glenn Greenwald (see his article "Sam Harris, the New Atheists, and Anti-Muslim Animus"), philosopher Michael Ruse (see his article "Why I Think the New Atheists Are a Bloody Disaster"), author Reza Aslan (see his article "Reza Aslan: Sam Harris and 'New Atheists' Aren't New, Aren't Even Atheists"), and writer Chris Hedges (see his book *When Atheism Becomes Religion*).

[8] Yet as sociologist Stephen LeDrew (an avowed atheist critical of the New Atheists) observes, "these atheists and right-wing Christians have much in common. Moving from metaphysics to politics, the line between the groups begins to blur" (LeDrew, *The Evolution of Atheism*, 187).

New Atheists featured in this book tend to portray the interpretations of Islam promoted by radicals such as bin Laden as literalistic and especially faithful to Islamic scripture. The central argument of this book is twofold: (1) among the most distinctive features of radicals such as bin Laden are not their alleged literal readings of the foundational texts of Islam – in some cases, they go to great lengths to circumvent such readings – but rather their aberrant, expansive conceptions of justifiable combat and retaliation and their particular, often crude assessments of geopolitical reality; and (2) on account of the New Atheists' overreliance on a limited array of sources and their apparent unfamiliarity with some of the prevailing currents of Islamic thought, they ultimately privilege anomalous interpretations of scripture. Yet not only do the New Atheists' conceptions of armed jihad conflict with those of the majority of Muslim scholars and laypeople, they even overstep what we find in the discourse of radicals.

PART I

JIHAD

Although the term *jihad* (literally, a "struggle" or "striving") conveys a myriad of meanings in Islamic religious culture, in Islamic law it typically signifies an armed struggle against outsiders, primarily non-Muslims. It is this understanding of jihad that concerns us here. But before examining the Islamic legal dimensions of jihad, we shall first consider how the primary sources of Islamic thought – the Qur'an and early Muslim accounts of the actions and sayings of the Prophet Muhammad and his followers – portray war and peace.

I

War and Peace in the Foundational Texts of Islam

Muslims generally take the Qur'an (Koran) to be the "word of God," a scripture that was revealed piecemeal to the Prophet Muhammad (570–632) over the last twenty-three years of his life. It contains passages that promote restraint and reconciliation and others that call for war. This parallels what we find in the popular biographies of Muhammad:[1] When he began his prophetic mission in the city of Mecca as a monotheistic preacher to mostly polytheistic tribespeople, he adopted a pacifistic approach – and adhered to it despite the persecution and even murder of some of his followers. It was only after he emigrated in 622 to the city of Medina (then called Yathrib), established a community of believers, and assumed direct responsibility for the well-being of his followers that he took up arms.

THE CONTEXT

By all accounts, seventh-century Arabia was a world in which tribes regularly clashed. "In this society," historian Fred Donner writes, "war (*harb*, used in the senses of both an activity and a condition) was in one sense a normal way of life." Indeed, "a 'state of war' was assumed to exist

---

[1] Examples of relatively early works that offer biographical accounts of Muhammad include the *Sira* ("Biography") of ibn Ishaq (d. 767) and ibn Hisham (d. 833), the *Maghazi* ("Expeditions") of al-Waqidi (d. 823), the *Tabaqat* ("Generations") of ibn Sa'd (d. 845), and the *Tarikh* ("History") of al-Tabari (d. 923). My concern here is not the extent to which these sources are authentic or historically accurate. For our purposes, all that matters is that most of the major episodes reported therein are widely accepted as true among Muslim scholars.

between one's tribe and all others, unless a particular treaty or agreement had been reached with another tribe establishing amicable relations."[2] In the absence of such treaties or agreements, the clans of Mecca and the surrounding region could only find reprieve from war in the Ka'ba sanctuary (throughout the year) and everywhere else during four "forbidden months" – the first, seventh, eleventh, and twelfth months of the Arabian lunar calendar. These forbidden months, recognized throughout Arabia, facilitated an annual pilgrimage to Mecca in the twelfth month and a "lesser pilgrimage" in the seventh, not to mention commercial trade. Beyond these restrictions, however, the pre-Islamic Meccans seem to have condoned and often engaged in tribal warfare and caravan raids.

The Qur'an attests to this reality:[3]

Can [the unbelievers] not see that [God has] made [them] a secure sanctuary [in Mecca] though all around them people are snatched away? (29:67)

Remember when you were few, victimized in the land, afraid that people might catch you, but God sheltered you and strengthened you with His help, and provided you with good things so that you might be grateful. (8:26)

For the security of Quraysh [the dominant tribe of Mecca] – security in their winter and summer journeys – let them worship the Lord of this House [the Ka'ba], who provides them with food to ward off hunger, safety to ward off fear. (106:1–4)

In such an environment, the withdrawal of tribal support could render persons "fair game" for all aggressors.[4] This explains why some individuals were reluctant to follow Muhammad during his early pacifistic years: "They say, 'If we were to follow guidance with you, we would be swept from our land'" (Qur'an 28:57).

THE QUR'AN, FROM MECCA TO MEDINA

Despite (or perhaps due to) the precarious environment of seventh-century Arabia, Meccan passages of the Qur'an – so called because they were revealed before the emigration (*hijra*) to Medina – generally promote restraint when dealing with adversaries. Consider the following examples:

The servants of the Lord of Mercy are those who walk humbly on the earth, and who, when aggressive people address them, reply with words of peace. (25:63)

---

[2] Donner, "Sources of Islamic Conceptions of War," 34.
[3] Unless otherwise indicated, my translation of the Qur'an, here and throughout the present book, loosely follows M. A. S. Abdel Haleem's *The Qur'an*.
[4] Jackson, "Jihad and the Modern World," 12.

Patiently endure what they say, ignore them politely. (73:10)

Good and evil cannot be equal. [Prophet], repel evil with what is better and your enemy will become as close as an old and valued friend, but only those who are steadfast in patience, only those who are blessed with great righteousness, will attain to such goodness. (41:34–35)

As such, the jihad of the Meccan passages entails "striving" through nonviolent means:

So [Muhammad] do not give in to the unbelievers: ardently *strive* [or do jihad] against them with [this Qur'an].[5] (25:52)

In Medinan passages – passages revealed after the emigration, when Muhammad had become the de facto chief and overseer of Medina – we encounter a call to armed self-defense:

Those who have been attacked are permitted to take up arms because they have been wronged – God has the power to help them – those who have been driven unjustly from their homes only for saying, "Our Lord is God." If God did not repel some people by means of others, many monasteries, churches, synagogues, and mosques, where God's name is much invoked, would have been destroyed. God is sure to help those who help His cause – God is strong and mighty.[6] (22:39–40)

Why should you not fight in God's cause and for those oppressed men, women, and children who cry out, "Lord, rescue us from this town whose people are oppressors! By your grace, give us a protector and give us a helper!"? (4:75)

The first of a series of battles against the Meccan polytheists – whom Muslim historians present as manifestly oppressive – took place in the second year after the emigration. A recurring theme in the Medinan passages involves the reluctance of some of Muhammad's followers to fight – a reluctance stemming not necessarily from concern that such fighting was immoral or gratuitous but from a fear of death and an abhorrence of the prospect of fighting relatives.[7] Thus we read,

---

[5] Emphasis added here and in all other instances where words are italicized in the English translation of the Qur'an. See Afsaruddin, *Striving in the Path of God*, 16–18, where Islamic studies scholar Asma Afsaruddin discusses the general preference among medieval Qur'anic commentators for nonviolent interpretations of Qur'an 25:52.

[6] There is some debate among Muslim scholars as to whether this passage is Medinan or late Meccan. According to one opinion, this passage was revealed around the time of the Prophet's emigration (see al-Qurtubi, *al-Jami' li-ahkam al-Qur'an*, 14:406 [commentary on Qur'an 22:39]; and Nasr [ed.], *The Study Quran*, 830, 839 [commentary on Qur'an 22:39]).

[7] To be sure, not everyone was reluctant to fight. And in a well-known prophetic report (or *hadith*) conveyed by (the scholar named) Muslim (d. 875), Muhammad calls for some

Fighting has been ordained for you, though it is hard for you. You may dislike something although it is good for you, or like something although it is bad for you: God knows and you do not. (2:216)

[Prophet], do you not see those who were told, "Restrain yourselves from fighting, perform the prayer, and pay the prescribed alms"? When fighting was ordained for them, some of them feared men as much as, or even more than, they feared God, saying, "Lord, why have You ordained fighting for us? If only You would give us just a little more time." Say to them, "Little is the enjoyment in this world, the Hereafter is far better for those who are mindful of God: you will not be wronged by as much as the fiber in a date stone." (4:77)

Accordingly, the Qur'an instructs the believers not to "lose heart and cry out for peace" when dealing with antagonistic unbelievers who "bar others from God's path" – it is the believers "who have the upper hand" (47:34–35). And as for those "killed in God's way," they "are alive with their Lord, well provided for" (3:169).

Yet even in the midst of the Medinan passages, we encounter statements that present peace and reconciliation as the ideal:

Those who remain steadfast ... who repel evil with good – these will have the reward of the [true] home: they will enter perpetual gardens ... (13:22–23)

God may still bring about affection between you and your [present enemies] – God is all powerful, God is most forgiving and merciful – and He does not forbid you to deal kindly and equitably with anyone who has not fought you for your faith or driven you out of your homes: God loves those who act equitably. (60:7–8)

Prepare against [the unbelievers] whatever forces you [believers] can muster, including warhorses, to frighten off [these] enemies of God and of yours[8] ... But if they incline toward peace, you [Prophet] must also incline toward it, and put your trust in God: He is the All Hearing, the All Knowing. (8:60–61)

In the sixth year after the emigration, Muhammad inclined toward peace when he agreed to what his followers initially regarded as an unfavorable armistice with their Meccan enemies: the truce of Hudaybiyya. Nearly two years later, however, following a Meccan violation of one of the truce's stipulations, Muhammad led his ever-growing

---

initial restraint: "Do not desire an encounter with the enemy; but when you encounter them, persevere."

[8] As Islamic studies scholar ElSayed Amin notes, some modern Muslims and non-Muslims – including Geert Wilders, the Dutch politician who produced the 2008 anti-Islam film *Fitna* – see in this verse (8:60) a specific call for terrorism. But through his analysis of classical and modern commentaries on the Qur'an, Amin argues that this verse was historically understood as a general call for "Muslims to prepare for defensive purposes sufficient forces to deter their enemies" (Amin, *Reclaiming Jihad*, 53; see chapter 2).

forces to Mecca and, with relative ease, conquered his home city; eventually, he designated it a haven for believers.

Clearly, the Medinan era presented Muhammad with the kinds of thorny decisions he had never had to grapple with during the early years of his mission. Not surprisingly, then, it is the Qur'an's Medinan passages that figure most significantly in contemporary debates on violence in Islam. Consider, for instance, the Medinan commandment that has often appeared in print, online, and on television in the days and years following the September 11 attacks: "Kill them wherever you find them."

Versions of this (variously translated) directive appear in the second (2:191), fourth (4:89, 91), and ninth (9:5) chapters of the Qur'an. Needless to say, it is not a stand-alone commandment. Here is how it appears in the second and fourth chapters:

Fight in God's cause against those who fight you, but do not overstep the limits. *Kill them wherever you encounter them*, and drive them out from where they drove you out, for persecution is more serious than killing. Do not fight them at the Sacred Mosque [in Mecca] unless they fight you there. If they do fight you, kill them – this is what such unbelievers deserve – but if they stop, then God is most forgiving and merciful. Fight them until there is no more persecution, and worship[9] is devoted to God. If they cease, there can be no [further] hostility, except toward oppressors. (2:190–193)

[The hypocrites] would dearly like you to reject faith, as they themselves have done, to be like them. So do not take them as patrons until they migrate [to Medina] for God's cause. If they turn,[10] then seize and *kill them wherever you encounter them*. Take none of them as a patron or supporter. But as for those who reach people with whom you have a treaty, or who come over to you because their hearts shrink from fighting against you or against their own people, God could have given them power over you, and they would have fought you. So if they withdraw and do not fight you, and offer you peace, then God gives you no way against them. You will find others who wish to be safe from you, and from their own people, but whenever they are back in a situation where they are tempted [to hostility], they succumb to it. So if they neither withdraw, nor offer you peace, nor restrain themselves from fighting you, seize and *kill them wherever you encounter them*: We give you clear authority against such people. (4:89–91)

Here we see violent directives surrounded by critical qualifications: those whom Muhammad's followers are to fight and kill are the very

[9] Qur'anic studies scholar M. A. S. Abdel Haleem maintains that "worship" here denotes "worship at the sacred mosque by those who were no longer persecuted" (Abdel Haleem, *The Qur'an*, 22, note a). See Qur'an 2:217, 8:39; and Chapter 7, note 49 in what follows.
[10] As Abdel Haleem notes, "That 'turn with aggression' is the intended meaning is clear from the context" (Abdel Haleem, *The Qur'an*, 59, note a). Abdel Haleem then refers to Qur'an 4:91, which I quote in what follows.

people trying to fight and kill them. And, again, "If they cease, there can be no [further] hostility, except toward oppressors" (2:193). But while it would be reasonable to take "cease" here to mean simply "cease hostilities" – and this is precisely the wording used in a well-known scholarly translation of the Qur'an[11] – various medieval Qur'anic commentators were of the view that it actually denotes the cessation of *both* the hostilities *and unbelief* of the Meccan polytheists referred to in this verse (2:193).[12] According to this contested reading, the Meccan polytheists could terminate the conflict they had initiated and perpetuated only through conversion to Islam; their particular beliefs, some scholars suggest, went hand in hand with their hostility against Muhammad and his community.[13] This would mean that they were excluded from the prohibition against forced conversion expressed later in the same chapter: "There is no compulsion in religion" (2:256).[14]

This takes us to the ninth chapter of the Qur'an, al-Tawba (Repentance). The prevailing view among Muslim scholars is that it is one of the last,

---

[11] Abdel Haleem, *The Qur'an*, 22. This particular reading is in line with that ascribed to, among others, the eighth-century Qur'anic commentators Mujahid (d. 722) and al-Suddi (d. 745) (see al-Tabari, *Tafsir al-Tabari*, 3:303–304 [commentary on Qur'an 2:193]).

[12] See, for instance, al-Tabari, *Tafsir al-Tabari*, 3:301–304 (commentary on Qur'an 2:193); and al-Razi, *Tafsir al-Fakhr al-Razi*, 5:143–144 (commentary on Qur'an 2:193). Cf. Al-Dawoody, *The Islamic Law of War*, 60–63; and Nasr (ed.), *The Study Quran*, 84 (commentary on Qur'an 2:193).

[13] See, for instance, al-Razi, *Tafsir al-Fakhr al-Razi*, 5:137–146 (commentary on Qur'an 2:190–194); and Asma Afsaruddin's discussion of al-Razi's Qur'anic commentary in *Striving in the Path of God*, 53–55, 273.

[14] On the historical range of interpretations of Qur'an 2:256, see Crone, "'No Compulsion in Religion'." Although some Muslim commentators hold that Qur'an 2:256 was abrogated by passages revealed later in time that call on Muslims to fight unbelievers (such as 9:5, which I discuss in the next paragraph), many other scholars maintain that this verse remains in effect (see Nasr [ed.], *The Study Quran*, 111–112 [commentary on Qur'an 2:256]; and Afsaruddin, *Striving in the Path of God*, 230, 240). Among Muslim jurists, the majority view has been that "[f]ighting non-Muslims solely because they do not believe in Islam contradicts" the "no compulsion" principle expressed in Qur'an 2:256 (Al-Dawoody, *The Islamic Law of War*, 78). As historian David Wasserstein observes, "One feature that has characterized the preaching of Islam and conversion to that faith over the last fourteen centuries is the general absence, other than in the cases of conversion of an entire state or group for political reasons, of compulsion. Justified by a sentence in the Qur'an (Q 2:256), 'there is no compulsion in religion' ... the prohibition thus implied has been largely honoured" (Wasserstein, "Conversion and the *ahl al-dhimma*," 200). The notion of "no compulsion in religion" is buttressed by other Qur'anic passages, for instance, "Had your Lord willed, all the people on earth would have believed. So can you [Prophet] compel people to believe?" (10:99); and "Say, 'Now the truth has come from your Lord: let those who wish to believe in it do so, and let those who wish to reject it do so'" (18:29).

if not the final chapter revealed (the Qur'an is not arranged chronologic-
ally) and that its revelation occurred sometime after the Meccan polytheists had violated the truce of Hudaybiyya. The chapter includes what
various scholars label the "sword verse,"[15] a passage calling for war
against the polytheists:

When the forbidden months are over, *wherever you encounter the polytheists,*[16]
kill them, seize them, besiege them, wait for them at every lookout post; but if
they repent, maintain the prayer, and pay the prescribed alms, let them go on their
way, for God is most forgiving and merciful. (9:5)

One well-known Muslim scholarly opinion is that this passage opened
the door to continual warfare against *all* polytheistic tribes and not
only the belligerent ones. According to this view, the "sword verse" abrogated the Qur'anic statements revealed earlier that present peace with
polytheists as the ideal.[17]

This abrogationist assertion has long been contentious.[18] It reflects an
expansionist paradigm that, at least during the formative centuries of
Islamic thought, was actively promoted by scholars living in the political
centers of the Muslim Umayyad (661–750) and Abbasid empires (750–
1258) but not by others "not known to be close to the ruling elites of
their time"[19] and thus not as likely to be driven by aspirations for empire
building. This dichotomy calls into question the view that "during the
first several centuries of Islam the interpretation of *jihad* was unabash-
edly aggressive and expansive."[20]

---

[15] Regardless of when the "sword verse" (*ayat al-sayf*) designation was first conceived, it
was not commonly used in popular Qur'anic commentaries until the fourteenth century
(see Afsaruddin, *Striving in the Path of God*, 276). Incidentally, a minority of Muslim
scholars reserve the "sword verse" label for other Qur'anic verses, such as 9:29, 36, and
41 (see al-Qaradawi, *Fiqh al-Jihad*, 1:286–287).

[16] "The polytheists" here are *al-mushrikin* (or *al-mushrikun*) in Arabic. A more precise but
wordier translation of this term would be "those who associate partners with God."

[17] See, for instance, al-Qurtubi, *al-Jami' li-ahkam al-Qur'an*, 10:108–112 (commentary on
Qur'an 9:5; al-Qurtubi [d. 1273] promotes the abrogationist assertion, though he never
uses the term "sword verse").

[18] Prominent scholars such as Abu Ja'far al-Nahhas (d. 949), ibn al-Jawzi (d. 1201), and al-
Suyuti (d. 1505) all accepted approximately twenty cases of scriptural abrogation, none
of which involved the "sword verse." Many contemporary scholars reject the doctrine of
abrogation altogether (see Blankinship, "Sword Verses").

[19] Afsaruddin, *Striving in the Path of God*, 4. Focusing on the expansionist paradigm, historian Patricia Crone asserts that the "holy war" of the early Arab Muslim conquerors was
comparable to earlier Near Eastern modes of "divinely enjoined imperialism" (Crone,
God's Rule, 366).

[20] Cook, *Understanding Jihad*, 30.

There is, in fact, good reason to question the abrogationist-expansionist paradigm: if we consider the passages surrounding the "sword verse" (9:5), we find that this particular call for war is congruous with the similarly worded, *qualified* directives of the second and fourth chapters. In the passage preceding the "sword verse," we read,

As for those polytheists who have honored the covenant you [believers] made with them and who have not supported anyone against you: fulfill your agreement with them to the end of their term. God loves those who are mindful of Him. (9:4)

Immediately following the "sword verse," we encounter the following qualifications and clarifications:

If any one of the polytheists should seek your protection [Prophet], grant it to him so that he may hear the word of God, then take him to a place safe for him, for they are people who do not know. How could there be a covenant with God and His Messenger for the polytheists? – But as for those with whom you made a covenant at the Sacred Mosque, so long as they remain true to you, be true to them; God loves those who are mindful of Him. – [How,] when, if they were to get the upper hand over you, they would not respect any tie with you, of kinship or of covenant? ... Where believers are concerned, they respect no tie of kinship or covenant. They are the ones who are committing aggression ... [I]f they break their oath after having made an agreement with you and revile your religion, then fight these leaders of unbelief – oaths mean nothing to them – so that they may stop. How could you not fight a people who have broken their oaths, who tried to drive the Messenger out, who attacked you first? (9:6–13)

Taken as a whole, these verses appear to be calling for war against bellicose polytheists, specifically those "who attacked you first."

Later in the same Qur'anic chapter, we encounter other critical passages, most notably the following:

Fight those of the People of the Book [Christians, Jews, and arguably others] who do not [truly] believe in God and the Last Day, who do not forbid what God and His Messenger have forbidden, who do not follow the religion of truth,[21] until they pay the tax (*jizya*) promptly and agree to submit. (9:29)

Fight the polytheists all together as they fight you all together.[22] (9:36)

---

[21] In the place of "who do not follow the religion of truth," M. A. S. Abdel Haleem opts for a less common translation: "who do not obey the rule of justice." As Abdel Haleem would have it, this refers to those who fail to pay the *jizya* tax, which I discuss in what follows (Abdel Haleem, *The Qur'an*, 118, note d).

[22] An alternative translation of this passage reads, "[Y]ou may fight the idolaters at any time, if they first fight you" (Abdel Haleem, *The Qur'an*, 119).

Prophet, *strive* [or do jihad] against the unbelievers and the hypocrites and be tough with them. (9:73)

You who believe, fight the unbelievers near you and let them find you standing firm: be aware that God is with those who are mindful of Him. (9:123)

In the eyes of various Muslim scholars, all such injunctions pertain to specific contexts – according to certain Qur'anic commentators, 9:29 refers to threatening Byzantines,²³ while 9:36, 9:73, and 9:123 concern Muhammad's nearby Arab enemies²⁴ – and are qualified by the afore-mentioned Qur'anic passages that present peace as the ideal and that limit fighting to "those who fight you" (2:190). From this perspective, all of Muhammad's battles and even conquests were ultimately defensive or protective in nature.²⁵ In the eyes of scholars representing the abro-gationist-expansionist paradigm, however, the Prophet plainly sought to conquer the lands of unbelievers, and the final Qur'anic verses revealed allow for the prospect of perpetual warfare: polytheists, or at least those of Mecca, must either convert or be fought, and Christians, Jews, and arguably many others have a third option: acceptance of Muslim rule and the payment of a tax called the *jizya*.²⁶

²³ See Nasr (ed.), *The Study Quran*, 5 1 3 (commentary on Qur'an 9:29).
²⁴ See Nasr (ed.), *The Study Quran*, 503, 5 16–5 17 (commentary on Qur'an 9:36), 526 (commentary on Qur'an 9:73), 540 (commentary on Qur'an 9:123); see also the commentary on the surrounding verses.
²⁵ Islamic studies scholar Ahmed Al-Dawoody, for instance, maintains that the Prophet's major battles and sieges – Badr, Uhud, the Ditch, Khaybar, Hunayn, and Ta'if – "were defensive" in nature and "just": "The first three, one of which, the Ditch, involved a number of Jewish tribes, were launched by the Meccans on the Muslims in Medina. The march to Khaybar was intended to put an end to its inhabitants' hostility after they had fought in the battle of the Ditch. The Hunayn and [Ta'if] incidents were initiated by the Hawazin and Thaqif tribes." As for Muhammad's expedition to Tabuk to face the Byzantines, "although no encounter took place, the Muslims marched as a result of a rumor circulated by Syrian traders about a Byzantine army camping in Tabuk on its way to make war upon the Muslims in Medina. Reading the context in this way, Muslims throughout history have seen the Muslims involved in these incidents as the victims of their enemies' aggression" (Al-Dawoody, *The Islamic Law of War*, 45–46; see pages 24–25, where Al-Dawoody discusses the lead-up to the Battle of Badr, and pages 63–66, where Al-Dawoody examines different interpretations of some of the critical passages of the Qur'an's ninth chapter pertaining to warfare). This perspective is to be contrasted with that of scholars such as Reuven Firestone, who maintains that "it was Muhammad and not the Meccan Quraysh who initiated the battles" between them (Firestone, *Jihad*, 1 10; cf. Al-Dawoody, *The Islamic Law of War*, 14, 23, 32–36, 46, 57, 66).
²⁶ Various medieval Muslim scholars affirmed the permissibility of entering into *jizya* contracts with polytheists, including Arab ones who did not belong to the Meccan tribe of Quraysh (see Peters [ed.], *Jihad in Classical and Modern Islam*, 40–41 [from Peters's

Some abrogationists went further than others by asserting that the "sword verse" (or other verses) abrogated *all* of the peaceful passages of the Qur'an, including "But if they incline toward peace, you [Prophet] must also incline toward it" (8:61). This, however, "remained a minority contested" position, at least among Qur'anic commentators.[27] Among the remaining majority of commentators, some allowed for a straightforward reading of the injunction above (8:61), while others restricted its meaning so that it precluded the possibility of establishing *permanent* peaceful relations with those who refused to submit to Muslim rule.[28] Owing to the obvious example of the Prophet and pragmatic considerations, however, the vast majority of scholars recognized the legitimacy of truces, even while differing on how long they should last.[29]

THE HADITHS

Although most revered, the Qur'an is by no means the only primary source utilized by scholars of Islam. I already mentioned the biographies of Muhammad as an important source. More significant than the biographies, at least in the context of Islamic law, are *hadiths*, reports of the Prophet's sayings, actions, and normative example. Compiled and standardized over the course of centuries, hadiths appear in numerous collections of varying degrees of authenticity. To be sure, the veracity (to say nothing of interpretation) of individual hadiths can be the subject of much scholarly debate. Suffice it to say that the hadith corpus (not to mention the biographies), taken as a whole, seldom

---

translation of ibn Rushd's (d. 1198) chapter on jihad in the legal handbook *al-Bidaya*]; and Brown, "Jizyah").

[27] Afsaruddin, *Striving in the Path of God*, 280. Incidentally, some early Muslim authorities reportedly maintained that Qur'an 9:5 was itself abrogated by the command in Qur'an 47:4 to "release" the unbelievers after combat "as a grace or for ransom" (see al-Qurtubi's discussion of this in *al-Jami' li-ahkam al-Qur'an*, 10:110 [commentary on Qur'an 9:5]).

[28] For an example of this "restricted" interpretation of Qur'an 8:61, see al-Tabari, *Tafsir al-Tabari*, 11:251–255 (commentary on Qur'an 8:61). On the range of popular medieval interpretations of Qur'an 8:61, see Afsaruddin, *Striving in the Path of God*, 90–93.

[29] See, for instance, Peters (ed.), *Jihad in Classical and Modern Islam*, 38–40 (ibn Rushd's *al-Bidaya*). A common view among medieval Muslim scholars was that truces should last ten years, which was the (most widely recognized) stated term of the truce of Hudaybiyya; however, some claimed it should be shorter than this, while others (including prominent scholars from three of the four major Sunni schools of legal thought) argued for no limit. Among those who imposed a term limit, some allowed for truces to be renewed (see al-Qurtubi, *al-Jami' li-ahkam al-Qur'an*, 10:64–65 [commentary on Qur'an 8:61]; and Reiter, *War, Peace and International Relations in Islam*, 20–22).

simplifies matters related to the topic of war and peace. Consider, for instance, the following two hadiths:

Do not attack the [Ethiopians] if they do not attack you, and do not attack the Turks unless they attack you.[30]

I have been commanded to fight against people until they testify [to] the fact that there is no god but [God], and believe (in me) that I am the Messenger (from the Lord), and in all that I have brought. And when they do it, their blood and [wealth] are guaranteed protection on my behalf except where it is justified by law, and their affairs rest with God.[31]

The first hadith appears in the collections of various eminent scholars, including Malik ibn Anas (d. 795), Abu Dawud (d. 889), and al-Nasa'i (d. 915); the second and its variants (including one that makes no reference to belief in the Messenger) appear in, among other sources, the two most widely accepted collections, those of al-Bukhari (d. 870) and Muslim (d. 875).[32] As one might surmise, scholars often qualify the meanings and implications of hadiths in light of other reports and considerations. In the case of the second hadith quoted, for instance, the prevailing view among Muslim scholars is that it refers only to Arab polytheists (not "people" in general), and some limit it further to the oppressive polytheists of Mecca.[33]

Using all of the available evidence from the Qur'an and reports about the Prophet and the earliest generations of Muslims, as well as other legal considerations, such as scholarly consensus (*ijma'*) and analogical reasoning (*qiyas*), Muslim scholars developed rules of armed jihad. Relevant for our purposes is their criteria for justifying warfare (in Latin, *jus ad bellum*) and criteria for conducting warfare justly (*jus in bello*).

---

[30] Translated and discussed in Ahmad, *Islam, Modernity, Violence, and Everyday Life*, 123. As indicated in what follows, this prophetic directive appears in multiple hadith collections.

[31] Translated and discussed in Peters (ed.), *A Reader on Classical Islam*, 154. The version of the hadith quoted here appears in the collection of (the scholar named) Muslim.

[32] One should be careful not to assume that all Sunni scholars accept every hadith compiled by al-Bukhari and Muslim (both Sunni). In the case of this particular hadith ("I have been commanded to fight against people ..."), even some early authorities questioned its authenticity (see ibn Hajar, *Fath al-bari*, 1:95–96).

[33] See Al-Dawoody, *The Islamic Law of War*, 79. Variants of this hadith that appear in the collection of al-Nasa'i replace "I have been commanded to fight against people" with "I have been commanded to fight against polytheists."

2

Jihad in Islamic Law

Considering the rapid expansion of the Muslim empire during the reigns of Muhammad's political successors, the caliphs, it should come as no surprise that medieval scholars would have much to say on the topic of armed jihad.[1] And these discussions were by no means monolithic: much like the Jewish rabbis, Muslim scholars developed a rich legal tradition marked by considerable diversity.

We shall now turn our attention to the medieval and modern Islamic legal discourse on jihad. What follows is not intended to be an exhaustive account of Muslim scholars' shared and conflicting rules of armed jihad but rather a survey of the principles most relevant to the subject of the present book. Accordingly, as both al-Qaeda and ISIS represent radical Sunni organizations, our focus here will be Sunni (as opposed to Shi'ite) Islamic law.

JUSTIFYING JIHAD

Medieval scholars delineated two major forms of armed jihad, one defensive, the other aggressive:

(1) Defensive jihad was an armed struggle against an invading force. All able-bodied Muslims – male and female, young and old – were

---

[1] To be clear, however, they were hardly obsessed with this topic: by one estimate, premodern Islamic legal works devote, on average, only 1.5 percent of their text to the subject of war and peace (Hallaq, *Introduction to Islamic Law*, 30).

generally required to partake in this form of jihad in some way, for their community's survival was at stake.

(2) Aggressive jihad was a highly regulated preemptive or offensive attack commissioned by a recognized political authority, such as a caliph. According to most scholars, this form of jihad was a collective requirement, incumbent not on each individual but on a Muslim community in general. Each year, a community's army of men was expected to set out from the "abode of Islam" to attack a neighboring people's army in the "abode of war," a non-Muslim-controlled country with which there was no truce.

Although Muslim scholars conceptualized aggressive jihad as a means of promulgating Islam (typically through influence and incentives, not mandatory conversion), there was nonetheless a widespread belief that such a jihad was necessary to protect and preserve Muslim communities. Thus, while various scholars saw the unbelief of neighboring non-Muslims as sufficient grounds for declaring war on them, a popular view was that even aggressive jihad was ultimately defensive in nature.[2] The assumed "state of war" in Arabia was not unlike the state of affairs throughout much of the premodern world: a premodern country, having no fixed territorial borders, was often as safe as it was aggressive. Thus, when Muslim scholars labeled non-Muslim-controlled countries with which there was no truce as the "abode of war," they were *describing* their reality; the labels "abode of Islam" and "abode of war" were far more descriptive than prescriptive.[3]

As the Muslim scholar and academic Sherman A. Jackson observes, in our current world order, our *assumed* (not necessarily actual) global state is generally one of peace. The United States and Mexico, for instance, need not sign a treaty or make special arrangements of any kind to establish or secure a nonviolent relationship: it is expected. This assumed state of peace is a product of modern institutions like the United Nations. Assuming that Islamic legal rulings must be context specific, Jackson maintains that it would be problematic for contemporary scholars to continue to uphold aggressive jihad, especially if an assumed state of peace persists.[4] In the words of the thirteenth-century Egyptian cleric al-Qarafi (d. 1285), "Holding to rulings that have been deduced on the basis of

---

[2] See Al-Dawoody, *The Islamic Law of War*, 78–81.
[3] Jackson, "Jihad and the Modern World," 18.
[4] Jackson, "Jihad and the Modern World," 18–20.

custom, even after this custom has changed, is a violation of Unanimous Consensus and an open display of ignorance of the religion."[5]

In affirming the desirability of a perpetual state of peace with non-Muslims, Jackson is hardly alone among modern Muslim thinkers. He himself cites supporting statements by other influential figures such as the Arab scholars Rashid Rida (d. 1935), Abdul Wahhab Khallaf (d. 1956), and Wahba al-Zuhayli (d. 2015).[6] Nevertheless, Jackson recognizes that some of his assumptions about jihad and the modern world are not universal among Muslims. The controversial Egyptian Islamist Sayyid Qutb (d. 1966), for instance, held that Jews and Christians have proven themselves to be inherently antagonistic toward Muslims, whether during the Prophet's era or in modern times, and this reality necessitates a communal obligation to permanent jihad. Furthermore, according to Qutb, the United Nations and other Western institutions have no bearing on Islamic law, in large part because they were established by non-Muslims.[7] As Jackson notes, such views were derived not from a strictly literal approach to scripture but rather a "dynamic" one – views colored by Qutb's particular conceptions of history and geopolitical reality. These are also views Jackson readily dismisses, as he draws attention to Qur'anic passages that portray certain Jews and Christians in a positive light[8] as well as instances from Muhammad's life when even he recognized institutions established by non-Muslims, such as the aforementioned forbidden months.[9]

As we shall see, debates over the continuing legitimacy of aggressive jihad have minimal bearing on the problem of contemporary Muslim terrorism, in part because the belligerent tactics employed by terrorists would be even more difficult to justify in the context of what is supposed to be a highly regulated war. In the case of Osama bin Laden,

---

[5] Al-Qarafi, *Kitab al-ihkam*, 231 (translated and discussed in Jackson, "Jihad and the Modern World," 9; see page 8).

[6] Jackson, "Jihad and the Modern World," 19.

[7] See Qutb's commentary on the Qur'an, specifically his discussion of 9:29 (Qutb, *In the Shade of the Qur'an*, 8:80–106; on page 95, we read, "Legal Islamic rulings have always been, and will continue to be, the result of action taken in accordance with the Islamic method and approach"). Interestingly, in 1945 (years before he composed his Qur'anic commentary and before he was imprisoned by the Egyptian government), Qutb stated, "When Islam commands war against polytheists, the command refers only to defensive war, which is aimed at stopping aggression" (Qutb, *Social Justice in Islam*, 118).

[8] As examples, Jackson cites Qur'an 5:82, a verse that portrays certain Christians as being "closest in affection toward the believers"; and 3:113–114, a passage that refers to "righteous" People of the Book.

[9] Jackson, "Jihad and the Modern World," 22–25.

for instance, although he defended the doctrine of aggressive jihad, he consistently presented his attacks on American targets, however aggressive they actually were, as part of a *defensive* jihad. Furthermore, even after 9/11, he affirmed the possibility of peaceful relations with certain Western countries, specifically those nations he deemed nonthreatening. Like many other influential Muslims, bin Laden often invoked security, political, and practical considerations when contemplating the prospect of either peace with or warfare against non-Muslim entities.

THE ROLE OF POLITICS IN JIHAD DISCOURSE AS DEMONSTRATED IN A FAMOUS MID-1990S DEBATE

Any assessment of jihad discourse – including that of radicals such as bin Laden – must account for the critical role played by politics and individual perceptions of the facts on the ground. To illustrate this, we shall now turn our attention to a famous scholarly dispute that took place several years before 9/11. This was an in-print debate on the permissibility of making peace with Israel – a topic, as we shall see, bin Laden would weigh in on. The debate featured two of the most prominent and controversial Arab Muslim scholars of the past few decades, the then grand mufti of Saudi Arabia (the nation's foremost state cleric) Abdulaziz bin Baz (d. 1999) and the Doha-based Egyptian cleric Yusuf al-Qaradawi.[10]

A surprising development precipitated the debate: in August 1993, after many years of intense conflict, representatives of the Israeli government and the Palestine Liberation Organization (PLO) agreed to meet face-to-face for the first time to hammer out a peace plan. The outcome of their negotiations, held in Oslo, was an agreement that each side would recognize the other officially and that Israel would withdraw from various territories. The formal signing of the Oslo Accords took place the next month, and this was followed by further negotiations in Cairo several months later. Before long, numerous Muslim scholars and leaders voiced concern over the legitimacy and merits of these negotiations.

---

[10] For a more extensive treatment of this bin Baz–Qaradawi debate, see Khalil, "War or Peace in Israel?" For discussions and translations of various Muslim scholarly statements and debates on the permissibility of making peace with Israel, see Reiter, *War, Peace and International Relations in Islam*. See also Sohail Hashmi's forthcoming essay on a Sadat-era Egyptian debate, tentatively entitled "A Complaint from God: Al-Azhar, the Muslim Brotherhood, and the Debate on the Legitimacy of the Egyptian–Israeli Peace Treaty."

In the December 24, 1994, issue of the Jeddah-based newspaper *al-Muslimun*, the paper's Editor-in-Chief Abdullah al-Rifa'i noted that many Muslim detractors of the peace plan had objected on the premise that wars against the "enemies" of Islam must be waged constantly and that peace treaties with such enemies are generally illegitimate. Turning to bin Baz, al-Rifa'i solicited the Saudi cleric's opinion on this matter.[11]

Just a few years earlier, bin Baz had called for an armed jihad against Israel and declared this jihad obligatory upon Palestinian Muslims.[12] Now as a state-affiliated cleric – perhaps recognizing the benefits of a more pragmatic approach as well as the new opportunities afforded by the latest Israeli concessions – bin Baz responded to al-Rifa'i with a *fatwa* (religious legal opinion) that surprised some of his followers: peace with Israel is not only permissible but also a matter of necessity.

In this fatwa, bin Baz argues that since the Israelis are now inclined toward peace, the Palestinians should be similarly inclined. This is in accordance with the Qur'anic commandment, "But if they incline toward peace, you [Prophet] must also incline toward it, and put your trust in God" (8:61). Bin Baz also points to Muhammad's precedent of entering into a truce with his oppressors, the Meccan polytheists. This, the truce of Hudaybiyya, was a pact that appeared to favor the polytheists because, among other things, it stipulated that the Prophet could not accept new converts (or at least male ones) from Mecca into his Medinan community (while Meccan Muslims who were already in Medina could freely choose to leave the Prophet and return to Mecca). Furthermore, bin Baz asserts that – at least for the time being – making peace with Israel benefits the Palestinians and serves the common good.[13]

A little more than two weeks after bin Baz's fatwa first appeared in print, the Kuwait-based newspaper *al-Mujtama'* published a response by al-Qaradawi.[14] In this rejoinder, al-Qaradawi insists that all religious legal opinions should take into account the facts on the ground; in this case, a cleric issuing a fatwa must consult political scientists and diplomats. After consulting such experts, it should become clear, he writes, that Israel is not truly inclined toward peace; this is evident in their refusal to return land they originally confiscated from Palestinians. Thus, one could not justifiably maintain that such a truce serves the common good, as

[11] *Al-Muslimun* 516.
[12] See Reiter, *War, Peace and International Relations in Islam*, 127–128.
[13] *Al-Muslimun* 516.
[14] *Al-Mujtama'* 1133.

it involves Palestinians surrendering territory – and not just any territory, but holy land – that was once theirs. As such, al-Qaradawi invokes
another Qur'anic commandment: "So [believers] do not lose heart and
cry out for peace. It is you who have the upper hand: God is with you"
(47:35). Ironically, al-Qaradawi also quotes a rhetorical question that
the Qur'an attributes to the Children of Israel: "How could we not fight
in God's cause when we and our children have been driven out of our
homeland?" (2:246).

Nearly a month and a half later (and toward the end of the Islamic
holy month of Ramadan), bin Baz published a response to al-Qaradawi
in *al-Mujtama'*.[15] In bin Baz's rejoinder, he reiterates his contention that
there already exists a prophetic precedent for the issue at hand. The truce
of Hudaybiyya, signed just a few years before the Prophet's death, was an
arrangement between Meccan polytheists and Muslims who were forced
out of their homes in Mecca. The Qur'an itself refers to the latter as
"the poor emigrants who were *driven from their homes and possessions*"
(59:8). And yet when the Meccan polytheists inclined toward peace,
Muhammad inclined toward peace and signed the Hudaybiyya truce.

Bin Baz then turns his attention to the Qur'anic commandment, "So
[believers] do not lose heart and cry out for peace. It is you who have the
upper hand: God is with you" (47:35). According to bin Baz, this directive applies to Muslims who are in a position of strength. Thus, given
the relative weakness of the Palestinians, they should seek peace; it is
best for the time being that they retrieve at least some of their land as an
outcome of the peace plan. Remarkably, bin Baz goes on to clarify that
when Muslims are in a superior position, it is *obligatory* that they fight
non-Muslims whenever they can until the latter either accept Islam or
agree to pay the *jizya* tax.

To this, al-Qaradawi produced a relatively lengthy rejoinder, which
was published in the next issue of *al-Mujtama'*.[16] In it he reiterates that
clerics should confer with experts who understand the facts on the ground
before issuing fatwas. He also restates his assertion that Israel is not truly
inclined toward peace: it continues to occupy Palestinian land, establish
new settlements, and amass weapons of mass destruction. And in addition to reaffirming the sanctity of Jerusalem, al-Qaradawi rehashes the
popular conspiracy claim that the Israelis are clandestinely digging tun-
nels in the proximity of the al-Aqsa Mosque in Jerusalem to prepare for

---

[15] *Al-Mujtama'* 1140.
[16] *Al-Mujtama'* 1141.

the rebuilding of the Third Temple. The Israelis, he adds, envision a day in which their nation will extend from the Euphrates to the Nile. Thus, he alleges, they are now calling for peace because they are troubled by Palestinian resistance movements.

Al-Qaradawi dismisses bin Baz's attempt to compare the current peace talks with Muhammad's truce of Hudaybiyya. Bin Baz had stated that the Prophet signed this truce with enemies who had driven him and his followers out of their homes in Mecca. According to al-Qaradawi, however, this is a mischaracterization of what occurred: when the Muslims left Mecca, they were compelled to do so *secretly*, for the Meccan polytheists did not, in fact, want them to leave. Although the Qur'an itself states that the poor Muslim emigrants were "driven from their homes and possessions" (59:8), al-Qaradawi insists that this passage was not intended to be interpreted literally: the Muslims were "driven" out of Mecca by persecution, not physical expulsion. As for the truce of Hudaybiyya, Muhammad's decision to sign this seemingly unfavorable pact was made under exceptional circumstances, in accord with divine inspiration to which only he had access.

Al-Qaradawi proceeds to address bin Baz's interpretation of the Qur'anic statement, "So [believers] do not lose heart and cry out for peace. It is you who have the upper hand: God is with you" (47:35). While bin Baz saw this verse as being addressed to Muslims who occupy a position of strength, al-Qaradawi argues that it actually speaks to Muslims who are in a state of weakness; when the Qur'an declares that Muslims "have the upper hand," it is simply reminding them that they have God on their side. To support this reading, al-Qaradawi points to a similar Qur'anic statement: "Do not lose heart or despair – if you are true believers you have the upper hand" (3:139). As al-Qaradawi observes, this verse appears in the third chapter of the Qur'an, Ali-Imran (The Family of Imran), which, according to Muslim commentators, was revealed after Muhammad's army had been defeated in the second major battle of Islamic history, the Battle of Uhud.

Al-Qaradawi also critiques bin Baz's conception of jihad: if Muslims must constantly fight even peaceable non-Muslim-controlled countries and not "cry out for peace" whenever they are in a position of power, as bin Baz asserts, then according to al-Qaradawi, this would render Muslims morally bankrupt "opportunists"; in this case, their primary objective would be the attainment of supremacy and not simply security. Al-Qaradawi clarifies that what he is calling for is defensive – not aggressive – jihad. Although he recognizes the legitimacy of aggressive jihad, he holds that warfare against nonthreatening, nonrepressive states is generally unjustifiable. Peace is the ideal. But it cannot be pursued if the other party inclines toward aggression and suppression.

What is intriguing about this modern exchange is that when we go beyond the actual positions taken by both scholars and examine their reasoning, we find that bin Baz is hardly the dove some might presume him to be. On account of his call for peace with Israel, bin Laden vehemently criticized bin Baz (in a December 1994 statement that I shall discuss later); so it is tempting to juxtapose these two.[17] But consider the implication of bin Baz's argument: if Muslims are in a position of strength, they must pursue aggressive jihad, presumably until they control the world.

In contrast, al-Qaradawi holds that jihad is only justifiable when the enemy is deemed threatening and/or repressive. This means that, unlike bin Baz, al-Qaradawi – here and elsewhere – effectively advances the argument (articulated by, among others, Sherman A. Jackson) that *conquest-driven* aggressive jihad should generally not be waged in a modern context.[18] Again, al-Qaradawi's call for war against Israel was inspired by his particular, admittedly conspiracy-theory-laden assessment of the facts on the ground – and not, say, the Qur'an's "sword verse."[19] Even his reference to the sanctity of Jerusalem stems from his concern that the holy sites are at risk. As he repeatedly states that clerics must

---

[17] For bin Laden's criticism of bin Baz, see his December 1994 statement on the "Betrayal of Palestine" in bin Laden, *Messages to the World*, 3–14.

[18] This is made clear in al-Qaradawi's two-volume set *Fiqh al-jihad* (Jurisprudence of Jihad). In the latter, however, al-Qaradawi clarifies that aggressive jihad is justifiable if tyrannical rulers prevent Muslims from proselytizing (see, for instance, al-Qaradawi *Fiqh al-jihad*, 1:259). But as Ahmed Al-Dawoody observes, "it seems inconceivable" that Muslims today would declare war on the basis of an inability to proselytize; in fact, "the freedom to practise Islam is more secure in some non-Muslim countries than in a few Muslim ones" (Al-Dawoody, *The Islamic Law of War*, 199).

[19] Although al-Qaradawi often refers to Israelis as simply "the Jews," he insists that his call to war has nothing to do with "Jewishness" (see Reiter, *War, Peace and International Relations in Islam*, 124-127); speaks of the salvation of various categories of non-Muslims, Jews and others (al-Qaradawi, *Fatawa mu'asira*, 3:154-156; see Khalil, *Islam and the Fate of Others*, 131-132); and states that the conflict with Zionism concerns justice and is not simply a religious war (al-Qaradawi, *Fatawa mu'asira*, 3:198-199). In a March 2007 statement, he indicated that he would only recognize the state of Israel if the Israelis recognized a truly sovereign Palestinian state. This statement was posted on al-Qaradawi's official website (www.qaradawi.net) and appears in translation in Reiter, *War, Peace and International Relations in Islam*, 124.

consult experts in political science and diplomacy before issuing fatwas that pertain to political policy, one can only wonder how different his own position might have been had he been exposed to alternative sources of information. In any case, as we shall see later (Chapter 4), what is particularly troubling about al-Qaradawi's doctrine of jihad is his rules for conducting warfare, particularly in the Palestinian context.

CONDUCTING JIHAD JUSTLY

In developing rules for conducting armed jihad, Muslim scholars rely heavily on hadiths and other material outside the Qur'an. This is because the latter makes mostly general statements, such as, "Fight in God's cause against those who fight you, but do not overstep the limits" (2:190). One of the "limits" widely recognized by Muslim scholars, medieval and modern, is that it "is not permissible to kill [the opponents'] women and [prepubescent] children if they are not in direct combat."[20] This prohibition comes directly from the hadith tradition (including, among other sources, the collections of al-Bukhari and Muslim). Muslim scholars invoke other statements ascribed to the Prophet and his followers when expanding on this prohibition, often including the elderly, the blind, the sick, the incapacitated, the mentally disabled, clergy, and individuals such as farmers, craftsmen, and traders who do not engage in fighting – even if they are paid to do services on the battlefield.[21]

As one might infer, however, these categories were not unanimously agreed upon. For instance, a minority of scholars maintained that it would be permissible to attack all non-Muslim men who were neither under Muslim rule nor protected by a truce.[22] The twelfth-century scholar al-Kasani (d. 1191) held that only enemy men who are capable of fighting may be targeted in battle; but even in the case of women and children, if civilians incite warfare against Muslim forces, reveal their hiding places, or occupy authoritative roles and benefit enemy forces with their judgment, they may be killed.[23] Meanwhile, various scholars belonging

[20] Al-Akiti, *Defending the Transgressed*, 20.

[21] See Peters (ed.), *Jihad in Classical and Modern Islam*, 33–35 (ibn Rushd's *al-Bidaya*); Nasr (ed.), *The Study Quran*, 84 (commentary on Qur'an 2:190–194); and Al-Dawoody, *The Islamic Law of War*, 112–116.

[22] See Peters (ed.), *Jihad in Classical and Modern Islam*, 33–35 (ibn Rushd's *al-Bidaya*); and Al-Dawoody, *The Islamic Law of War*, 81, 111.

[23] Al-Kasani, *Bada'i' al-sana'i'*, 9:399 (cited and discussed in Syed, "Jihad in Classical Islamic Legal and Moral Thought," 148–149).

to the Sunni Maliki school of thought maintained that even women who directly aid and abet enemy forces and attack Muslim soldiers by throwing stones at them may not be targeted.[24]

We encounter additional tensions in modern jihad discourse. As we shall see, radicals such as bin Laden and some controversial clerics expand the category of "combatants" beyond medieval standards to include all male and female citizens of nations deemed threatening.[25] Meanwhile, the Oxford-based Malaysian scholar Muhammad Afifi al-Akiti asserts that, according to a popular Islamic legal opinion, even in the midst of a "valid war," one must not attack hostile enemy soldiers who are "off-duty," not engaged in combat, and not occupying a "valid military target," that is, a battlefield or military base.[26]

When fighting enemy combatants who are intermingled with civilians, however, the most popular opinion has long been that the responsibility for the "collateral" deaths falls on the enemy, not on the Muslim fighters. This position is grounded in a well-known hadith (versions of which appear in the collections of al-Bukhari and Muslim) in which one of Muhammad's companions asks him whether it would be permissible to attack an enemy force at night, when its affiliated noncombatants could be harmed collaterally. The Prophet responds in the affirmative: "they are of them." Interestingly, however, some scholars hold that this hadith was abrogated, and according to another widely accepted hadith (recorded by al-Bukhari), "whenever the Prophet reached a people by night, he never started an attack until it was morning."[27]

Another precedent invoked for the legitimization of collateral damage comes from a biographical account of Muhammad's siege of a fortress in the Arabian city of Ta'if in 630. According to this account, when Muslim forces were unable to penetrate the walls protecting the enemy Thaqif tribe, the Prophet permitted the use of a mangonel (a catapult used to throw large stones); however, this turned out to be a brief, ineffectual attempt to breach the well-guarded fortifications. In fact, it is not clear that the mangonel the Muslims constructed was put to use in the first place, and some of the individuals attempting to operate it were killed

---

[24] See al-Dardir, *al-Sharh al-kabir*, 2:176; and Al-Dawoody, *The Islamic Law of War*, 113.

[25] The term "combatant" (*al-muqatila*) has long been used in the Islamic tradition and appears in certain hadiths and prophetic biographies. See, for instance, note 35 in what follows.

[26] Al-Akiti, *Defending the Transgressed*, 33–34.

[27] Both of these hadiths are translated and discussed in Al-Dawoody, *The Islamic Law of War*, 119. My translation of the Prophet's response in the first hadith differs slightly from that of Al-Dawoody, who renders it, "they are *from* them" (*minhum*) (emphasis added). On the abrogation claim, see al-Qaradawi, *Fiqh al-jihad*, 1:751–752.

when the forces of Thaqif attacked them with hot iron and arrows.[28] The Muslim army subsequently continued to lay siege to Ta'if (without the use of mangonels), and the Thaqif eventually surrendered. Considering that our sources portray Muhammad as having generally avoided using weapons of mass destruction, various Muslim scholars only permitted their use in cases of self-defense and "necessity" (*darura*).[29]

The principle of necessity is widely recognized in Islamic law, though scholars disagree on its precise conditions and parameters. If Muslim forces feel threatened – as they would in a defensive jihad – they could justifiably invoke necessity to legitimize *certain* actions that would otherwise be forbidden. According to many scholars, one such action would be to attack – but not exclusively target – noncombatants (including Muslim ones) who are used as human shields by a threatening enemy.[30] Returning to weapons of mass destruction, necessity could also be invoked to justify their use if this might deter an enemy force that has already resorted to using such weapons – a case of reciprocity.

Proponents of reciprocal retaliation typically point to Qur'anic statements such as, "So if anyone commits aggression against you, attack him as he attacked you" (2:194); "fight the polytheists all together as they fight you all together" (9:36); "God will help those who retaliate against an aggressive act merely with its like and are then wronged again" (22:60); and "If you [believers] respond to an attack, make your response proportionate" (16:126). For various medieval scholars, this principle of reciprocity, predicated on necessity, "not only permitted but *required* Muslims to resort to rather indiscriminate and destructive

---

[28] See al-Waqidi, *The Kitab al-Maghazi of al-Waqidi*, 3:927–928; ibn Kathir, *al-Sira al-nabawiyya*, 3:658–659; Peters (ed.), *Jihad in Classical and Modern Islam*, 36 (ibn Rushd's *al-Bidaya*); Al-Dawoody, *The Islamic Law of War*, 123–124; and Hashmi, "Ethics and Weapons of Mass Destruction," 328. In al-Waqidi's classical record of the Prophet's battles (the *Maghazi*), we read that it was Muhammad's Persian companion Salman al-Farisi who initially suggested the use of a mangonel at Ta'if; he reportedly told the Prophet that mangonels were used in Persia to shoot at enemy fortresses (al-Waqidi, *The Kitab al-Maghazi of al-Waqidi*, 3:927).

[29] See Abou El Fadl, "The Rules of Killing at War," 156. Here the Muslim scholar and academic Khaled Abou El Fadl notes that the use of fire was especially controversial among medieval Muslim jurists (for more on this point, see Peters [ed.], *Jihad in Classical and Modern Islam*, 35–36 [ibn Rushd's *al-Bidaya*]). Incidentally, Abou El Fadl also observes that although Muslim scholars generally regarded wars against fellow Muslims as police actions, there exist "remarkable similarities in the discursive practice of the classical jurists on fighting Muslims and non-Muslims."

[30] See, for instance, al-Tabari, *Kitab al-jihad*, 5–7; and Al-Dawoody, *The Islamic Law of War*, 116–118.

methods" – this *excludes* the specific targeting of innocents – "if the enemy initiated their use."[31]

The scriptural basis for this particular notion of obligatory reciprocity, however, is not as firm as one might think. For instance, the final passage cited in the previous paragraph (16:126) continues, "but it is best to stand fast. So [Prophet] be steadfast: your steadfastness comes only from God. Do not grieve over them; do not be distressed by their scheming, for God is with those who are mindful of Him and who do good" (16:126–128). According to most of the classical commentaries on the Qur'an, this passage was revealed after the Meccan polytheists had killed and muti-lated many Muslims, including Muhammad's beloved uncle Hamza, in the Battle of Uhud. In a moment of anger, Muhammad is said to have made an oath to kill and mutilate many of the polytheists; some of his followers made similar oaths. It was in response to such oaths that the passage was reportedly revealed: it was intended both to *limit* any pos-sible retaliation so that it would be proportionate and to encourage the Prophet to be patient so that he would *refrain* from revenge altogether. Indeed, Muhammad subsequently atoned for his oath and even forgave Hamza's killer.[32] Incidentally, he also reportedly issued general prohib-itions against the mutilation of humans and animals and even instructed his followers to try to avoid striking the enemy's face during battle.[33]

---

[31] Hashmi, "Ethics and Weapons of Mass Destruction," 330 (emphasis added). Islamic pol-itical philosophy scholar Sohail Hashmi opines, "The use in war of any WMD [weapon of mass destruction] should be rejected by Muslims, even as purely second-strike weap-ons. Retaliating with chemical, biological, and nuclear weapons against an unscrupulous enemy who initiates their use is not likely to deter the enemy from further use ... Their use in retaliation can only be seen as an inhumane punishment ... The attitude common-place among early Muslim theorists that the responsibility for the death of enemy non-combatants lies with the enemy commanders who refused to remove them from harm's way cannot be validly applied in the age of WMD" (Hashmi, "Ethics and Weapons of Mass Destruction," 335).

[32] See Nasr (ed.), *The Study Quran*, 691–692 (commentary on Qur'an 16:126–128).

[33] These prohibitions appear in numerous hadith collections. Most scholars of Islamic law held that torture of enemy soldiers is also generally forbidden (see Abou El Fadl, "The Rules of Killing at War," 156). For surveys of the various scholarly views concerning the destruction of enemy property and possessions, see Peters (ed.), *Jihad in Classical and Modern Islam*, 36–37 (ibn Rushd's *al-Bidaya*); and Al-Dawoody, *The Islamic Law of War*, 126–129. As Al-Dawoody notes, Muslim sources offer "two conflicting incidents": (1) a report of Muhammad cutting down the palm trees of an enemy tribe during a siege to compel them to surrender and (2) a report of Muhammad's companion and first polit-ical successor (or caliph) Abu Bakr instructing his army commander not to destroy build-ings, harm palm and other fruit-bearing trees, or slaughter animals "except for food."

The notion that Muslims should not blindly imitate the wartime practices of their enemies is made explicit in a well-known account involving
the first caliph (the political successor to Muhammad), Abu Bakr (r. 632 to
634). When one of his followers presented him with the decapitated head
of a Byzantine leader, Abu Bakr rebuked him. When the follower com-
mented that such was the practice of their enemies, Abu Bakr retorted,
"Do you take your guidance from the Persians and the Byzantines?"[34] It
is, therefore, *in spite of* such sentiments and likely owing to pragmatic
considerations that reciprocity became a widely invoked legal principle.

As for the treatment of prisoners of war – at least those not found
guilty of any major crime, such as treason – some scholars held that
"under no circumstances" could they be executed and that this was the
consensus view of Muhammad's companions. Most scholars, however,
gravitated toward a "functional approach" that left this decision to the
discretion of the Muslim ruler.[35] But although lying to the enemy is generally permitted during warfare,[36] if enemy combatants are offered security
in return for their surrender, this offer must be honored, and they cannot
be harmed.[37]

---

[34] Al-Bayhaqi, *al-Sunan al-kubra*, 9:223. See al-Qarafi, *al-Dhakhira*, 3:408; and Abu Id,
al-'Alaqat al-kharijiyya fi dawlat al-khilafa, 222.

[35] Abou El Fadl, "The Rules of Killing at War," 152–153. Also see Peters (ed.), *Jihad in
Classical and Modern Islam*, 31–32 (ibn Rushd's *al-Bidaya*); and Al-Dawoody, *The
Islamic Law of War*, 136–139. As Abou El Fadl notes, "The ruler is granted discretion over the execution of male prisoners of a fighting age because of the risk that such
males pose to Muslims. Arguably, people who are capable of fighting pose a continuing
threat to Muslims, and the ruler is entrusted to evaluate that risk and act on it" (Abou
El Fadl, "The Rules of Killing at War," 153). According to hadiths appearing in, among
other sources, the collections of al-Bukhari and Muslim, following the perilous Battle of
the Ditch, Muhammad oversaw the execution of the "combatants" (*muqatila*) – some
accounts say "men" (*rijal*) – of the Jewish tribe of Banu Qurayza who were taken as
prisoners after they had betrayed and "fought" (*harabat Qurayza*) the Prophet. (Some of
Banu Qurayza's men sought Muhammad's protection and were spared; we are informed
that they converted to Islam.) In their treatment of the same incident, the classical biographies of the Prophet claim that hundreds (the precise numbers vary widely) of imprisoned Banu Qurayza males of a fighting age were executed – a claim that is disputed by
some modern scholars (see, for instance, Ahmad, *Muhammad and the Jews*, chapter 4;
and Arafat, "New Light on the Story of Banu Qurayza and the Jews of Medina"; cf.
Kister, "The Massacre of the Banu Qurayza").

[36] There is, of course, nothing particularly "Islamic" about the tactic of deceiving the enemy
in battle. This age-old war tactic is promoted in, among other works, the famous ancient
Chinese military treatise *The Art of War*, attributed to Sun Tzu (d. 544 BCE): "All warfare is based on deception" (chapter 1, verse 18).

[37] See Peters (ed.), *Jihad in Classical and Modern Islam*, 32–33 (ibn Rushd's *al-Bidaya*); and
Abou El Fadl, "The Rules of Killing at War," 156.

One final rule of armed jihad worth mentioning here pertains to the prelude to war. In line with the example of the earliest Muslims, various scholars held that, before launching a military campaign, Muslim forces must give a notice of attack and offer their non-Muslim enemies an opportunity to convert to Islam or – in the case of Jews, Christians, and arguably many others – to accept Muslim rule and enjoy limited rights by paying the *jizya* tax.[38]

Notwithstanding such particularities, to quote Islamic legal scholar Ahmad Atif Ahmad, "jihad theories address the same puzzling issues that engaged non-Muslim theorists of war in ancient, medieval, and modern times." To Ahmad's mind, however, because Muslim scholars were often not directly tied to state apparatuses, "jihad jurisprudence provides an example of lesser degrees of comfort with violence than many other examples of war theorization."[39] And yet Ahmad recognizes an unfortunate reality: a study of the past reveals that "theories of legitimate war hardly regulate the practice of actual wars or adequately describe historical wars."[40] Nevertheless, these "theories" – the rules of jihad in the case of Muslims – remain critical, for they offer a finite spectrum of criteria for assessing the moral and/or legal status of armed conflicts.

---

[38] See Peters (ed.), *Jihad in Classical and Modern Islam*, 37–38 (ibn Rushd's *al-Bidaya*); and Ahmad, *Islam, Modernity, Violence, and Everyday Life*, 124–125, 128–129, 135.

[39] Ahmad, *Islam, Modernity, Violence, and Everyday Life*, 8. For a general comparison of Muslim and Western conceptions of "just war," see Blankinship, "Parity of Muslim and Western Concepts of Just War."

[40] Ahmad, *Islam, Modernity, Violence, and Everyday Life*, 118.

PART II

VIOLENT RADICALISM: BIN LADEN, 9/11, AND ISIS

Before the recent atrocities committed by ISIS, there were the haunting events of Tuesday, September 11, 2001. On a day when nearly three thousand civilians were killed in the Twin Towers of the World Trade Center, the Pentagon, and a field in Pennsylvania, we learned that the perpetrators of the tragedy were Muslims who claimed to be acting in the name of Islam. What is more, televised images of some Muslims overseas rejoicing in the streets left indelible imprints in the minds of countless Westerners. Many were left to wonder how adherents of one of the world's largest religions could condone and even celebrate such barbarity and evil. English translations of the Qur'an quickly became bestsellers, and politicians and pundits throughout the world had much to say about the violent – or peaceful – nature of Islam. Occupying center stage in this global drama was the figure behind 9/11, Osama bin Laden.

3

"So We Kill Their Innocents"

Bin Laden and 9/11

I shall lead my steed
and hurl us both at the target.
Oh Lord, if my end is nigh,
may my tomb not be draped
in green mantles.
No, let it be the belly of an eagle,
perched up on high with his kin.
So let me be a martyr,
dwelling in a high mountain pass
among a band of knights who,
united in devotion to God,
descend to face armies.
When they leave this world,
they leave trouble behind,
and meet their Day of Judgment,
as told in the Scriptures.[1]

    – *Osama bin Laden, Eid al-Adha sermon,*
    February 14, 2003

On May 2, 2011, shortly after midnight, a United States special forces military unit penetrated the secret residence of Osama bin Laden in Abbottabad, Pakistan. Following an intense firefight, the unit achieved its objective of killing the previously elusive bin Laden. Less than twenty-four hours later, the body of one of the most wanted figures in modern history was buried at sea.

---

[1] Bin Laden, *Messages to the World*, 205.

As he presumably imagined it, bin Laden achieved his objective of martyrdom. In the eyes of many of his countrymen and coreligionists, however, this was the inglorious final chapter of a disturbing life story. The purpose of the present chapter is to examine relevant aspects of this life story, paying special attention to bin Laden's statements regarding his most infamous scheme.

OSAMA

Osama bin Muhammad bin Awad bin Laden was born in Riyadh on March 10, 1957. His father Muhammad was a Yemeni laborer who had spent most of his life in Saudi Arabia and, despite his humble origins, established both a successful construction company and close ties with the Saudi royal family. When his plane tragically crashed in 1967, he left behind a fortune worth billions of dollars. Having married and divorced dozens of women, he fathered well over fifty children. Osama's mother was a Syrian woman named Hamida Ibrahim (also known as Alia Ghanem), and her association with Muhammad was short lived, Osama being their only shared child. She subsequently married another Yemeni and gave birth to four other children.

Although he was close to his mother, Osama seemed destined to follow in his father's footsteps. After spending some time in Jeddah at the Management and Economics School at King Abdulaziz University (he evidently never graduated), he joined his family's construction business and proved to be an effective manager and amassed some wealth.

Religion was undoubtedly an important dimension of bin Laden's life, and not simply because he spent much of his youth residing in the sacred cities of Mecca and Medina. Although he was never formally trained in Islamic studies, he was in frequent contact with various scholars of Islam, particularly those of the conservative Salafi and Wahhabi traditions, and came to acquire a reputation of being devout and knowledgeable. Aside from the Prophet Muhammad and his companions, bin Laden was greatly inspired by Salah al-Din al-Ayyubi (also known as Saladin; d. 1193), the famous warrior who reclaimed Jerusalem from the Crusaders, and ibn Taymiyya (d. 1328), an influential scholar-warrior whose controversial views led to his imprisonment in Egypt and Syria. Bin Laden revered and sought to emulate those willing to sacrifice their well-being for the sake of the truth and in defense of their fellow Muslims.[2]

---

[2] My biographical sketch of bin Laden in this chapter draws much from Michael Scheuer's 2011 book *Osama Bin Laden*. Although not without its shortcomings, this is an

THE AFGHAN STRUGGLE

It was precisely this spirit of sacrifice that inspired bin Laden to relocate to Pakistan to support his Muslim brethren in neighboring Afghanistan shortly after the 1979 Soviet invasion. Making use of his wealth, Saudi connections, and technical and managerial skills, bin Laden went to great lengths to support the Afghan *mujahidin* (literally, "those who engage in jihad"). In 1984, he joined forces with Abdullah Azzam (d. 1989), a Palestinian Islamist and scholar of Islamic law.[3] Together they founded Maktab al-Khadamat ("Services Bureau"), an organization that recruited foreign *mujahidin* and raised both awareness and funds in support of the Afghan Muslim struggle against communism – a struggle, incidentally, that did not involve suicide missions. Although bin Laden and Azzam did not always see eye to eye, it would appear that they continued to support each other until Azzam's mysterious assassination in 1989.

The year 1989 also marked the official end of the failed Soviet occupation of Afghanistan. The outcome of this decade-long struggle contributed to bin Laden's growing belief that armed jihad was necessary for the future of Islam. After all, bin Laden had just finished "fighting Soviets who had no interest in negotiations and left Afghanistan only because victory was not in sight and their economy was being ravaged by the cost of war."[4] And the victors included not only Afghans (the obvious majority) but also Muslims of different ethnicities and nationalities – Muslims united under the banner of Islam.

But this struggle also attracted "a wide variety of radicals from Muslim antigovernmental and resistance movements and fused them

---

important study, one that builds upon and serves as a corrective to earlier works on bin Laden, including Lawrence Wright's *The Looming Tower* and Scheuer's own *Through Our Enemies' Eyes*. In the latter (92–93, 114, 392), Scheuer makes the common assertion that bin Laden was profoundly influenced by the Egyptian Islamist thinker Sayyid Qutb (d. 1966) (erroneously identified as Qutb's brother Muhammad, whom bin Laden knew personally). Scheuer convincingly repudiates this idea in *Osama Bin Laden*, 41–42. According to Fawaz Gerges, although bin Laden and his associate Ayman al-Zawahiri praised Qutb, they "twisted" his ideas "to suit their purposes ... Qutb never called for a confrontation with the West and instead exhorted [his followers] to strike at Arab rulers who conspired with Islam's external enemies and allowed them to infiltrate Muslim lands ... [H]e showed no interest in ... the targeting of Western powers" (Gerges, *The Rise and Fall of Al-Qaeda*, 31–32).

[3] Although bin Laden may have encountered Azzam in Saudi Arabia before the Afghan war, there is no concrete evidence of such an encounter (see Scheuer, *Osama Bin Laden*, 53).

[4] Scheuer, *Osama Bin Laden*, 70.

together."[5] It would seem that shortly before the formal conclusion of the war, bin Laden and other Islamists laid the ideological foundations for an insurgent organization that eventually came to be known as al-Qaeda ("the Base").[6] Building on the success of the Afghan struggle, bin Laden now sought to promote, sponsor, and facilitate armed jihad throughout the world, wherever it was needed. In a 1989 interview, bin Laden proclaimed,

> It is due to God's blessing that we are returning to jihad after long years of negligence and after the Islamic holy sites have been taken; Muslim women were taken prisoner; and their land and honor were violated ... God has blessed us with taking jihad in our hands in order to make up for our misdeeds when we abandoned religion in the past ... I would like to advise my brother Muslims in all parts of the East and West to take the initiative and leave what they are doing to assist in raising the banner of jihad for the cause of God ... May God accept our and your prayers and our urging of believers to perform jihad in order to deter the infidel forces and be truthful.[7]

Here we encounter themes that would reappear in bin Laden's later statements, including the idea that Muslims can only blame themselves for their failings and that they must partake in defensive jihad for the sake of protection and in order to reclaim lands – most notably sacred ones – that were taken from them.[8] (Given that bin Laden made this statement in the late 1980s, before the 1991 Gulf War, we can assume that his reference to "Islamic holy sites" pertains, at the very least, to Jerusalem, home of al-Aqsa Mosque and the Dome of the Rock.)

By the end of the 1980s, with reports circulating about the wealthy bin Laden's sacrifices and heroics in war, he had become renowned in Saudi Arabia. Having completed his mission in Pakistan and Afghanistan, he returned to his home country a star. And yet, just a few years later, he was stripped of his Saudi citizenship.

---

[5] Cook, *Understanding Jihad*, 128.

[6] As Gerges notes, "Although the evidence is sketchy and inconclusive, in 1988 in Peshawar, bin Laden and a dozen or so close associates appeared to have set up al-Qaeda al-Askariya, or 'a training base' – as bin Laden subsequently recalled – 'and that is where the name came from'." In any case, the "formal launch" of the organization known as al-Qaeda was in 1998 (Gerges, *The Rise and Fall of Al-Qaeda*, 50, 56).

[7] Scheuer, *Osama Bin Laden*, 76–77. As Scheuer notes, this statement was made by bin Laden in an interview appearing in a 1989 documentary film called *The Arab Ansar in Afghanistan*. This film was issued in 2006 by Islamic Muhajirun Network.

[8] Scheuer, *Osama Bin Laden*, 77.

DEFENDING ARABIA

Despite their different perspectives, bin Laden had remained loyal to the Saudi royal family. Throughout the early 1990s, however, that loyalty was replaced by animosity. Bin Laden began to view the Saudi establishment – including state-affiliated religious scholars – as hypocritical, misguided, corrupt, and greedy: while the Saudis lauded and supported the fight against communism in Afghanistan, they refused to do the same in Yemen; when certain scholars of Islam decried what they perceived to be corruption of the Saudi regime, they were imprisoned; and despite the royal family's enormous wealth (acquired in part through means bin Laden considered usurious and therefore sinful), government social services often proved to be inadequate.

What truly infuriated bin Laden, however, was the regime's response to the Iraqi invasion of neighboring Kuwait in August 1990. Bin Laden offered to protect his home country, as he was confident in his ability to mobilize fellow veterans of the Soviet–Afghan War and manage the Saudi defense. But not only did the royal family turn him down, they invited the United States military in his stead – a decision that was legitimized by the then Saudi grand mufti Abdulaziz bin Baz (d. 1999). Before long, the United States had set up various bases throughout the Saudi kingdom and other parts of the Arabian peninsula.

To understand why the Saudi grand mufti – a cleric – felt compelled to address this issue in the first place, one must appreciate the religious significance of Arabia. A segment of the Muslim population considers the entirety of the Arabian peninsula to be an Islamic sanctuary. This idea can be traced back to a hadith in which – according to one popular version of the account – Muhammad expresses his intention to permit only Muslims to reside in the "peninsula of the Arabs" (*jazirat al-'Arab*).[9] Considering the understanding and precedent of the early caliphs, however, the prevailing view of Muslim scholars is that this "peninsula" corresponds roughly to the Hijaz, a sensitive region in the western part of the Arabian peninsula that encompasses Mecca and Medina.[10]

Be that as it may, in a 1997 interview, bin Laden declared, "In our religion, it is not permissible for any non-Muslim to stay in our country."[11]

---

[9] This particular account appears in, among other sources, the hadith collection of (the scholar named) Muslim.

[10] On the prevailing medieval Muslim understanding of the "peninsula of the Arabs," see Brown, *Misquoting Muhammad*, 127.

[11] Bin Laden, *Messages to the World*, 47.

Given that non-Muslim civilians had long resided in various parts of Saudi Arabia (and other countries of the Arabian peninsula), it would seem that what most bothered bin Laden was the introduction of American soldiers to the region.[12] And although most of these soldiers operated near the eastern coast of the Arabian peninsula immediately before, during, and long after the 1991 Gulf War (most left in 2003), over several months in 1990 and 1991, the American armed forces made use of air bases in the Hijaz, not far from Mecca and Medina. According to the Saudi regime, this was a temporary, religiously permissible accommodation, and one that was justified on the basis of necessity.[13]

In any case, shortly after the monarchy's 1990 decision to invite the United States to Saudi Arabia, an increasingly vocal bin Laden warned the regime that the American forces would never leave.[14] Around this time, the Saudi military raided a farm near Jeddah owned by bin Laden, who was by then something of a nuisance to the monarchy. Dismayed and disillusioned, bin Laden decided to leave his home country. Perhaps he envisioned himself one day returning a hero once again; but there would be no homecoming after this.

He made his way back to Pakistan only to find dissension and disorder among the Afghan insurgents. He quickly realized he would need to plant roots elsewhere. Toward the end of 1991, he and his family relocated to Sudan and remained there until 1996. Welcomed by the controversial Islamist leader Hasan al-Turabi (d. 2016), bin Laden wasted little time creating new wealth using the skills he first acquired working in his father's business. He also began planning attacks on the United States military.

ANTAGONISM

Bin Laden came to loathe the United States, largely because of its foreign policy. As we shall soon see, bin Laden compiled a laundry list of

[12] In a 2004 statement, bin Laden criticized the Saudi regime for allowing "Muhammad's peninsula to be occupied by the Jews and Christians, letting them take control and giving them military bases" (bin Laden, *Messages to the World*, 264).

[13] The notion that non-Muslims may enter the Hijaz can be traced back to early Islam. During the reign of the second caliph Umar (who ruled from 634 to 644), for instance, Jewish, Christian, and Zoroastrian merchants were reportedly permitted to remain in Medina for up to three days every year (Brown, *Misquoting Muhammad*, 127).

[14] Scheuer, *Osama Bin Laden*, 81.

grievances against the world's lone remaining superpower. From his personal experience, he felt that the United States had misled and taken advantage of the Afghan *mujahidin*: after arming and supporting them,[15] once the Soviets left Afghanistan, the United States pushed for a non-Islamist regime that would include former Afghan communists. In short, the United States came to prefer former enemies over former allies; from bin Laden's perspective, this was a manifest betrayal. And now with the United States positioned inside Saudi Arabia, bin Laden held that the former was influencing and manipulating the latter. Drawing on lessons he learned from the Soviet–Afghan War, bin Laden became convinced that violence was necessary to curb American imperialism.

In 1992, the United States commenced a multinational initiative called Operation Restore Hope in war-torn Somalia. The stated objective of this operation was to establish security and facilitate the delivery of humanitarian relief. Ever distrustful of America's intentions, bin Laden began assisting anti-American forces in the country. He also commissioned unsuccessful attacks on Somalia-bound American soldiers staying in hotels in Aden, Yemen – bombings that nonetheless led to civilian casualties, including the death of an Austrian tourist and a hotel employee.[16]

To be sure, bin Laden was still deeply troubled by his "near enemy," the Saudi establishment.[17] But he clung to the hope that his fellow Saudis would eventually mend their country. In 1994, he established the Advice and Reform Committee (ARC) and, through a London office, disseminated ARC communiqués that were extremely critical of Saudi leaders. It was around this time that King Fahd revoked bin Laden's Saudi citizenship.

---

[15] This support included strong words of encouragement: at the turn of the 1980s, for instance, the then United States National Security Advisor Zbigniew Brzezinski (d. 2017) told a group of *mujahidin* at the Afghan–Pakistan border, "your cause is right and God is on your side" (Glad, *An Outsider in the White House*, 212; "CNN Presents: Soldiers of God"; "Zbigniew Brzezinski to the Mujahideen").

[16] Several years later, in March 1997, bin Laden declared, "Muslims do not believe the US allegations that they came to save the Somalis. A man with human feelings in his heart does not distinguish between a child killed in Palestine or in Lebanon, in Iraq or in Bosnia. So how can we believe your claims that you came to save our children in Somalia while you kill our children in all of those places?" (bin Laden, *Messages to the World*, 54).

[17] The terms "near enemy" and "far enemy" were popularized by the Egyptian radical Islamist Muhammad Abdul Salam Faraj (d. 1982), author of the infamous pamphlet *al-Farida al-gha'iba* (The Neglected Duty). For Faraj, the "near enemy" was local Muslim regimes – Faraj's primary targets – whereas the "far enemy" included entities such as the United States and Britain.

In the ARC's communiqués, bin Laden reproaches prominent Saudi figures for their stances concerning non-Muslim enemies. Consider, for instance, bin Laden's open letter to the grand mufti bin Baz, dated December 29, 1994. In response to bin Baz's backing of the Oslo Accords between Israel and the Palestine Liberation Organization – a reversal of his 1989 call for armed jihad against Israel – bin Laden declares that the "current Jewish enemy is not an enemy settled in his own original country fighting in its defense until he gains a peace agreement, but an attacking enemy and a corrupter of religion and the world." Thus, the "legal duty" is to wage jihad in defense of the "poor men, women, and children" of Palestine "who have nowhere to go," so that their homeland "may be completely liberated and returned to Islamic sovereignty."[18]

Furthermore, with American forces still in Saudi Arabia, years after the conclusion of the 1991 Gulf War, bin Laden offers the following message of warning to Saudi clerics:

This aggression has reached such a catastrophic and disastrous point as to have brought about a calamity unprecedented in the history of our *umma* [Muslim community], namely the invasion ... of the Arabian peninsula and Saudi Arabia, the home of the Noble Ka'ba, the Sacred House of God, the Muslim's direction of prayer, the Noble Sanctuary of the Prophet, and the city of God's Messenger, where the Prophetic revelation was received.

This momentous event is unprecedented both in pagan and Islamic history. For the first time, the Crusaders have managed to achieve their historic ambitions and dreams against our Islamic *umma*, gaining control over the Islamic holy places and the Holy Sanctuaries, and hegemony over the wealth and riches of our *umma*, turning the Arabian peninsula into the biggest air, land, and sea base in the region.[19]

Bin Laden goes on to call for a defensive jihad and reminds his audience of the adversities of this life: "*jihad* will go on until the Day of Judgment."[20]

Having recognized the threat bin Laden was becoming, in 1996, the United States pressured Sudan to expel him. With his options limited, bin

[18] Bin Laden, *Messages to the World*, 9.
[19] Bin Laden, *Messages to the World*, 15–16. This undated statement was issued sometime in the mid-1990s. It was during this period that radicals bombed American targets in the Saudi cities of Riyadh and Khobar. Although bin Laden was not implicated in these bombings, he celebrated the attackers and referred to them as martyrs (see, for instance, bin Laden, *Messages to the World*, 36–38).
[20] Bin Laden, *Messages to the World*, 19.

Laden chose to return to the site of his wartime glory, Afghanistan, and revive his relationships with the *mujahidin*. Having come to the conclusion that little progress could be made in Muslim-majority countries as long as the United States continued to exert its influence, bin Laden was now determined to devote much of his attention to the source of his problem.

Shortly after his arrival in Jalalabad, Afghanistan, bin Laden issued "A Declaration of *Jihad* against the Americans Occupying the Land of the Two Holy Sanctuaries." In this August 1996 statement, typically called the "Ladenese Epistle" and originally published by the London-based Arabic newspaper *al-Quds al-'Arabi*, bin Laden makes the case for a defensive jihad against the United States – "occupiers" of Saudi Arabia, home of Islam's most sacred cities, Mecca and Medina – as well as America's close ally, Israel – "occupiers" of a third sacred city, Jerusalem.

BIN LADEN'S CASE FOR WAR

Before considering the steps bin Laden took to justify 9/11, we shall flash forward to October 2002, when a widely circulated statement attributed to bin Laden and addressed to Americans appeared online. Although its authenticity is contested, this statement offers an adequate summary of bin Laden's grievances – as expressed in various proclamations and interviews – against the United States:

(1) The United States military occupies various Muslim-majority countries.

(2) The United States strongly supports unjust Muslim leaders who oppress their own people and fail to uphold Islamic law.

(3) The United States steals Muslim wealth and oil "at paltry prices" because of its "international influence and military threats" – the "biggest theft ever witnessed by mankind."

(4) American foreign policy tends to support the oppression and killing of Muslims, and American sanctions against Iraq have led to the deaths of "more than 1.5 million Iraqi children." (While this figure is likely exaggerated, it is widely recognized that a great many Iraqi children passed away during the course of the 1990–2003 United Nations Security Council sanctions on Saddam Hussein's Iraq. Of course each side points to the other as the ultimate cause of these deaths.)

(5) The United States is wholly devoted to Israel and supports its occupation of Palestinian land, oppression of Palestinians, and aggression against neighboring countries, most notably Lebanon.[21]

Some of these grievances appear in the 1996 Ladenese Epistle:

It is no secret to you, my brothers, that the people of Islam have been afflicted with oppression, hostility, and injustice by the Judeo-Christian alliance and its supporters. This shows our enemies' belief that Muslims' blood is the cheapest and that their property and wealth is merely loot. Your blood has been spilt in Palestine and Iraq, and the horrific image of the [April 1996 Israeli] massacre in Qana in Lebanon[22] are still fresh in people's minds. The massacres that have taken place in Tajikistan, Burma, Kashmir, Assam, the Philippines, [Patani], Ogaden, Somalia, Eritrea, Chechnya, and Bosnia-Herzegovina send shivers down our spines and stir up our passions. All this has happened before the eyes and ears of the world but the blatant imperial arrogance of America, under the cover of the immoral United Nations, has prevented the dispossessed from arming themselves.[23]

Several weeks after the publication of the Ladenese Epistle, bin Laden was interviewed by the Australian Muslim journal *Nida'ul Islam*. While denying that he and his associates were engaging in terrorist activity, bin Laden presented the United States and Israel as the "real" terrorists. In his words, they accuse "others of their own affliction in order to fool the masses." He then pointed to "the recent Qana massacre," the sanctions against Iraq, and "their withholding of arms from the Muslims of Bosnia-Herzegovina, leaving them prey to the Christian Serbians who massacred and raped in a manner not seen in contemporary history." He also mentioned "the deliberate, premeditated dropping" of atomic bombs "on cities with their entire populations of children, elderly, and women, as was the case with Hiroshima and Nagasaki." In contrast, he proclaimed, the Afghan jihad "was unstained with any blood of innocent people, despite

---

[21] Bin Laden, *Messages to the World*, 162–164. On the dubious authenticity of the October 2002 Internet statement (which was published in English in November 2002), see Bergen, *The Osama bin Laden I Know*, xxxii. Bruce Lawrence (ed.) seems to regard the statement as genuine but speculates that bin Laden's "associates may have contributed to its composition" (bin Laden, *Messages to the World*, 160).

[22] This is a reference to the Israeli shelling of a United Nations base in southern Lebanon, which occurred during heavy fighting between Israel and Hezbollah and resulted in more than a hundred civilian deaths.

[23] Bin Laden, *Messages to the World*, 25. This passage comes from an abbreviated translation of the Ladenese Epistle. For a complete English transcript, see bin Laden, *Osama Bin Laden*, 32–58.

the inhuman Russian campaign against our women, our children, and our brothers."[24]

In a December 1998 interview with the Doha-based television network Al Jazeera, bin Laden elaborated, insisting that there is nothing uniquely Islamic about defending one's people:

It is not acceptable in such a struggle as this that he [the Crusader][25] should attack and enter my land and holy sanctuaries, and plunder Muslims' oil, and then when he encounters any resistance from Muslims, to label them terrorists. This is stupidity, or considering others stupid. We believe that it is our legal duty to resist this occupation with all our might, and punish it in the same way as it punishes us ...

[W]hat is wrong with resisting those who attack you? All religious communities have such a principle, for example these Buddhists, both the North Koreans and Vietnamese who fought America. This is a legal right ...[26]

As such, resistance to the American "occupation" of the Arabian peninsula should be expected, whatever the religion of the peninsula's inhabitants:

[I]f God had not blessed us with Islam then our ancestors in the pagan age would not have let these people come either – not so that these infidel asses can come using as their excuse this invitation that wouldn't even fool a child ... [W]e are now in the ninth year, and the Americans are all lying, saying "We have interests in the region, and we will not move before we can guarantee them."[27]

Along these lines, back in March 1997, in an interview with Cable News Network (CNN) journalist Peter Arnett, bin Laden asserted that although peaceful relations with non-Muslims are part of the Islamic tradition, peace is not an option when dealing with the "unjust, criminal, and tyrannical" United States government – a government that has "transgressed all bounds and behaved in a way not witnessed before by any power or any imperialist power in the world." It is for this reason that bin Laden chose to target the United States as opposed to its much weaker "agent," the Saudi regime. "Our people in the Arabian peninsula," he stated, "will send him [the United States] messages with no words because he does not know any words." But lest one assume that his only true concern was the

---

[24] Bin Laden, *Messages to the World*, 40. In 2004, on account of the American sanctions against Iraq, bin Laden accused the United States of having committed "the greatest slaughter of children that mankind has known" (bin Laden, *Messages to the World*, 267).
[25] Brackets in the original.
[26] Bin Laden, *Messages to the World*, 73–76.
[27] Bin Laden, *Messages to the World*, 89–90.

role of the United States in the Saudi kingdom, he went on to say that "the defensive *jihad* against the US does not stop with its withdrawal from the Arabian peninsula; rather, it must desist from aggressive intervention against Muslims throughout the whole world ... Wherever we look, we see the US as the leader of terrorism and crime in the world."[28] Furthermore, bin Laden declared, "the American people ... are not exonerated from responsibility": they elected their government officials "despite their knowledge" of their government's "crimes in Palestine, Lebanon, Iraq, and in other places."[29] And yet bin Laden was careful to clarify that he was not targeting civilians – a criminal practice he ascribed to the United States.

TARGETING AMERICAN CIVILIANS

Bin Laden's patience with American civilians did not last much longer. Less than a year after his CNN interview, bin Laden issued a joint fatwa with four other individuals calling on all Muslims to seize American money and "kill the Americans and their allies – civilians and military" so that "their armies leave all the territory of Islam, defeated, broken, and unable to threaten any Muslim."[30] The other signatories of the fatwa were Ayman al-Zawahiri, bin Laden's close associate and a leader of the

---

[28] Bin Laden, *Messages to the World*, 48–56.

[29] Bin Laden, *Messages to the World*, 47.

[30] Bin Laden, *Messages to the World*, 61. The journalist Peter Bergen holds that the February 1998 fatwa derived inspiration and legitimacy from another fatwa that had just been issued, apparently, by the controversial Egyptian cleric Omar Abdel Rahman (popularly known as "the Blind Sheikh"; d. 2017). It is difficult to ascertain the authenticity of the fatwa, which had been circulating among al-Qaeda members in Afghanistan; at the time, Abdel Rahman was imprisoned in solitary confinement in the United States. (Following the February 1993 World Trade Center bombing, the Federal Bureau of Investigation began to keep a more careful eye on the New York–based Abdel Rahman out of concern that he was involved in the attack and was planning future operations; although he claimed his innocence, he was eventually found guilty of numerous charges, including seditious conspiracy.) In any case, the fatwa ascribed to Abdel Rahman warns that America is attempting to undermine Muslims and wipe out clerics "who speak the truth." And so it calls on "all Muslims everywhere" to "tear [the Americans] to pieces, destroy their economies, burn their corporations, destroy their peace, sink their ships, shoot down their planes and kill them on air, sea, and land. And kill them wherever you may find them" (Bergen, *The Osama bin Laden I Know*, 202–209). What makes this fairly brief fatwa peculiar is that it was attributed to a cleric who had received a doctorate in Islamic studies from the prestigious al-Azhar University in Cairo. Regardless of whether he actually authored the fatwa, he had already stood out among al-Azhar alumni for his radical views and had previously been involved with extremist organizations in Egypt, including al-Gama'a al-Islamiyya and the Egyptian Islamic Jihad.

Egyptian Islamic Jihad;[31] Abu Yasir Rifa'i Ahmad Taha (d. 2016), a representative of Egypt's al-Gama'a al-Islamiyya (also known as the Islamic Group); Mir Hamzah, secretary-general of Pakistan's Jamiat-e-Ulema (also known as the Assembly of Pakistani Clergy); and Fazlur Rahman, a leader of the Jihad Movement in Bangladesh. Released in February 1998 under the name of a newly formed alliance called the World Islamic Front,[32] the fatwa rearticulates a case for war against the United States and presents three "well acknowledged and commonly agreed facts":

(1) America has "occupied the holiest parts of the Islamic lands, the Arabian peninsula, plundering its wealth, dictating to its leaders, humiliating its people, terrorizing its neighbours and turning its bases there into a spearhead with which to fight the neighbouring Muslim peoples."

(2) America has brought about "great devastation" in Iraq through "horrific massacres" and sanctions that have led to "over one million" deaths.

(3) America's wars, waged "for religious and economic purposes," benefit Israel, "the petty Jewish state," and divert attention from the latter's "occupation of Jerusalem and its murder of Muslims there."

"All of these American crimes and sins," the fatwa states, "are a clear proclamation of war against God, his Messenger, and the Muslims. Religious scholars throughout Islamic history have agreed that *jihad* is an individual duty when an enemy attacks Muslim countries."[33]

---

[31] For a response to the popular claim that al-Zawahiri brainwashed and manipulated bin Laden, see Scheuer, *Osama Bin Laden*, 11–14, 91–92. See also Gerges, *The Rise and Fall of Al-Qaeda*, 58, in which Gerges quotes one of al-Zawahiri's cohorts: al-Zawahiri "has always believed in the primacy and urgency of battling the near enemy. He joined bin Laden out of necessity and desperation not choice or belief."

[32] In a December 1998 interview, bin Laden indicated that one of the other signatories of the February 1998 fatwa, Taha of al-Gama'a al-Islamiyya, had actually chosen not to join the newly formed World Islamic Front (bin Laden, *Messages to the World*, 88–89). According to a member of al-Gama'a al-Islamiyya named Osama Rushdi, the formation of the World Islamic Front was "random." When Taha was asked about his signing of the Front's February 1998 fatwa, "he said that he was informed by telephone about the intention of the group to issue a statement expressing their support to the Iraqi people against the aggression that they were suffering. He agreed to the inclusion of his name in the statement. He was surprised later to discover that the statement referred to the establishment of a new front and that it included a very serious *fatwa* that all Muslims would be required to follow" (al-Zayyat, *The Road to Al-Qaeda*, 88–89). As Scheuer observes, the World Islamic Front "never gelled as an organization" (Scheuer, *Osama Bin Laden*, 114).

[33] Bin Laden, *Messages to the World*, 59–60.

Nearly six months later, on August 7, 1998, radicals linked to al-Qaeda bombed American embassies in Kenya and Tanzania, killing more than 200 people. In response, the United States launched a missile attack on a training camp in Khost, Afghanistan, in an unsuccessful attempt to kill bin Laden, now a "Most Wanted Terrorist."

In the aforementioned December 1998 interview with Al Jazeera, bin Laden denied his direct involvement in the embassy bombings but celebrated the attacks nonetheless. He also reaffirmed his call for the killing of American civilians, this time offering a clarification: "Every American is our enemy, whether he fights directly or whether he pays taxes." This would suggest that American children should not be harmed. (As we shall see, bin Laden actually sent mixed messages about the targeting of American women and children.) Meanwhile, the United States and Israel were "not only killing innocents, but children as well!" They "preach one thing and do another."[34]

The next major al-Qaeda attack took place on October 12, 2000, when radicals bombed the USS *Cole* while it was harbored in Aden, Yemen, killing seventeen American sailors. It seems that bin Laden was attempting to lure the United States into a protracted, costly war on Afghan terrain in the hope that the world's lone superpower would ultimately suffer the fate of the Soviets. But it took an even more tragic event to draw the United States into Afghanistan.

9/11 AND ITS AFTERMATH

On September 11, 2001, nineteen al-Qaeda operatives hijacked four American passenger airplanes, crashing one into the Pentagon and two into New York City's World Trade Center, leading to the eventual destruction of the Twin Towers; the fourth aircraft crashed into a field in Pennsylvania following a scuffle between the hijackers and some of the passengers. In all, nearly 3,000 people perished in the deadliest terrorist attack on American soil.

In response, then American president George W. Bush launched the War on Terror, famously declaring, "Either you are with us, or you are with the terrorists." When the Taliban government of Afghanistan refused to turn bin Laden over to the United States, the latter commenced an aerial bombing campaign on Taliban and al-Qaeda targets as part of Operation Enduring Freedom.

---

[34] Bin Laden, *Messages to the World*, 70.

On the first night of the operation, October 7, 2001, Al Jazeera aired a short video message from bin Laden, recorded a few days earlier. In it bin Laden is seen celebrating 9/11: "God has struck America at its Achilles heel and destroyed its greatest buildings ... America has been filled with terror from north to south and from east to west ... What America is tasting today is but a fraction of what we have tasted for decades."[35]

THE "CLASH": INTERVIEWS IN THE IMMEDIATE AFTERMATH OF 9/11

Approximately two weeks after the United States launched Operation Enduring Freedom, bin Laden was interviewed by the well-known Al Jazeera reporter Taysir Alluni – an interview that was not aired until late January 2002. In this conversation, "the most revealing exchange with bin Laden on record,"[36] bin Laden presented the September 11 attacks as a case of "self-defense" – "defense of our brothers and sons in Palestine, and in order to free our holy sanctuaries." And, he proclaimed, if killing those who "kill our sons is terrorism, then let history witness that we are terrorists."[37] If anything, he asserted, the American response to 9/11

proved very clearly the magnitude of the terrorism America inflicts in the world. Bush admitted that there can only be two kinds of people: one kind being Bush and his followers; and any nation that doesn't follow the Bush government, or the World Crusade, is guaranteed to be included with the terrorists. What kind of terrorism is more terrifying and evident than this?[38]

Thus, he added, whoever among Muslims "walks behind Bush or his plan" and takes the Jews or Christians as allies at the expense of fellow

---

[35] Bin Laden, *Messages to the World*, 104.
[36] Bruce Lawrence (ed.) in bin Laden, *Messages to the World*, 106.
[37] Bin Laden, *Messages to the World*, 107.
[38] Bin Laden, *Messages to the World*, 113. In this same interview, bin Laden drew attention to the fact that in a September 16, 2001, speech, Bush referred to what would be known as the War on Terror as a "crusade" against terrorism. Bush later apologized for the use of this term in that context. Bin Laden exclaimed, "The odd thing about this is that he has taken the words right out of our mouth [that this war is a Crusade] ... [W]hen Bush speaks, people make apologies for him and they say that he didn't mean to say that this war is a Crusade, even though he himself said that it was! So the world today is split in two parts, as Bush said: either you are with us, or you are with terrorism. Either you are with the Crusade, or you are with Islam. Bush's image today is of him being in the front of the line, yelling and carrying his big cross" (bin Laden, *Messages to the World*, 121–122; see pages 135, 215).

Muslims "has become an apostate."[39] For the Qur'an states, "You who believe, do not take the Jews and Christians as patrons" (5:51). (We shall revisit this accusation of apostasy in the next chapter and Qur'an 5:51 in Chapter 7.)

To bin Laden's mind, "the situation is straightforward: America won't be able to leave this ordeal unless it pulls out of the Arabian peninsula, and it ceases its meddling in Palestine, and throughout the Islamic world."[40] But these are not things bin Laden imagined America would actually do. Thus, fully embracing a "clash of civilizations" worldview, and assuming that the United States was set on a path of perpetual warfare against Muslims and Islam, he presented global jihad as the only viable response to the "World Crusade." Furthermore, citing a statement attributed to the Prophet about a future Muslim–Jewish battle that presages Judgment Day, he dismissed the utopian illusion of everlasting peace in this world.[41]

As for the notion that the 9/11 hijackers had killed innocent civilians, bin Laden remarked,

It is very strange for Americans and other educated people to talk about the killing of innocent civilians. I mean, who said that our children and civilians are not innocents, and that the shedding of their blood is permissible? Whenever we kill their civilians, the whole world yells at us from east to west, and America starts putting pressure on its allies and puppets. Who said that our blood isn't blood and that their blood is blood? What about the people that have been killed in our lands for decades? More than 1,000,000 children died in Iraq, and they are still dying, so why do we not hear people that cry or protest, or anyone who reassures or anyone who sends condolences? ... [We kill] the civilians among the disbelievers, in response to the amount of our sons they kill: this is correct in both religion and logic.[42]

Here the interviewer, Alluni, interjected:

So you say that this is an eye for an eye? They kill our innocents, so we kill theirs?

[39] Bin Laden, *Messages to the World*, 122–123.
[40] Bin Laden, *Messages to the World*, 127.
[41] Bin Laden, *Messages to the World*, 124–129. Various versions of this prophetic statement appear in, among other sources, the hadith collections of al-Bukhari and Muslim. For a contemporary Muslim discussion of and response to a popular anti-Semitic interpretation of this prophecy, see Suleiman et al., "The Myth of an Antisemitic Genocide in Muslim Scripture."
[42] Bin Laden, *Messages to the World*, 117–118.

[BIN LADEN]: Yes, so we kill their innocents – this is valid both religiously and logically. But some of the people who talk about this issue, discuss it from a religious point of view ...

[ALLUNI]: *What is their proof?*

[BIN LADEN]: They say that the killing of innocents is wrong and invalid, and for proof, they say that the Prophet forbade the killing of children and women, and that is true. It is valid and has been laid down by the Prophet in an authentic Tradition ...

[ALLUNI]: *This is precisely what I'm talking about! This is exactly what I'm asking you about!*

[BIN LADEN]: ...but this forbidding of killing children and innocents is not set in stone, and there are other writings that uphold it.

Bin Laden proceeded to quote the Qur'anic injunction, "If you [believers] respond to an attack, make your response proportionate" (16:126). Recall that this verse appears in a passage (16:126–128) that, according to most of the classical commentaries on the Qur'an, actually encourages restraint. Bin Laden continued,

The scholars and people of knowledge, amongst them Sahib al-Ikhtiyarat [this is ibn Taymiyya, d. 1328][43] and ibn al-Qayyim [d. 1350], and [al-Shawkani, d. 1834], and many others, and [al-]Qurtubi [d. 1273] – may God bless him – in his Qur'an commentary, say that if the disbelievers were to kill our children and women, then we should not feel ashamed to do the same to them, mainly to deter them from trying to kill our children and women again. And that is from a religious perspective, and those who speak without any knowledge of Islamic law, saying that killing a child is not valid and whatnot, and in the full knowledge that those young men, for whom God has cleared the way, didn't set out to kill children, but rather attacked the biggest center of military power in the world, the Pentagon, which contains more than 64,000 workers, a military base which has a big concentration of army and intelligence ...

---

[43] "Sahib al-Ikhtiyarat" can be translated as "author of *al-Ikhtiyarat.*" Bin Laden and some of his associates occasionally described ibn Taymiyya as the author of a work called *al-Ikhtiyarat* (The Selections). When affirming the obligation of defensive jihad in their February 1998 fatwa, for instance, bin Laden and the other signatories cite "Shaykh al-Islam [this is ibn Taymiyya's well-known honorific title] and his *Ikhtiyarat*" (Cook, *Understanding Jihad*, 174 [from Cook's translation of the February 1998 fatwa]; cf. Bin Laden, *Messages to the World*, 60, in which *ikhtiyarat* is translated as "chronicles"). And in a 2002 statement, the al-Qaeda spokesperson Sulayman Abu Ghayth refers to "*al-Ikhtiyarat* and *al-Fatawa*" of ibn Taymiyya when discussing the principle of reciprocity (Cook, *Understanding Jihad*, 193 [from Cook's translation of Abu Ghayth's 2002 statement *Under the Shadow of the Spears*]). Strictly speaking, however, ibn Taymiyya never authored a work called *al-Ikhtiyarat*; rather, this was the title of a collection of some of his statements from *al-Fatawa* (The Fatwas) that were compiled after his death.

[ALLUNI]: *What about the World Trade Center ...?*

[BIN LADEN]: As for the World Trade Center, the ones who were attacked and who died in it were part of a financial power. It wasn't a children's school! Neither was it a residence. And the general consensus is that most of the people who were in the towers were men that backed the biggest financial force in the world, which spreads mischief throughout the world. And those individuals should stand before God, and rethink and redo their calculations. We treat others like they treat us. Those who kill our women and our innocent, we kill their women and innocent, until they stop doing so.[44]

While America and Israel practice "ill-advised terrorism," bin Laden explained, "we [practice] good terrorism, because it deters [them] from killing our children in Palestine and other places."[45]

In an early November 2001 interview with Pakistani journalist Hamid Mir of the *Daily Ausaf*, bin Laden was once again questioned about the killing of innocent people on 9/11. According to bin Laden,

This is a significant issue in Islamic jurisprudence. According to my information, if the enemy occupies an Islamic land and uses its people as human shields, a person has the right to attack the enemy. In the same way, if some thieves broke into a house and took a child hostage to protect themselves, the father has the right to attack the thieves, even if the child gets hurt. The United States and their allies are killing us ... That's why Muslims have the right to carry out revenge attacks on the US.

... The targets of September 11 were not women and children. The main targets were the symbol of the United States: their economic and military power. Our Prophet Muhammad was against the killing of women and children. When he saw the body of a non-Muslim woman during a war, he asked what the reason for killing her was. If a child is older than thirteen and bears arms against Muslims, killing him is permissible. The American people should remember that they pay taxes to their government and that they voted for their president. Their government makes weapons and provides them to Israel, which they use to kill

---

[44] Bin Laden, *Messages to the World*, 118–119 (the text here mistakenly lists al-Shawkani as Shawaani).

[45] Bin Laden, *Messages to the World*, 120. Within the same interview, and referring to the American government's call for censorship of al-Qaeda's recorded statements ("which don't exceed a few minutes"), bin Laden alleged that American officials "felt that the truth started to appear to the American people ... that we aren't really terrorists in the way they want to define the term, but rather ... we are being violated ... throughout the world, and ... this is a reaction from the young men of our *umma* [Muslim community] ..." (bin Laden, *Messages to the World*, 112–113). Eleven days earlier, White House press secretary Ari Fleischer had criticized Al Jazeera for airing unedited al-Qaeda messages: "At best, this is a forum for prerecorded, [pretaped] propaganda inciting people to kill Americans. At worst, the broadcasts could contain signals to 'sleeper' agents" (quoted and discussed in Samuel-Azran, *Al-Jazeera and US War Coverage*, 57).

Palestinian Muslims. Given that the American Congress is a committee that represents the people, the fact that it agrees with the actions of the American government proves that America in its entirety is responsible for the atrocities that it is committing against Muslims. I demand the American people to take note of their government's policy against Muslims. They described the government's policy against Vietnam as wrong. They should now take the same stand that they did previously. The onus is on Americans to prevent Muslims from being killed at the hands of their government.

... [W]e are following our Prophet's mission. That mission is spreading the message of God, not killing people. We ourselves are the victims of murder and massacres. We are only defending ourselves against the United States. This is a defensive *jihad* to protect our land and people. That's why I have said that if we don't have security, neither will the Americans. It's a very simple equation that any American child could understand: live and let others live.

... The Israeli forces are occupying our land and the American forces are sitting on our territory. We no longer have any choice but *jihad*.⁴⁶

Bin Laden conceded, "Many in the West are polite and good people. The American media are inciting them against Muslims, but some of these good people are demonstrating against the American attacks [in Afghanistan] because human nature is against cruelty and injustice." Yet, he noted, while "good people are everywhere," the "pro-Jewish lobby has taken the United States and the West hostage."⁴⁷

Before turning to bin Laden's subsequent statements, I would like to draw attention to his ostensibly contradictory justifications for the method of fighting employed on 9/11:

(1) American adult civilians could be treated as enemy combatants on account of the fact that they paid taxes and elected government leaders who then made belligerent foreign policy decisions.

(2) The 9/11 attacks were directed at the "symbol" of the United States, that is, "their economic and military power." Innocents were never targeted; if they were killed, then they were collateral casualties.

(3) "They kill our innocents, so we kill theirs." Reciprocal retaliation is *necessary* for the survival of the *umma* (Muslim community) and serves the common good.

---

⁴⁶ Bin Laden, *Messages to the World*, 140–141. Bin Laden's conception of justifiable collateral damage parallels what we find in an undated, seemingly pre-9/11 treatise issued by al-Zawahiri (see Ibrahim [ed.], *The Al Qaeda Reader*, 137, 139–140, 161–171 [from Ibrahim's translation of al-Zawahiri's treatise *Jihad, Martyrdom, and the Killing of Innocents*]).

⁴⁷ Bin Laden, *Messages to the World*, 142–143.

In the next chapter, we shall see how various scholars and clerics responded to these justifications. For now, I would like to discuss bin Laden's third justification. Even in terms of reciprocity, there is a distinction between using destructive methods that could lead to collateral casualties and *intending* to target innocents. Without explicitly affirming his role in 9/11 (he would do so later), bin Laden effectively indicated that he *intended* to kill American innocents ("so we kill their innocents"). And this effectively discredits his claim that they were not targeted.

In his interview with Alluni, bin Laden suggested that "many" scholars of the past – including ibn Taymiyya, his student ibn al-Qayyim, the nineteenth-century reformer al-Shawkani, and the eminent thirteenth-century Qur'anic commentator al-Qurtubi – justified the intentional killing of women and children in retaliation for an enemy's targeting of noncombatants. (The scholars, he tells us, "say that if the disbelievers were to kill our children and women, then we should not feel ashamed to do the same to them.") In a 2002 statement, the al-Qaeda spokesperson Sulayman Abu Ghayth invoked these same four scholars and a fifth, al-Nawawi (d. 1277), when claiming that, on the basis of reciprocity, Muslims "have the right to kill four million Americans, among them one million children."[48]

The reality, as noted earlier, is that various scholars legitimized – in cases of necessity – collateral damage and the use of certain destructive methods in response to an enemy's use of such methods, in order to deter the enemy; they generally did not condone the *intentional* killing of innocents as a means of retaliation. In fact, the Qur'anic commentator bin Laden invoked to justify this practice, al-Qurtubi, *explicitly* rejected it in his exegetical writings: he stated that even if enemy forces "killed our women and children and made us grieve on account of this, then it is (still) not permissible for us to kill them intentionally in a similar manner to cause them to grieve and be sad."[49] This statement comes from al-Qurtubi's commentary on the Qur'anic directive, "do not let hatred

---

48 Cook, *Understanding Jihad*, 194 (Abu Ghayth's *Under the Shadow of the Spears*).
49 Al-Qurtubi, *al-Jami' li-ahkam al-Qur'an*, 7:372 (commentary on Qur'an 5:8). Like various other scholars, al-Qurtubi acknowledged the legitimacy of reciprocity when it comes to, for example, the types of weapons one may use (see, for instance, *al-Jami' li-ahkam al-Qur'an*, 3:252–256 [commentary on Qur'an 2:194] and 12:463 [commentary on Qur'an 16:126]). Incidentally, the only Qur'anic commentary cited in bin Laden's February 1998 fatwa is that of al-Qurtubi (bin Laden, *Messages to the World*, 60). And as Islamic studies scholar Rosalind Gwynne shows, the use of this commentary in the fatwa is highly selective (Gwynne, "Usama bin Ladin, the Qur'an and Jihad").

of others lead you away from justice, but adhere to justice, for that is closer to awareness of God" (5:8). The available writings of the other scholars invoked by bin Laden and Abu Ghayth reveal no obvious departure from al-Qurtubi on this issue.

Now there was at least one prominent modern Saudi scholar who seemed to justify the intentional killing of innocents as a means of retaliation: Muhammad ibn al-Uthaymeen (he died in 2001, several months before 9/11).[50] According to some of his defenders, however, his was a theoretical opinion that applied only to women and children related to enemy forces threatening Muslim-controlled lands; it would not allow for a foreign operation such as 9/11.[51] Be that as it may, we know that bin Laden occasionally invoked ibn al-Uthaymeen as an authority on jihad.[52] One might speculate that the leadership of al-Qaeda was swayed by ibn al-Uthaymeen's opinion on reciprocity, appropriated and modified it for their own purposes, and came to view the writings of earlier, more prominent scholars such as al-Qurtubi through a distorted lens.

ELABORATIONS

Over the course of the three years following 9/11, bin Laden issued various statements elaborating on the purpose of the operation without explicitly acknowledging his own role in the attacks. In a December 26, 2001, video that aired on Al Jazeera, for instance, bin Laden celebrated the nineteen hijackers – "nineteen post-secondary students" – who "shook America's throne, struck its economy right in the heart and dealt the biggest military power a mighty blow."[53] He also insisted that 9/11 was "merely a response to the continuous injustice inflicted upon our sons" and that people "need to wake up from their sleep and try to find a solution to this catastrophe that is threatening *all of humanity*."[54]

---

[50] See, for instance, "Fiqh of Jihad by Sheikh ibn Uthaymeen." See also Maher, *Salafi-Jihadism*, 51.

[51] See "Can Terrorism Be Justified by the Fatwah of ibn Uthaymeen?"; and "Intentional Killing of Non Combatants Is Not Permitted." I should note that ibn al-Uthaymin condemned suicide bombing, describing the act as damnable suicide, not martyrdom (see Wiktorowicz, "A Genealogy of Radical Islam," 93).

[52] Scheuer, *Osama Bin Laden*, 82; Khatab, *Understanding Islamic Fundamentalism*, 102.

[53] Bin Laden, *Messages to the World*, 149.

[54] Bin Laden, *Messages to the World*, 148–149 (emphasis added).

Incredibly, while condemning the "deliberate killing" of Palestinian children by Israeli soldiers, bin Laden also declared that "one issue on which people are agreed, even if they themselves have been the victims of oppression and hostility, is that you cannot kill innocent children."[55] This is an odd statement to make when defending a massive attack that claimed the lives of American children and when he himself had openly justified the reciprocal killing of innocents. This illustrates precisely how troubling bin Laden's thinking was: he could virtually do no wrong, and all blame fell on the shoulders of his enemies, whom he consistently portrayed as ill-intentioned.

But just as it would be crude to portray bin Laden's foes as one-dimensional caricatures, it would be simplistic to assume that bin Laden and al-Qaeda declared war on them simply because – as George W. Bush claimed in a September 20, 2001, address to the United States Congress – they "hate our freedoms" and seek to "end a way of life." In a February 2003 sermon – an audio recording of which was circulated online – bin Laden responded to this assertion. He excoriated what he called the

gang of criminals in the White House misrepresenting the truth, whose idiotic leader claims that we despise their way of life – although the truth that the Pharaoh of the age is hiding is that we strike them because of their injustice towards us in the Islamic world, especially in Palestine and Iraq, and their occupation of Saudi Arabia.[56]

But bin Laden went further than this: although Bush, in his aforementioned address to Congress, had presented Islam as a "religion of peace" – one that terrorists were trying "to hijack" – bin Laden alleged that Bush and his ally, the then British prime minister Tony Blair, wanted to "annihilate Islam."[57]

While bin Laden's specific call for war against the United States was not *primarily* predicated on a deep-seated hatred for the American way of life, we have good reason to think that he came to despise it,

---

[55] Bin Laden, *Messages to the World*, 147. Bin Laden continued, "History knows that one who kills children, even if rarely, is a follower of Pharaoh ... [Y]et the sons of Israel have done the same thing to our sons in Palestine. The whole world has witnessed Israeli soldiers killing Muhammad al-Durreh and others like him." Al-Durreh was a twelve-year-old boy who was tragically shot and killed during a standoff between Israeli and Palestinian security forces in Gaza in September 2000. Video footage of the attack was broadcast throughout the world, and it was widely believed that al-Durreh was killed by Israeli fire.

[56] Bin Laden, *Messages to the World*, 193.

[57] Bin Laden, *Messages to the World*, 188.

or at least aspects of it.[58] In fact, he occasionally expressed revulsion at Americans in general. In his aforementioned 1998 interview with Al Jazeera, for instance, when asked to respond to suspicions that the United States Central Intelligence Agency (CIA) was secretly funding him and al-Qaeda, bin Laden went to great lengths to discredit this myth: "Every Muslim, from the moment they [realize] the distinction in their hearts, hates Americans, hates Jews, and hates Christians. This is a part of our belief and our religion."[59] To be sure, this "very defensive" response served a purpose: it allowed bin Laden to distance himself from the potentially dangerous suspicion that he was secretly colluding with the United States.[60] Yet assuming he was indeed speaking his mind,[61] the reality is that as a devout young Muslim, bin Laden did not appear to be anti-American (and apparently had no scruples about owning an American Chrysler).[62] According to international relations scholar Fawaz Gerges,

---

[58] For instance, in the aforementioned October 2002 Internet statement ascribed to bin Laden and addressed to Americans, we see that, in addition to criticizing American foreign policy, the statement refers to America as "the worst civilization witnessed in the history of mankind" and condemns, among other things, its human-made laws, immorality, destruction of nature, exploitation of women, and acceptance of usury, intoxicants, gambling, and adult entertainment (bin Laden, *Messages to the World*, 166–168). Although Peter Bergen indicated in 2006 that he did not consider this statement authentic, I assume even if he did, he would continue to hold that bin Laden was "pretty consistent" about why he attacked the United States: "It's because of American foreign policy." It is "all about" what America was "doing in his backyard," as he saw it. Thus, from bin Laden's perspective, his was "a defensive war responding to a record of humiliation that began after the end of World War I when the Ottoman Empire was carved up by the British and the French." "His war" was "about humiliation and reclaiming Muslim pride" (Bergen, *The Osama bin Laden I Know*, 182).

[59] Bin Laden, *Messages to the World*, 87.

[60] Brahimi, *Jihad and Just War in the War on Terror*, 111.

[61] Consider the words of a February 2002 open letter popularly ascribed to bin Laden (and addressed to Saudi leaders): "Battle, animosity, and hatred – directed from the Muslim to the infidel – is the foundation of our religion" (Ibrahim [ed.], *The Al Qaeda Reader*, 43 [from Ibrahim's translation of the February 2002 open letter]; see my comments on this letter in the next chapter). The same section of the letter indicates that the proper relationship between Muslims and unbelievers is "summarized" by the Qur'anic statement, "You have a good example in Abraham and his companions, when they said to their people, 'We disown you and what you worship beside God. We renounce you! Until you believe in God alone, the enmity and hatred that has arisen between us will endure'" (60:4). This passage seems to concern the pagans who were *hostile* to God's prophets, first Abraham and then Muhammad. Not surprisingly, then, the open letter all too easily downplays the significance of a verse that appears later in the same chapter, Qur'an 60:8, which encourages kindness and equitable dealings with peaceable non-Muslims. See Chapter 6, note 112 in what follows.

[62] Bergen, *The Osama bin Laden I Know*, 22.

"there exists no hard evidence for bin Laden entertaining or expressing anti-American sentiments before 1990-91"; the "catalyst for change was American military intervention in the Gulf and its permanently stationing troops in Saudi Arabia."[63] Nevertheless, the seeds of bin Laden's extreme hatred of America were probably planted several years earlier. As we shall soon see, by his own testimony, his desire to "punish" the United States was precipitated by the 1982 Israeli invasion of Lebanon.

As for the unqualified claim that "every Muslim" hates Jews and Christians, there is no denying that such hatred exists among violent radicals.[64] This hatred, however, runs counter to Qur'anic passages such as 5:5, which permits marriage – a relationship of "love and kindness" (30:21) – to certain Jews and Christians. In any case, assuming bin Laden genuinely felt a general sense of enmity toward non-Muslims, as we shall soon see, he was still willing to affirm – in speech and action – a state of peace with non-Muslim-majority nations he deemed nonthreatening.

Now it is true that bin Laden often pejoratively referred to American forces as "Crusaders." But, to quote terrorism specialist Alia Brahimi, "in the context of his entire case for war, the fact of America's Christianity is principally emphasized in conjunction with its alleged bellicosity," as manifested in its attacks on and occupation of Muslim-majority lands.[65] It could be said, then, that bin Laden was, to a large extent, "driven by

---

[63] Gerges, *The Rise and Fall of Al-Qaeda*, 47–49 (interestingly, here Gerges notes that in the 1980s, the CIA nicknamed bin Laden a "good-gooder" on account of his efforts to support the Afghan jihad). In a 2016 interview for al-Qaeda in the Arabian Peninsula's *Inspire* magazine, the longtime al-Qaeda member Abu-Khubeyb As-Sudani (né Ibrahim al-Qosi) indicated that bin Laden only began to think "seriously about targeting and confronting America when its armies set foot in the land of the two holy mosques" in 1991 (*Inspire* 15 [May 2016], 52; "Interview with Abu-Khubeyb As-Sudani" runs from pages 50–59).

[64] As researcher Shiraz Maher observes, an uncompromising "loyalty" toward and "love" of Muslims and "disavowal" and "hatred" of non-Muslims (*al-wala' wa-l-bara'*) is one of the "defining characteristics" of "Salafi-Jihadi" radicals (Maher, *Salafi-Jihadism*, 15; see chapters 6–7). See, for instance, Ayman al-Zawahiri's December 2002 treatise on "loyalty and enmity," in which al-Zawahiri defends the idea that Muslims must be loyal to fellow believers and hostile toward "the Americans, Jews, and their alliance of hypocrites and apostates" (Ibrahim [ed.], *The Al Qaeda Reader*, 66-115 [from Ibrahim's translation of al-Zawahiri's treatise *Loyalty and Enmity*]).

[65] Brahimi, *Jihad and Just War in the War on Terror*, 112. As Brahimi notes, bin Laden "argues that 'these people [jihadis] are resisting global unbelief that has *occupied our lands*' and speaks of 'the brutal crusader *occupation* of the peninsula' underlining that 'it is not acceptable in such a struggle that the crusader should *attack and enter my land* and holy sanctuaries and plunder Muslims' oil'."

the same sort of anti-imperialism that motivates other religious and non-religious groups in the Middle East and around the world."[66]

WAR/PEACE

Bin Laden considered fighting necessary for the survival of *both* Muslims and the United States. In an audiotape that aired on Al Jazeera in January 2004, he averred,

Although our enemy lies, our religion tells the truth when it stipulates: You fight, so you exist. This is what they teach their children, but they tell us the contrary. Moreover, fighting comes about through the big powers' need for survival. Just read history if you want – including the history of America, which has ignited dozens of wars throughout only six decades. This is because this was one of its most pressing needs. When the United States makes a sincere decision to stop wars in the world, it knows before anyone else that that day will mark the beginning of its collapse and the disintegration of its states. This day is coming, God willing. So, beware of any call for laying down arms on the pretext of achieving peace. This is because this will be a call to humiliate us. Only a hypocrite or an ignorant person can promote such calls.[67]

Yet despite these assertions, approximately one month after the March 11, 2004, Madrid train bombings, which were carried out by terrorists inspired by al-Qaeda, Al Jazeera and the Dubai-based television network Al Arabiya broadcast a call for peace by bin Laden addressed to Europeans. In his words, this "peace proposal"

is essentially a commitment to cease operations against any state that pledges not to attack Muslims or intervene in their affairs ... This peace can be renewed at the end of a government's term and the beginning of a new one, with the consent of both sides. It will come into effect on the departure of its last soldier from our lands ...

Whoever chooses war over peace will find us ready for the fight.

Whoever chooses peace can see that we have responded positively.

Therefore, stop spilling our blood in order to save your own. The solution to this equation, both easy and difficult, lies in your own hands.[68]

Several months later, in a videotape aired by Al Jazeera on October 29, 2004, bin Laden addressed the "people of America." Remarkably, this statement marked the first time bin Laden publicly and explicitly claimed

[66] Hashmi, "9/11 and the Jihad Tradition," 155.
[67] Bin Laden, *Messages to the World*, 231.
[68] Bin Laden, *Messages to the World*, 235.

responsibility for 9/11. Aired just a few days before the American presidential election, bin Laden criticized both the incumbent George W. Bush and his Democratic challenger John Kerry; however, he reserved most of his venom for Bush:

I tell you that security is one of the pillars of human life. Free men do not underestimate the value of their security, despite Bush's claim that we hate freedom. Perhaps he can tell us why we did not attack Sweden, for example?

... We have been fighting you because we are free men who cannot acquiesce in injustice. We want to restore security to our *umma* [Muslim community]. Just as you violate our security, so we violate yours. Whoever encroaches upon the security of others and imagines that he will himself remain safe is but a foolish criminal.[69]

Bin Laden went on to explain how he got the idea to attack the Twin Towers of the World Trade Center:

Bush is still practicing his deception, misleading you about the real reason behind it. As a result, there are still motives for a repeat [attack]. I will explain to you the reasons behind these events, and I will tell you the truth about the moments when this decision was taken, so that you can reflect on it. God knows that the plan of striking the towers had not occurred to us, but the idea came to me when things went just too far with the American–Israeli alliance's oppression and atrocities against our people in Palestine and Lebanon.

The events that made a direct impression on me were during and after 1982, when America allowed the Israelis to invade Lebanon ... They started bombing, killing, and wounding many, while others fled in terror. I still remember those distressing scenes: blood, torn limbs, women and children massacred. All over the place, houses were being destroyed and tower blocks were collapsing, crushing their residents, while bombs rained down mercilessly on our homes. It was like a crocodile devouring a child, who could do nothing but scream. Does a crocodile understand anything other than weapons? The whole world heard and saw what happened, but did nothing. In those critical moments, many ideas raged inside me, ideas difficult to describe, but they unleashed a powerful urge to reject injustice and a strong determination to punish the oppressors.

As I looked at those destroyed towers in Lebanon, it occurred to me to punish the oppressor in kind by destroying towers in America, so that it would have a taste of its own medicine and would be prevented from killing our women and children. On that day I became sure that the oppression and intentional murder of innocent women and children is a deliberate American policy. It seemed then that "freedom" and "democracy" are actually just terror, just as resistance is labelled "terrorism" and "reaction." Imposing lethal sanctions on millions of people, as [George] Bush [Senior] did, and carrying out the mass butchering of children, is the worst thing that humanity has ever known. So is dropping millions of pounds

[69] Bin Laden, *Messages to the World*, 238.

of bombs and explosives on millions of children in Iraq, as [George] Bush Junior did, to remove a former collaborator, and install a new one who will help steal Iraq's oil, as well as commit other atrocities.

Against the background of these and similar images, the events of September 11 came as a response to these great injustices. Can you blame someone for protecting his own? Self-defense and punishing the oppressor in kind: is this shameful terrorism? Even if it is, we have no other option. This is the message that we have repeatedly tried to convey to you in words and deeds, years before September 11 ...

... For if you could avoid perpetrating these injustices, you Americans would be on the right path towards the security you enjoyed before September 11.[70]

In the years leading up to his death, bin Laden continued to release statements in which he referred to 9/11, criticized American foreign policy, and warned of future attacks. At the same time, he also expressed an openness to making peace with the United States. In January 2006, for instance, with the Iraq War becoming increasingly unpopular among Americans, he offered the United States a conditional "long-term" truce (an offer that was quickly rejected by the White House).[71] In the end, he would tell us little more about the thinking behind his most disastrously successful plot. In the next chapter, we shall see how various influential Muslims – including many who have been and still are extremely critical of American foreign policy – responded to the tragedy.

---

[70] Bin Laden, *Messages to the World*, 239–240. Of course bin Laden was not the first Muslim radical to attack the World Trade Center; the February 1993 bombing was executed by a group of terrorists supported by bin Laden's future al-Qaeda associate Khalid Sheikh Mohammed. Although Mohammed played a critical role in developing and carrying out al-Qaeda's plan of attack on 9/11, it was bin Laden who financed it, selected the pilots of the hijacked planes, and oversaw the entire operation (Gerges, *The Rise and Fall of Al-Qaeda*, 84–90).

[71] See Whitaker and MacAskill, "Bin Laden Talks of Truce but Threatens US with New Attacks."

4

"Our Hearts Bleed"

9/11 and Contemporary Muslim Thought

Contrary to popular belief, numerous prominent Muslim scholars, clerics, leaders, and organizations throughout the world publicly, explicitly, and fairly quickly condemned the September 11 attacks, often on Islamic grounds. Many of the condemnations came from some of the most outspoken critics of the United States, including controversial Egyptian cleric Yusuf al-Qaradawi, Hamas founder Ahmed Yassin (d. 2004), and Iranian Supreme Leader Ali Khamenei.[1] If one were to study Georgetown University's 2009 list of the 500 most influential Muslims in the world – an imperfect yet useful list – one would find that the overwhelming majority of those individuals were opposed to the attacks.[2]

According to a major 2008 Gallup poll, the same is true for Muslims in general: after interviewing tens of thousands of Muslims across dozens of Muslim-majority countries from 2001 to 2007, Gallup found that a disturbing yet relatively small percentage of respondents – 7 percent to be precise – thought the September 11 attacks were "completely" justified; the overwhelming majority thought they were objectionable to varying degrees. Interestingly, in the case of Indonesia, the country with the world's largest Muslim population, the minority of respondents who defended the attacks never once cited the Qur'an when justifying

---

[1] For an archive of various Muslim condemnations of 9/11, see Kurzman (ed.), "Islamic Statements Against Terrorism."

[2] See Esposito and Kalin (eds.), *The 500 Most Influential Muslims 2009*. Not surprisingly, there were "a few radical scholars who condoned the attacks" (Peters [ed.], *Jihad in Classical and Modern Islam*, 178). One example is the radical Saudi scholar Hamud ibn Abdullah al-Shu'aybi (d. 2002), who essentially reproduced bin Laden's justifications for 9/11 (see Peters [ed.], *Jihad in Classical and Modern Islam*, 178–180).

their stances, advancing instead "secular" and "worldly" arguments; meanwhile, many of the respondents who condemned the attacks offered "humanitarian or religious justifications."[3]

As international relations scholar Fawaz Gerges observes, the *umma* (Muslim community) "did not respond the way bin Laden had expected, and like-minded jihadist groups accused him of heresy and treachery."[4] The many "ordinary" Arabs and Muslims with whom Gerges conversed shortly after the attacks – "from bank tellers to fruit vendors and taxi drivers to small shop owners" and including "those who voiced strong anti-American foreign policy views" – "concurred that the attacks were a crime."[5] This parallels my own experiences in post-9/11 visits to Cairo: while some of the Cairenes I spoke to insisted that America "deserved" what it got on 9/11, the general feeling was that innocent civilians were horrifically and wrongfully murdered that day.

Although numerous Americans witnessed select images of Palestinian Muslims and others overseas singing and rejoicing in the streets after the attacks, few even heard about the more solemn Muslim responses, including a major candlelight vigil in Iran. Fewer still were aware of the same-day condemnation of 9/11 issued by none other than the Taliban government of Afghanistan.[6]

Indeed, although the Taliban did not publicly denounce Osama bin Laden, whom they maintained was innocent until proven guilty, tension had been brewing between the two sides. As late as June 2001, the then Taliban supreme commander Mullah Omar (d. 2013) had maintained that any fatwa issued by bin Laden declaring war against the United States and ordering Muslims to kill Americans was "null and void." This, he said, was because bin Laden was "not entitled to issue fatwas as he did not complete the mandatory 12 years of Koranic studies to qualify for the position of mufti [one who issues fatwas]."[7] As we now know, the Taliban objected not only to 9/11 but also to the 2000 bombing of the USS *Cole*.[8] Shortly before 9/11, Mullah Omar reportedly made it clear to bin Laden

---

[3] Esposito and Mogahed, *Who Speaks for Islam?*, chapter 3.
[4] Gerges, *The Rise and Fall of Al-Qaeda*, 103.
[5] Gerges, *The Rise and Fall of Al-Qaeda*, 93.
[6] Brahimi, *Jihad and Just War in the War on Terror*, 99–100. The then Afghan ambassador to Pakistan, Mullah Abdul Salam Zaeef, stated, "We strongly condemn the attacks and condemn those who have carried out these blasts" ("Taliban Condemn Attacks in United States"; see Brahimi, *Jihad and Just War in the War on Terror*, 100).
[7] De Borchgrave, "Mullah Omar."
[8] Rosenberg, "In Osama bin Laden Library."

that he opposed "any attack against the United States." Although bin Laden's senior advisors "urged him to heed Omar's warning," bin Laden is said to have responded defiantly: "I will make it happen even if I do it by myself."[9] Although the Taliban refused to comply with the post-9/11 American demand to hand over bin Laden – still technically their "guest," and one who had supported his hosts for years – they were reportedly willing to put him on trial.[10]

REVISITING BIN LADEN'S DECLARATION OF JIHAD

Countless Muslims, scholars and laypeople, were appalled by bin Laden's *method* of fighting the United States. Less controversial (though controversial nonetheless) was bin Laden's initial call for a defensive jihad against the United States. In the case of the latter, leaving aside the widespread belief that bin Laden lacked the requisite authority to declare war in the first place (he was neither a head of state nor a certified scholar), it is not difficult to understand why many Muslims (including some clerics) and even certain non-Muslims would, to varying degrees, sympathize with his call for jihad. His propaganda effectively identified and exploited grievances stemming from America's preferential treatment of Israel and its support for repressive, authoritarian governments in certain Muslim-majority countries, despite its advocacy for democracy and human rights. By showing that he and al-Qaeda were "willing to take on the world's greatest power in order to redress widely felt injustices," they garnered "the support of many ordinary Muslims."[11]

Ultimately, bin Laden's call for a global jihad against the United States hinged on two critical assumptions: (1) he assumed an "expansive conception of 'self'" – the entire Muslim community (*umma*), rather than simply Saudi Arabia and/or the other countries in which he had resided; and (2) he assumed an "expansive conception of 'attack'" when describing America's actions. Thus, to his mind, the Saudi-invited Americans were "occupiers" and "invaders" who threatened the Ka'ba itself.[12] As for some of the other items on bin Laden's laundry list of grievances, terrorism specialist Alia Brahimi writes,

---

[9] Gerges, *The Rise and Fall of Al-Qaeda*, 90 (on the "complex and fractious" relationship between the Taliban and bin Laden, see pages 60–63).
[10] Mashal, "Taliban 'offered bin Laden trial before 9/11'."
[11] Hashmi, "9/11 and the Jihad Tradition," 156.
[12] Brahimi, *Jihad and Just War in the War on Terror*, 115–118.

It is difficult to divine how America might be held to account for issues like the Burmese ethnic cleansing or the Eritrean independence struggle, and the charge that America "supported the Serbs massacring the Muslims in Bosnia" is contradicted by the fact that the US intervention in 1995 swung the balance of power back in favour of the Muslims. The flimsiness of bin Laden's argument is crudely apparent when he lists the aforementioned massacres in the "Declaration of *Jihad*" and must conclude, with a relatively anticlimactic flourish, that the United States "has prevented the dispossessed from arming themselves." In order to gloss over the fact that no flagrant aggression has been committed (arguably, at least, until the 2003 invasion of Iraq), he resorts to rhetorical flourishes that emphasize the religiosity of the Americans.[13]

Islamic political philosophy scholar Sohail Hashmi makes an analogous observation:

As in all propaganda, the 1996 and 1998 declarations of war against the United States and its allies contain many distortions and half-truths … A concerted Western campaign to destroy Islam and to exterminate Muslims in a latter-day crusade is of course nonsense. Those who subscribe to this view have a hard time explaining why NATO intervened on behalf of the Muslims of Kosovo.[14]

ASSESSING BIN LADEN'S METHODS

One might think an attack on American soil would necessarily constitute an aggressive – rather than a defensive – jihad, even in the absence of immediate aspirations for foreign land acquisition, and even if such an attack was considered necessary for the security and liberty of Muslims. (As noted earlier, many Muslim scholars conceptualized aggressive jihad as being ultimately a means of protection.) And all indications suggest that bin Laden believed in the enduring legitimacy of aggressive jihad. For instance, in a February 2002 open letter popularly attributed to him and addressed to and critical of Saudi leaders who "prostrate" to the West in the name of "moderation," we encounter a passionate endorsement of aggressive jihad and the abrogationist-expansionist paradigm, a paradigm not acknowledged by some "defeatist" Saudis.[15]

But while the letter presents aggressive jihad as a means of self-preservation, at no point does it indicate that bin Laden's own violent operations constituted such a jihad. The fact of the matter is that bin Laden only ever called for defensive jihad; his armed struggle was

---

[13] Brahimi, *Jihad and Just War in the War on Terror*, 117.
[14] Hashmi, "9/11 and the Jihad Tradition," 156.
[15] See Ibrahim (ed.), *The Al Qaeda Reader*, 22–62 (February 2002 open letter).

intended to be immediately protective and retributive, not preemptive and expansionist. This explains why bin Laden declared war on certain Western nations but not others. His belief in the doctrine of aggressive jihad did not compel him to call for and engage in incessant warfare against any and all non-Muslim-controlled nations, if only because of obvious practical limitations, and especially since he deemed defensive jihad against specific foreign entities as being more pressing than any expansionist project. We read in the same February 2002 open letter that "Muslim hostilities" depend "on the harm [inflicted] by this or that nation against Islam and Muslims"; this is why Muslims must now combat "Crusading America, backed by Britain, Germany, France, Canada, and Australia," as opposed to "Japan, both Koreas, China, and others."[16]

---

[16] Ibrahim (ed.), *The Al Qaeda Reader*, 36 (February 2002 open letter). The author Raymond Ibrahim claims that bin Laden was deceptive in describing his intentions: before Western audiences, he asserted that his attacks on the United States were reciprocal and defensive in nature; before Muslim audiences, he revealed the truth: that his hostility was ultimately rooted in conquest-driven aggressive jihad. Ibrahim justifies this claim by pointing to the aforementioned February 2002 open letter, a letter that champions the abrogationist-expansionist paradigm and is addressed to Saudi leaders, "that is," Ibrahim writes, "for Islamic eyes only" (Ibrahim [ed.], *The Al Qaeda Reader*, 19 [see pages 1–10, 17–21]; see Ibrahim's articles "An Analysis of Al-Qa'ida's Worldview," "How Taqiyya Alters Islam's Rules of War," "Islam's Doctrines of Deception," and "The Two Faces of Al Qaeda"). I do not find Ibrahim's claim convincing. At no point does the open letter (or any other document we have that is widely attributed to bin Laden and addressed to fellow Muslims) present bin Laden's own violent operations as part of an aggressive jihad. Furthermore, it would be unreasonable to assume that bin Laden would author an *open* letter, a self-described "declaration" addressed to his Muslim opponents (the full title of the open letter, as translated by Ibrahim, is "Al-Qaeda's Declaration in Response to the Saudi Ulema: It's Best You Prostrate Yourselves in Secret"), and then expect it to be or remain "for Islamic eyes only." In fact, although the open letter is not geared toward a Western audience, it has nothing to hide: it repeatedly implores Saudi leaders to tell Westerners "the truth" about Islam and its doctrine of aggressive jihad. With all this in mind, see Michael Scheuer's critique of Ibrahim's assertion that al-Qaeda's specific war with the West is "existential, transcending time and space," in Scheuer, *Osama Bin Laden*, 192, note 43; see Ibrahim [ed.], *The Al Qaeda Reader*, xii (cf. page 140, where Ibrahim acknowledges that al-Qaeda invokes defensive jihad to justify its extreme tactics). Incidentally, in a September 2007 article published in *The Chronicle of Higher Education*, Ibrahim attempts to buttress his depiction of al-Qaeda as "two-faced" by quoting extensively from a British man named Hassan Butt (Ibrahim, "The Two Faces of Al Qaeda"). Butt claimed to be a former al-Qaeda "insider" and declared that although the organization used Western foreign policy and the principle of reciprocity to justify its terrorist attacks, in reality, its operations were primarily the product of Islamic theology. It was later revealed, however, that Butt was never a "jihadi" and had never met bin Laden or any member of al-Qaeda and was, by his own admission, a "professional liar" (Dodd, "Al-Qaida fantasist tells court: I'm a professional liar").

As we saw earlier in the case of the Oslo Accords debate, the Saudi grand mufti Abdulaziz bin Baz endorsed the doctrine of aggressive jihad while still ("opportunistically") calling for potentially long-term harmony with peaceable non-Muslim Israelis. For all bin Baz knew, the Palestinians might have renewed or extended their state of peace with Israel for decades, if not centuries, especially if alternative courses of action would have seemed detrimental. It is noteworthy, then, that bin Laden's primary disagreement with bin Baz on the Oslo Accords revolved around the question of whether the Israelis were truly inclined toward peace: bin Laden saw them as an "attacking enemy" and an immediate threat, thus necessitating a defensive jihad. Similarly, in the case of the United States and certain other Western nations, the consistently stated goal of bin Laden's jihad was to repulse, undermine, and retaliate against forces that had occupied and threatened Muslim-majority nations.[17] To his mind, the American threat warranted extreme tactics and a call for the participation of "all Muslims," as he indicated in his February 1998 declaration of war against the United States.[18]

Given that bin Laden was not a widely recognized authority and that he employed belligerent methods, he would actually have further undermined himself had he declared an aggressive jihad. As Hashmi explains,

Bin Laden is careful in all his statements to invoke the notion of defensive jihad, not just because self-defense is the timeworn justification for most acts of violence, but also because it provides a number of important Islamic grounds for bin Laden's particular war. In a defensive jihad, various restraints imposed on the expansionist jihad are relaxed. All able-bodied Muslims, male and female, are required as an individual obligation to rush to the defense of the Muslim victims. If some Muslims are not close to the fighting and they cannot travel to the battlefield, they are required to assist the Muslim defenders in other ways. Requirements relating to proper authority – that is, who may declare and under whose leadership the jihad may be fought – become more ambiguous. If the leaders of the Islamic state are incapable or unwilling to lead the defensive struggle, other Muslims must assume this responsibility. And finally, the normal constraints

---

[17] A few years after bin Laden's death and fifteen years after 9/11, Ayman al-Zawahiri issued a statement that appeared in the November 2016 issue of al-Qaeda in the Arabian Peninsula's online magazine *Inspire*. In al-Zawahiri's words, "our message to the Americans is as clear as the sun, and as cutting as the edge of the sword: the events on the 11th of September were a direct result of your crimes against us – your crimes in Palestine, Afghanistan, Iraq, [the Levant], Mali, Somalia, Yemen, Islamic Maghrib, and Egypt – and the result of your occupations of the lands of the Muslims, and your plundering of their fortunes, and your support for the criminal, corrupt killers who exercise control over them" (*Inspire* 16 [Nov. 2016], 13 [article runs from pages 12–15]).

[18] Bin Laden, *Messages to the World*, 61.

on how Muslims may fight to repulse the aggression are loosened under claims of necessity ...[19]

Yet however compelling bin Laden's call for a defensive jihad might have seemed, various influential scholars, including the then grand imam of al-Azhar, Mohammed Tantawi (d. 2010), and organizations, including Hezbollah, labeled the September 11 attacks an unjustifiable act of "aggression."[20] In a statement issued on September 13, 2001, the prominent cleric Yusuf al-Qaradawi proclaimed that, despite his "strong" opposition to American foreign policy with regard to Israel, the 9/11 "aggressor" must be punished. What is more, he declared, "Our hearts bleed for the attacks ... I categorically go against a committed Muslim's embarking on such attacks. Islam never allows a Muslim to kill the innocent and the helpless." Al-Qaradawi apparently could not even believe that Muslims could carry out "such attacks," referring to this as a claim of "some biased groups"; yet even if this were true, he added, "then we, in the name of our religion, deny the act and incriminate the perpetrator."[21]

Such words might seem odd coming from the controversial al-Qaradawi. On other occasions he has publicly countenanced suicide missions in Palestinian territories against Israeli adults, viewing them all as actual or potential soldiers representing an occupying force and an oppressive state.[22] But to al-Qaradawi's mind, the difference between such missions and 9/11 "is huge" since the hijackers "were not fighting an invasion" when they conducted their attack on American soil.[23] Thus, he condemned the hijackers despite his belief that the United States is the "preeminent example of 'international terrorism'."[24] Leaving aside for a moment al-Qaradawi's problematic views on suicide attacks on Israelis, to which I shall return shortly, what his and many other condemnations demonstrate is that even if al-Qaeda is "not especially radical when we confine our attention to its stated grievances or goals ... it is on

[19] Hashmi, "9/11 and the Jihad Tradition," 154–155.

[20] Brahimi, *Jihad and Just War in the War on Terror*, 120.

[21] "Sheikh Yusuf Al-Qaradawi Condemns Attacks Against Civilians." In a fatwa issued on September 27, 2001, al-Qaradawi went a step further: he averred that it would be religiously permissible for American Muslim soldiers – bound by their duty to justice, country, and the armed forces – to participate in United States military efforts directed against the 9/11 perpetrators, even if this involved combat against other Muslims. For a translation and discussion of this statement, see Nafi, "Fatwa and War."

[22] See, for instance, BBC, "Al-Qaradawi Full Transcript."

[23] Bunting, "Friendly Fire."

[24] Zaman, *Modern Islamic Thought in a Radical Age*, 271; see al-Qaradawi, *Fiqh al-jihad*, 2:1078–1082.

the fringes of the jihad tradition when we shift our attention to the means it employs to realize its objectives."[25]

Ultimately, "almost all" of the post-9/11 "uproar" of Muslim scholars and clerics "took its starting point from the deaths of civilians."[26] Now I should pause to note that throughout the twentieth century, radical Muslim discourse on jihad tended to focus more on the criteria for justifying jihad (*jus ad bellum*) than on the criteria for conducting warfare justly (*jus in bello*). One explanation for this is that radicals were generally "not actively engaged with military affairs in such a way that the kind of cases that would lead to a fuller development of *jus in bello* considerations [became] the object of reflection."[27] Yet so robust is the notion of civilian immunity in Islam that "many of the Muslims sympathetic to al-Qaeda's cause," such as Algeria's Salafist Group for Preaching and Combat, "could only reconcile their support for bin Laden with the events of 9/11 by denying that he was in fact the culprit."[28]

As journalist Peter Bergen observes, bin Laden has enjoyed "a large degree of personal popularity in the Muslim world for his stance against the United States"; yet al-Qaeda has failed to win over the Muslim "masses." This is because "the average Muslim knows that killing civilians is explicitly prohibited by the Koran, and al Qaeda presents no positive vision of the world it wants to create."[29] In the words of the former Bosnian grand mufti Mustafa Ceric, "there is not one normal man on this planet who can justify what happened in New York and Washington."[30]

Bin Laden claimed that the primary victims, American adult civilians, could be treated as enemy combatants because they paid taxes and elected malevolent government leaders. For the generality of contemporary scholars and clerics, however, it takes more than voting and paying taxes for individuals living in a democracy to be deemed legitimate targets.

Perhaps the closest analogous ruling to bin Laden's claim in premodern Sunni thought is the opinion of ibn Taymiyya (d. 1328), namely that innocents should not be killed "unless they actually fight with words

---

[25] Hashmi, "9/11 and the Jihad Tradition," 150.
[26] Brahimi, *Jihad and Just War in the War on Terror*, 177.
[27] Kelsay, *Islam and War*, 73–74.
[28] Brahimi, *Jihad and Just War in the War on Terror*, 189.
[29] Bergen, *The Osama bin Laden I Know*, 392. On the relative unpopularity among Muslims of al-Qaeda's ideology and tactics, see Charles Kurzman's *The Missing Martyrs*.
[30] "Head of Bosnia's Muslims Urges Bush to Exercise Caution" (cited in Brahimi, *Jihad and Just War in the War on Terror*, 99).

[e.g. by propaganda] and acts [e.g. by spying or otherwise assisting in the warfare]."[31] But even then, there is quite a gap between ibn Taymiyya and bin Laden. Whereas an act such as generating threatening propaganda ("fighting with words") or spying ("fighting with acts") reflects direct antagonism, secret ballot voting reveals a spectrum of anonymous stances, and paying taxes is a legal obligation, one that might even be accompanied by active protest against the policies and actions of one's own government. Here I should note that ibn Taymiyya makes the above statement in his famous work *al-Siyasa al-shar'iyya* (Governance According to God's Law). He goes on to demonstrate that mere support for an enemy does not render someone a viable target: he cites a well-known hadith in which the Prophet rebukes his soldiers for killing a woman affiliated with an enemy force (despite her obvious support for the latter) and then commands his followers not to slay innocents, including hired servants (despite their allegiance and physical contributions to enemy forces). Thus, ibn Taymiyya stresses, "we may only fight those who fight us."[32]

Although bin Laden was well aware of this hadith,[33] he did not deem it relevant when calling for the killing of American citizens. As he saw it, the democratic social contract rendered all Americans culpable for their government's actions. This view, however, sidesteps the fact that in democracies, political dissent is ubiquitous. Bin Laden himself affirmed this in November 2001 when – perhaps not recognizing his own logical inconsistency – he conceded that there were many "good people" in the West who objected to the American operation in Afghanistan.[34] One cannot justifiably claim, therefore, that *all* American adult citizens support – let alone fight for – *any* American foreign policy measure, simply on account of decisions made by *certain* American leaders who were *not* unanimously elected or because citizens pay taxes that are *required by law.* Accordingly, a condemnation of 9/11 issued shortly after the attacks and signed by forty-six prominent Muslims – including al-Qaradawi and various other clerics and Islamist leaders critical

---

[31] Peters (ed.), *Jihad in Classical and Modern Islam*, 49 (from Peters's translation of ibn Taymiyya's chapter on jihad in *al-Siyasa al-shar'iyya*).

[32] Peters (ed.), *Jihad in Classical and Modern Islam*, 49 (ibn Taymiyya's *al-Siyasa*). Various versions of the abovementioned hadith (some of which make no reference to hired servants) appear in the collections of, among others, Ahmad ibn Hanbal (d. 855), al-Bukhari, Muslim, ibn Maja (d. 887), and Abu Dawud.

[33] See bin Laden, *Messages to the World*, 140.

[34] Bin Laden, *Messages to the World*, 142.

of the United States – invokes the Qur'anic declaration, "No soul will bear another's burden" (17:15).[35]

Bin Laden also maintained that the killing of American civilians on 9/11 could be justified on the basis of reciprocity: "They kill our innocents, so we kill theirs"[36] – this is "mainly to deter them from trying to kill our children and women again."[37] And although American leaders may claim that they do not target civilians, again, as bin Laden saw it, they "preach one thing and do another."[38]

Recall that when one of the followers of the first caliph Abu Bakr presented him with the decapitated head of a Byzantine leader in imitation of their enemies' wartime custom, a disappointed Abu Bakr rhetorically asked, "Do you take your guidance from the Persians and the Byzantines?"[39] Muslim clerics might pose a similar question to bin Laden: "Do you take your guidance from the Americans, at least as you portray them?" Even the controversial Islamist Sayyid Qutb (d. 1966) held that the Islamic tradition "does not recommend [that we] resort to the same obscene methods used by its detractors."[40]

As suggested earlier, it is extremely difficult to locate clear examples of prominent Sunni (or Shi'ite) scholars, especially premodern ones, who condoned the intentional killing of innocents as a means of retaliation. (Recall that bin Laden could not offer a single good example of a premodern scholar who allowed for this.) It is significantly easier to locate scholars who held that, in cases of necessity, Muslims may (or should) employ somewhat indiscriminate and destructive methods (*excluding* the specific targeting of innocents) in response to an enemy's use of such methods, if this would likely deter the enemy. Yet even with the most extreme, most expansive conception of reciprocity, bin Laden's attacks

---

[35] *Al-Quds al-'Arabi*, 2; "A Clear Criterion." Although several children and hundreds of foreign nationals perished on 9/11, all indications suggest that this condemnatory statement pertains to *all* civilians (including American adults) killed that day: it does not distinguish between the casualties of the "massive killing" and concludes with the signatories offering their "sincerest condolences to the families of the innocent victims and the American people."

[36] Bin Laden, *Messages to the World*, 118. Technically, these are the words of the Al Jazeera reporter Taysir Alluni; the quote here was posed in the form of a question to bin Laden in their aforementioned interview. Bin Laden responded in the affirmative: "Yes, so we kill their innocents."

[37] Bin Laden, *Messages to the World*, 119.

[38] Bin Laden, *Messages to the World*, 70.

[39] Al-Bayhaqi, *al-Sunan al-kubra*, 9:223; see Abu Id, *al-'Alaqat al-kharijiyya fi dawlat al-khilafa*, 222.

[40] Qutb, *In the Shade of the Qur'an*, 1:279 (commentary on Qur'an 2:217).

could only be legitimized if (1) it could be shown that the United States truly did, as a general practice, intend to kill innocents – here, again, the interpretations of the facts on the ground are critical; and (2) there was good reason to think that such retaliatory attacks would prevent or discourage the United States from threatening Muslims in the future.

Without the benefit of hindsight, I imagine that someone with even a basic understanding of international politics could see that Muslim terrorist operations against the United States would likely lead to greater American intervention in Muslim-majority countries. As bin Laden saw it, however, 9/11 would help bring about the eventual downfall of the United States, just as the efforts of the *mujahidin* of Afghanistan brought down the Soviet Union; and previous al-Qaeda attacks had exposed the vulnerability of the United States. But in reality, the war in Afghanistan was but one factor in the downfall of the Soviets; and in 2001, the United States possessed a military that far surpassed that of the Soviet Union at its height. Bin Laden's strategy was, at best, a gamble. And although it is true that the United States suffered major financial and other setbacks as a result of al-Qaeda's various attacks, in many ways, these attacks proved to be especially detrimental to Muslims themselves. Anti-Muslim sentiments became more prevalent (and not just in the West), the United States increased its military presence and activities in Muslim-majority countries, and the subsequent destabilization of various regions was accompanied by an escalation in sectarian violence. Thus, in a televised address to bin Laden around the time of the sixth anniversary of 9/11, the Saudi cleric Salman al-Oadah, once deeply admired by bin Laden, rebuked the al-Qaeda leader, posing the following rhetorical questions to his "Brother Osama": "How much blood has been spilled? How many innocent children, women, and old people have been killed, maimed, and expelled from their homes in the name of 'al-Qaeda'?" Indeed, "What have all these long years of suffering, tragedy, tears, and sacrifice actually achieved?"[41]

Further muddling matters is the fact that although bin Laden justified the killing of American civilians and explicitly called for it in his February 1998 fatwa, he asserted that the innocents killed on 9/11 were collateral casualties; the targets of the attacks were "the symbol of the United States," not a "children's school." But most observers found this claim to be "obviously disingenuous; hijacking civilian airliners and crashing them into the Twin Towers when they were known to hold *thousands* of civilians makes human beings and not buildings 'the real targets'."[42]

---

[41] Al-Oadah, "A Ramadan Letter to Osama bin Laden."
[42] Hashmi, "9/11 and the Jihad Tradition," 160 (emphasis added).

Indeed, if al-Qaeda were truly interested in attacking symbols while min-
imizing civilian casualties, why would it direct passenger airplanes to
buildings teeming with people on a weekday during work hours? (I shall
say more on the topic of collateral damage in the next chapter.)

Another point of controversy was the suicidal method employed by the
9/11 hijackers, a method reminiscent of the Japanese kamikazes of World
War II. Contrary to popular belief, suicide attacks by Sunni Muslims
were rare until the 1990s.[43] And although common these days, prior to
the early 1980s, there was no such thing as a Muslim suicide *bomber*.
Even in the 1980s, the *mujahidin* of Afghanistan and various militant
groups shunned the kamikaze method altogether. Yet now, unfortunately,
it is remarkable *not* to hear or read about Muslim suicide attacks in a
given month.

Muslim clerics differ as to whether the kamikaze method in and of
itself constitutes suicide (since the attackers are directly responsible
for their own deaths) or heroic martyrdom (since the attackers sacrifice their lives for the sake of others).[44] The Qur'an warns, "Do not kill
yourselves" (4:29),[45] and various hadiths prohibit and strongly condemn
suicide. Combatants are not exempt from this prohibition: according to
the hadith tradition (including the collection of al-Bukhari), the Prophet
denounced a man from his own army who fought valiantly but killed
himself using his own sword to hasten his death after he was wounded.
Yet even among those scholars who see not suicide but heroic martyrdom
in the kamikaze method, most hold that (1) the target must be legitimate, and (2) the attack could only be "carried out during a valid war
when there is no ceasefire." According to Islamic legal scholars such as
Muhammad Afifi al-Akiti, the 9/11 attacks failed on both counts and
thus constitute a clear breach of "the scholarly consensus."[46]

As indicated earlier, scholars such as al-Qaradawi strongly condemned
9/11 yet endorsed suicide attacks in Palestinian territories against Israeli
adults. According to al-Qaradawi, Israeli adult civilians forfeit their protected status because not only are they active "occupiers" of Palestinian

---

[43] Cook, *Understanding Jihad*, 142.
[44] For a defense of the kamikaze method by al-Qaeda's Ayman al-Zawahiri, see Ibrahim
(ed.), *The Al Qaeda Reader*, 146–161 (al-Zawahiri's *Jihad, Martyrdom, and the Killing
of Innocents*). On al-Qaeda's portrayal of suicide attacks as noble acts of sacrifice, see
Finn, *Al-Qaeda and Sacrifice*.
[45] An alternative translation reads, "Do not kill each other" (Abdel Haleem, *The
Qur'an*, 53).
[46] Al-Akiti, *Defending the Transgressed*, 24.

land and supporters of Israel's military (as demonstrated simply by their decision to remain in Israel), they themselves – men and women – are required to join the military. This, however, is a bewildering assessment: many Israeli citizens actively object to its government's treatment of Palestinians, and, whatever their past or future, the majority of Israelis currently do not serve in the military, and some, such as yeshiva students, are exempt from such service altogether. As al-Akiti would have it, "No properly schooled jurists" would say – "as a legal judgement" – that Israeli women may be targeted; "if they faithfully followed the juridical processes of the orthodox schools" of Sunni thought, they would realize this ruling is "outright wrong."[47] In fact, he adds, "[o]ur jurists agree" that even in the course of a valid war, "off-duty" soldiers – be they women or men – are to be treated as noncombatants.[48]

To be sure, numerous prominent scholars besides al-Akiti have expressed their unequivocal opposition to the suicide attacks condoned by al-Qaradawi. The condemners include, among many others, the Fiqh Council of North America, the Saudi Wahhabi establishment, the (Shi'ite) cleric and former Iranian president Mohammad Khatami, and the foremost (Sunni) cleric of Bangladesh.[49] In the words of British Sunni scholar T. J. Winter (Abdal-Hakim Murad), "Targeting civilians is a negation of every possible school of Sunni Islam. Suicide bombing is so foreign to the Quranic ethos that the Prophet Samson" – who in the Bible (Judges 16:26–31) engages in what could be called a suicide attack – "is entirely absent from our scriptures."[50]

Al-Akiti recognizes that we live in a world replete with injustice. But he cautions his fellow Muslims against losing "hope in Allah" when "the military option is not a legal one" for them. He reminds them of the widely reported words of the Prophet: "The best *jihad* is a true (*i.e.*,

---

[47] Al-Akiti, *Defending the Transgressed*, 32. As religious studies scholar John Kelsay notes, al-Qaradawi "seems to have been saying that the 'potential combatancy' presented by the fact that all Israelis of a certain age are eligible for military service justifies attacks in public places. Such an argument would involve a considerable stretch of, if not an outright departure from, Shari'a precedents." Perhaps, Kelsay speculates, this is why al-Qaradawi also invoked "necessity" when justifying such attacks (Kelsay, *Arguing the Just War in Islam*, 141).

[48] Al-Akiti, *Defending the Transgressed*, 33–34.

[49] See Brahimi, *Jihad and Just War in the War on Terror*, 173; and Kurzman (ed.), "Islamic Statements Against Terrorism." One particularly outspoken critic of suicide terrorism is the Pakistani scholar Muhammad Tahir-ul-Qadri, who attracted international media attention several years ago with the publication of his fairly lengthy *Fatwa on Terrorism and Suicide Bombings*.

[50] Kurzman (ed.), "Islamic Statements Against Terrorism."

brave) word in the face of a tyrannical ruler." Al-Akiti adds, "it is possible still, and especially today, to fight injustice" through other forms of
jihad: "through your tongue and your words and through the pen and
the courts."[51]

ASSESSING BIN LADEN

While conceding that bin Laden "is not in the mainstreams of Islam
and Salafism," the former chief of the United States Central Intelligence
Agency's bin Laden unit, Michael Scheuer (whose work on bin Laden I
find generally insightful), makes the problematic claim that the al-Qaeda
mastermind

was, and continues to be seen as, a legitimate and good Muslim by his coreligionists. Many disagree with al-Qaeda's martial acts, but that bin Laden was a
good Muslim they have no doubt. Even his purest and politico rivals in the Salafi
movement (and recall that many are paid and controlled by Muslim regimes) do
not disown him. They have given him the benefit of the doubt and called on him
to repent.[52]

Leaving aside for a moment the fact that some Sunni scholars have indeed
labeled bin Laden an apostate,[53] Scheuer's assessment does not account for
the fact that declarations of apostasy in Sunni contexts are typically predicated on specific theological stances and not necessarily deeds, however violent and heinous they might be. As such, a Sunni might strongly condemn
and even call for the execution of bin Laden while at the same time deeming
him a "brother," albeit a fallen and possibly hell-bound one.

Calling on bin Laden to repent does not in any way suggest he is a
"good" Muslim. To the contrary, his rivals and critics would not entreat
him to repent if they were not troubled by his actions. There are also
obvious practical reasons for these entreatments. And as there are numerous hadiths that speak of sinners – and even unbelievers – repenting and
rectifying themselves before passing away, appeals for repentance were to
be expected in the case of bin Laden.

Be that as it may, I am not surprised by Scheuer's claim. If one were to
focus on statements by bin Laden and other individuals who inspired him

---

[51] Al-Akiti, *Defending the Transgressed*, 50. Versions of the prophetic report cited here
appear in the hadith collections of, among others, Ahmad ibn Hanbal, ibn Maja, Abu
Dawud, al-Tirmidhi (d. 892), and al-Nasa'i.
[52] Scheuer, *Osama Bin Laden*, 176–177.
[53] See, for example, Pingree, "Spanish Muslims Decry Al Qaeda."

and/or shared many of his views, one might imagine it easy for Sunnis to label other Sunnis apostates. Scheuer insists that bin Laden was not a *takfiri*, or one who accuses other Muslims of being unbelievers. Yet bin Laden deemed various Sunni leaders apostates because of their alignment with non-Muslim entities – recall his assessment of any Muslim who "walks behind Bush"[54] – and their acceptance of certain human-made laws.[55] In these claims one can see at least the indirect influence of the eighteenth-century Arabian reformer and eponym of Wahhabism, Muhammad ibn Abdul Wahhab (d. 1792), who taught that "judging by non-Islamic laws" and "supporting or helping non-believers against Muslims" are among the "voiders" (or "nullifiers") of Islam.[56] All in all, although bin Laden did not reach the level of some other *takfiris* (including some who tried to kill him on more than one occasion),[57] his practice of openly declaring Muslim leaders apostates on account of their deeds as he interpreted them – and making these declarations despite the fact that he was neither a state authority nor a formally trained scholar – cannot be taken to be representative of the broader Sunni tradition.[58]

In short, bin Laden's Islam was aberrant. It was neither mainstream nor predicated on a consistently literal reading of Islamic texts (recall, for instance, his treatment of the prophetic prohibition against killing women and children). And any serious discussion of his jihad must adequately account for his anti-imperialist politics. In the final analysis, his worldview was an amalgamation of, among other things, a radical interpretation of

---

[54] Bin Laden, *Messages to the World*, 122.

[55] Scheuer acknowledges this in *Osama bin Laden* (see, for instance, pages 95–96, 149). For a critique of bin Laden's apostasy charge against Saudi rulers, see Gwynne, "Usama bin Ladin, the Qur'an and Jihad."

[56] Wiktorowicz, "A Genealogy of Radical Islam," 81–82. For a contemporary Muslim scholarly rejoinder to this "voiders"-of-Islam paradigm, see Al-Yaqoubi, *Refuting ISIS*, chapters 4 and 8. Arguably, this paradigm can be traced back to ibn Taymiyya, who declared Muslim Mongol rulers apostates because, as he saw it, they considered Genghis Khan to be "of the same rank as the Prophet," took "unbelievers as allies against Muslims," and failed to apply Islamic law (Peters [ed.], *Jihad in Classical and Modern Islam*, 162). Nevertheless, ibn Taymiyya also maintained that, with the exception of the unusual case of the Mongols, the practice of *takfir* (accusing Muslims of apostasy) among Sunnis (at least) is generally "deplorable" (Afsaruddin, *The First Muslims*, 195).

[57] See Scheuer, *Osama bin Laden*, 88, 109–110.

[58] See Cook, *Understanding Jihad*, 139. As researcher Shiraz Maher notes, the tendency, exhibited by bin Laden, to accuse Muslims of apostasy is one of the "defining characteristics" of "Salafi-Jihadi" radicals (Maher, *Salafi-Jihadism*, 15; see chapters 4–5).

Islam and a conception of reality in which true believers are constantly threatened by callous, often Western enemies.

It is evident that bin Laden was "deeply rooted in faith."[59] We may presume that his faith in Islam led him to revere certain holy sites and their surrounding territories, to regard persecuted individuals living in far-off countries as "brothers and sisters" worthy of protection, and to glorify jihad and life after death. Of course the same is true for many of the Muslim scholars and clerics who condemned him, not to mention the multitudes of believers who strongly disapproved of 9/11. The fact of the matter is that in Saudi Arabia, Afghanistan, and many other Muslim-majority countries, Islam is the medium through which countless individuals – from persevering advocates of peace to menacing terrorists – view the world. And for the many believers who see gross distortions in violent radical Muslim discourse, the words of British rabbi Jonathan Sacks must surely resonate: "Religion is like fire. It warms, but it also burns; and we are the guardians of the flame."[60]

[59] Ibrahim (ed.), *The Al Qaeda Reader*, xii; cf. Scheuer, *Osama Bin Laden*, 192, note 43.
[60] Sacks, "The Future of Religion Is at Stake Today."

5

"We Will Take Revenge"

A Word on ISIS

Osama bin Laden has been replaced by ISIS in today's headlines. And although the Iraqi branch of al-Qaeda was the precursor to the Islamic State of Iraq and Syria (ISIS, formed in 2013) – also known as the Islamic State of Iraq and the Levant (ISIL), Daesh (an Arabic acronym), or simply the Islamic State (IS) – the dissimilarities between ISIS and al-Qaeda central are profound. For example, ISIS, which was disowned by al-Qaeda under the leadership of Ayman al-Zawahiri, has attempted to establish a caliphal state apparatus; while bin Laden's al-Qaeda generally eschewed videotaped executions (instead opting for sensational terrorist attacks), ISIS, for some time at least, seemed to be using videotaped executions to entice potential recruits and project an aura of strength;[1] and while the "face" of al-Qaeda, bin Laden, recorded and published numerous statements, the self-proclaimed caliph of ISIS, known as Abu Bakr al-Baghdadi (né Ibrahim Awwad Ibrahim al-Badri), has, as of this writing, been quieter.

Born in 1971 in the Iraqi city of Samarra, al-Baghdadi was raised in a lower-middle-class farming family. He earned a PhD in Islamic studies in 2007 from a university in Baghdad established by Saddam Hussein.[2] (Both his master's thesis and doctoral dissertation were on the subject of Qur'anic recitation, not Islamic law.) His path to

---

[1] On the topic of ISIS propaganda, see Stern and Berger, *ISIS*.

[2] The university, founded in 1989, was originally called Saddam University for Islamic Studies. It was renamed Islamic University in 2003 and then Al-Iraqia (or Iraqi) University in 2010.

a doctorate, however, was complicated. In February 2004, he was detained by American forces and held for roughly ten months after visiting a friend who was wanted by the United States. Following his release, al-Baghdadi's move toward radicalism became more obvious: he joined al-Qaeda in 2006 and, later that year, was assigned the task of overseeing the implementation of Islamic law in the newly formed, al-Qaeda-affiliated Islamic State of Iraq (ISI). He became the leader of ISI in 2010 and then ISIS when it was established three years later. In 2014, he declared himself caliph of the world's lone "Islamic state."[3]

In the eyes of those who recognize al-Baghdadi's authority, he is in a position to sanction and call for aggressive jihad. (All indications suggest that the overwhelming majority of Sunnis reject al-Baghdadi's claim to the caliphate.) Even before al-Baghdadi's reign, the leadership of ISI embraced aggressive jihad and directed it mainly against neighboring Shi'ites (whom ISI and now ISIS members generally regard as unbelievers). According to the former ISI leader known as Abu Umar al-Baghdadi (né Hamid Dawud al-Zawi; d. 2010), one desired outcome of aggressive jihad is the eradication of "polytheism" (*shirk*).[4]

When it comes to its justifications for declaring war on the United States and many other nations and killing their civilians through terrorist attacks, however, ISIS largely follows the line of thinking adopted by al-Qaeda. Consider Abu Bakr al-Baghdadi's first widely broadcast audio message as caliph of ISIS, a speech released on July 1, 2014 (less than two months before ISIS circulated footage of its execution of American journalist James Foley). Having glorified jihad, al-Baghdadi painted a dramatic and tragic scene:

[Y]ou have brothers in many parts of the world being inflicted with the worst kinds of torture. Their honor is being violated. Their blood is being spilled. Prisoners are moaning and crying for help. Orphans and widows are complaining of their plight. Women who have lost their children are weeping. [Mosques] are desecrated and sanctities are violated. Muslims' rights are forcibly seized in China, India, Palestine, Somalia, the Arabian Peninsula, the Caucasus, [the Levant], Egypt, Iraq, Indonesia, Afghanistan, the Philippines, [Ahvaz in Iran, by the Shi'ites], Pakistan, Tunisia, Libya, Algeria and Morocco, in the East and in the West.

So raise your ambitions, O soldiers of the Islamic State! For your brothers all over the world are waiting for your rescue, and are anticipating your brigades. It

---

[3] My biographical sketch of al-Baghdadi draws much from chapter 4 of terrorism specialist William McCants's recent book *The ISIS Apocalypse*.

[4] See Bunzel, "From Paper State to Caliphate," 10–11.

is enough for you to just look at the scenes that have reached you from Central Africa, and from Burma before that. What is hidden from us is far worse.

So by [God], we will take revenge! By [God], we will take revenge! Even if it takes a while, we will take revenge, and every amount of harm against the [*umma* (Muslim community)] will be responded to with multitudes more against the perpetrator.[5]

Al-Baghdadi went on to quote a passage from the Qur'an, 42:39, which describes believers as those who "defend themselves when they are oppressed." Al-Baghdadi added, "And the one who commences is the more oppressive."

To al-Baghdadi's mind, the oppressors include "the camp of the [J]ews, the crusaders, their allies, and with them the rest of the nations and religions of kufr [unbelief], all being led by America and Russia, and being mobilized by the [J]ews." In this civilizational clash, the "camp of the Muslims" must defend themselves, take revenge, and restore their honor, dignity, and superiority.[6]

Al-Baghdadi proceeded to rebuke critics who describe ISIS as a terrorist organization. If the acts of ISIS qualify as "terrorism," he asserted, then terrorism "is to refuse humiliation, subjugation, and subordination." He sarcastically added,

But terrorism does not include the killing of Muslims in Burma and the burning of their homes. Terrorism does not include the dismembering and disemboweling of the Muslims in the Philippines, Indonesia, and Kashmir. Terrorism does not include the killing of Muslims in the Caucasus and expelling them from their lands. Terrorism does not include making mass graves for the Muslims in Bosnia and Herzegovina, and the slaughtering of their children. Terrorism does not include the destruction of Muslims' homes in Palestine, the seizing of their lands, and the violation and desecration of their sanctuaries and families.

... Terrorism does not include the slaughtering of Muslims in Central Africa like sheep, while no one weeps for them and denounces their slaughter.

All this is not terrorism. Rather it is freedom, democracy, peace, security, and tolerance! Sufficient for us is [God], and He is the best Disposer of affairs.[7]

Al-Baghdadi then quoted the Qur'anic statement, "Their only grievance against them was their faith in God, the Mighty, the Praiseworthy" (85:8).

5 "Islamic State Leader Abu Bakr al-Baghdadi Encourages Emigration, Worldwide Action."
6 "Islamic State Leader Abu Bakr al-Baghdadi Encourages Emigration, Worldwide Action."
7 "Islamic State Leader Abu Bakr al-Baghdadi Encourages Emigration, Worldwide Action."

According to various Qur'anic commentators, this passage refers to a pre-Islamic king who ordered his subjects to kill believers who refused to abandon their monotheistic religion.[8]

In the same speech, al-Baghdadi promised world domination to those who would heed his words: "If you hold to [my advice], you will conquer Rome and own the world."[9] And yet al-Baghdadi's call here was primarily for a defensive jihad against the United States and other nations that, to his mind, were responsible for the suffering of Muslims in various parts of the world: "today," he told his followers, "you are the defenders of the religion and the guards of the land of Islam."[10] Again, his was a message of retaliation: "we will take revenge!"

Such sentiments parallel what we find in the ISIS online magazine *Dabiq*. An October 2014 issue, for instance, quotes from a speech given the previous month by the then spokesperson of ISIS, Abu Mohammad al-Adnani (d. 2016):

O Americans, and O Europeans, the Islamic State did not initiate a war against you, as your governments and media try to make you believe. It is you who started the transgression against us, and thus you deserve blame and you will pay a great price ... You will pay the price when this crusade of yours collapses, and thereafter we will strike you in your homeland, and you will never be able to harm anyone afterwards ...

So O muwahhid [true believer in the one God], do not let this battle pass you by wherever you may be ... Strike their police, security, and intelligence members, as well as their treacherous agents. Destroy their beds. Embitter their lives for them and busy them with themselves. If you can kill a disbelieving American or European – especially the spiteful and filthy French – or an Australian, or a Canadian, or any other disbeliever from the disbelievers waging war, including the citizens of the countries that entered into a coalition against the Islamic State, then rely upon Allah, and kill him in any manner or way however it may be ... Kill the disbeliever whether he is civilian or military, for they have the same ruling.

---

[8] See Nasr (ed.), *The Study Quran*, 1497 (commentary on Qur'an 85:4–9).

[9] In an audio message released by ISIS in May 2015 and ascribed to al-Baghdadi, presumably the latter can be heard declaring, "Islam was never a religion of peace. Islam is the religion of fighting" (BBC [British Broadcasting Corporation], "Islamic State Releases 'al-Baghdadi Message'"). Along these lines, the February 2015 issue of the ISIS online magazine *Dabiq* features an article entitled "Islam Is the Religion of the Sword Not Pacifism." The article promotes the abrogationist-expansionist paradigm and rejects the possibility of everlasting peace with unbelievers (*Dabiq* 7 [Feb. 2015], 20–24).

[10] "Islamic State Leader Abu Bakr al-Baghdadi Encourages Emigration, Worldwide Action."

So O muwahhid ... will you leave the American, the Frenchman, or any of their allies to walk safely upon the earth while the armies of the crusaders strike the lands of the Muslims not differentiating between a civilian and fighter?[11]

If we consider such statements in conjunction with the targeting of innocents in terrorist operations that ISIS has either coordinated – such as the November 2015 Paris attacks that claimed the lives of 130 people and reportedly served as retaliation for French airstrikes against ISIS[12] – or seemingly inspired and certainly celebrated – such as the June 2016 Orlando Pulse nightclub shooting that resulted in forty-nine deaths and reportedly served as a reprisal for American-led airstrikes in Iraq and Syria that had killed "innocent women and children" and an ISIS leader named Abu Waheeb[13] – we find that there is indeed much overlap between the retributive, indiscriminate "defensive jihad" of ISIS and that of bin Laden's al-Qaeda.[14] And because of the precarious state of ISIS at the time of this writing – it has been losing ground in Iraq and Syria, and its fighters seem to be dispersing to various parts of the world – we should expect the organization to abandon altogether its somewhat more regulated, conquest-driven aggressive form of jihad and devote much of its resources toward defensive and terrorist operations.

Nevertheless, in the July 2016 issue of *Dabiq*, in an article entitled "Why We Hate You & Why We Fight You," we find not only a celebration

---

[11] *Dabiq* 4 (Oct. 2014), 8–9. An emphasis on defensive jihad also appears in later online publications by ISIS. For instance, an April 2016 article states that just as God shamed the hypocrites for abandoning aggressive jihad during the Prophet's time, so too may He shame "those who abandon the defensive jihad today without any valid excuses" (*Dabiq* 14 [April 2016], 47). And we read in a September 2016 piece, "the scholars have concluded that jihad – even if it is offensive jihad – is the best of deeds ... How is it then if it is defensive jihad and it becomes obligatory on every Muslim, as is the case today?!" (*Rumiyah* 1 [Sept. 2016], 33).

[12] Elgot et al., "Paris Attacks."

[13] Doornbos, "Transcripts of 911 Calls Reveal Pulse Shooter's Terrorist Motives"; see Goldman, "FBI Has Found No Evidence That Orlando Shooter Targeted Pulse because It Was a Gay Club." Although there is no conclusive proof that Mateen targeted the Pulse nightclub, a self-described gay bar, because of a hatred of homosexuals, there is much speculation that such hatred was indeed a contributing factor (see, for instance, Williams et al., "Gunman Omar Mateen Described as Belligerent, Racist and 'Toxic'").

[14] In recent years, al-Qaeda under Ayman al-Zawahiri has called for more restraint than in the past. In a document posted online in September 2013, for instance, al-Zawahiri instructs his followers not to attack noncombatant women and children, religious minorities in Muslim-majority countries, and large gatherings where Muslims may be present (see MacDonald, "Al Qaeda Leader Urges Restraint in First 'Guidelines for Jihad'").

of terrorists such as the Orlando shooter Omar Mateen (d. 2016) but also a strong endorsement of the abrogationist-expansionist paradigm. This article, anonymously authored,[15] was published shortly after the Orlando shooting, at a time when ISIS was already losing much ground and was reportedly "quietly preparing its followers for the eventual collapse of the caliphate."[16] But one would not sense this from the triumphalist tone of the article.

The *Dabiq* author rebukes those who claim that there is "no logic behind [their] course of action" and that what they are doing is not truly "Islamic." In fact, the author proclaims, ISIS members will always hate and fight non-Muslims – here the focus is Westerners[17] – for six reasons:

(1) They are unbelievers.

(2) Their "secular, liberal societies" permit what God has forbidden, and forbid what He has permitted. They make it their "mission to 'liberate' Muslim societies; we've made it our mission to fight off your influence and protect mankind from your misguided concepts and your deviant way of life."

(3) Their "atheist fringe" rejects God despite the clear signs of His existence.

(4) They have committed "crimes against Islam," such as mocking the faith, insulting God's prophets, burning Qur'ans, and denouncing Islamic (Sharia) law.

(5) They have committed "crimes against the Muslims," such as the bombing, killing, and maiming of believers throughout the world, and they have propped up "puppets in the usurped lands of the Muslims [who] oppress, torture, and wage war against anyone who calls to the truth."

(6) They have invaded Muslim-majority countries, and so they must be fought, repelled, and driven out.

The *Dabiq* author provocatively stresses that the *primary* reason that ISIS members hate and fight Westerners is because they are non-Muslim.[18] But the non-Muslimness of Westerners in and of itself does not explain why ISIS fights them *today* and its indiscriminate *methods* of attack. Accordingly,

---

[15] The journalist Graeme Wood maintains that this article was probably written by the American recruit Yahya Abu Hassan (né John Georgelas) (Wood, *The Way of the Strangers*, 171).

[16] Warrick and Mekhennet, "ISIS Quietly Braces Itself for the Collapse of the 'Caliphate'."

[17] This is made clear in the foreword to the issue (*Dabiq* 15 [July 2016], 4–7).

[18] *Dabiq* 15 (July 2016), 30–33.

it is important to take into account the *entirety* of the above list. It is also critical to be mindful of other, more authoritative ISIS statements, including al-Baghdadi's call for revenge and al-Adnani's declaration that it was Americans and Europeans who commenced the war against ISIS and not the other way around. It bears repeating that al-Adnani specifically called for the killing of Americans and other "disbelievers waging war, including the citizens of the countries that entered into a coalition against the Islamic State"; and he had rhetorically asked his audience whether they would actually let the "crusaders" be while their armies attack Muslims, "not differentiating between a civilian and fighter." Thus, for the leadership of ISIS, those who are to be fought immediately as part of its terroristic "defensive jihad" are those deemed direct threats. As such, the foreign policies of Western nations (at least as they are perceived) might not be a primary reason for at least some ISIS members' general sense of hostility toward non-Muslims, but they are ISIS's primary justification for its terrorist operations against Western powers.[19]

Bearing some resemblance to the aforementioned February 2002 open letter popularly ascribed to bin Laden (and addressed to Saudi leaders), the "Why We Hate You" article declares that ISIS will continue to fight Western nations until the latter are "ready to leave the swamp of warfare and terrorism through the exits" of conversion to Islam, submission to Muslim rule, or a temporary truce. (Even in the latter two scenarios, the author clarifies, ISIS members would continue to hate such non-Muslims; they simply would not harm them.) "Thus," we read,

even if you were to stop fighting us, your best-case scenario in a state of war would be that we would suspend our attacks against you – if we deemed it necessary – in order to focus on the closer and more immediate threats, before eventually resuming our campaigns against you.[20]

In this hypothetical scenario, "resuming our campaigns" against peaceable Western nations would presumably entail launching a more regulated aggressive jihad – unless ISIS would choose to redefine aggressive jihad altogether – after ISIS had fended off all immediate threats. Of course considering ISIS's limitations and state of decline when

---

[19] The same is generally true for Ayman al-Zawahiri's al-Qaeda. In his December 2014 "Letter to the American People," al-Zawahiri criticizes American foreign policy and proclaims that al-Qaeda is fighting the United States simply because America "attacked us and continue[s] to do so" (*Inspire* 13 [Dec. 2014], 12 [article runs from pages 12–14]).

[20] *Dabiq* 15 (July 2016), 31, 33.

the "Why We Hate You" article was published, this particular warning comes across as both defiant and delusional.

As it turns out, this piece appeared in the final issue of *Dabiq*. The online magazine was named after a northern Syrian village that held great symbolic value to ISIS: in a hadith (recorded by the scholar named Muslim), the Prophet foretells an apocalyptic battle in Dabiq that is to take place between Muslim and non-Muslim, "Roman" forces; the Muslim victors, the hadith tells us, would be the "conquerors of Constantinople." This prophecy explains why, in the summer of 2014, ISIS soldiers "fought ferociously" to capture Dabiq: they wanted to partake in the foretold battle, which they imagined would involve the United States and many other nations. (The first issue of *Dabiq* was published in July 2014.) Of course it is not easy to reconcile the prophecy concerning Dabiq with the fact that Constantinople, or Istanbul, is in the hands of Turkish Muslims and that many Muslims are united against ISIS. But to quote terrorism specialist William McCants, "in the apocalyptic imagination, inconvenient facts rarely impede the glorious march to the end of the world."[21] Significantly, as of this writing, ISIS no longer controls Dabiq, as Turkish-backed Syrian rebels captured it in October 2016.

In September 2016, just before the fall of Dabiq, ISIS began publishing a new online magazine called *Rumiyah*, an Arabic name for Rome. Why the fixation on Rome? In addition to prophetic reports that foretell victory over the "Romans," one hadith (recorded by Ahmad ibn Hanbal [d. 855]) prophesies the future conquest of Constantinople and Rome, in that order.

Rumiyah reveals the cruel logic behind some of ISIS's rules of war. In the September 2016 issue, for instance, in an article entitled "The Kafir's [Unbeliever's] Blood Is Halal for You, So Shed It," an anonymous author avers that *all* non-Muslim men who are neither under Muslim rule nor protected by a truce may be killed. These would include noncombatant men, be they elderly or mentally disabled, be they priests or "merry Crusader citizen[s] selling flowers to passersby." The *Rumiyah* author justifies this, in part, by invoking the aforementioned hadith in which Muhammad declares that he has been "commanded to fight against people" until they affirm faith in Islamic monotheism and Muhammad's prophethood. According to the *Rumiyah* author, the wording of this hadith – he renders the key line, "I have been ordered to fight mankind" – leaves "no room for debate, as mankind includes every person in the world." (The author suggests that "fighting" noncombatant

[21] McCants, *The ISIS Apocalypse*, 102–105.

women and children entails enslaving, not killing, them.) Yet still within the same sentence, and presumably recognizing an obvious problem with his/her push for literalism, he/she backs off and offers a qualification: "and the only ones excluded from this order to fight are those who submit or surrender to the rule of Islam," such as non-Muslims who agree to pay the *jizya* tax.²² In other words, "mankind" does *not* include "every person in the world."

As mentioned earlier, this hadith was widely understood to be in reference specifically to Arab polytheists, with some limiting it further to the oppressive Meccan polytheists. The *Rumiyah* author never discusses this and never clarifies why his/her preferred, qualified interpretation of "people" (or "mankind") should be favored over others. (The author also makes no mention of the aforementioned hadith in which the Prophet commands his followers not to attack the Ethiopians or the Turks unless they attack first.) Instead, the article leaves the reader with the impression that what is being presented is the "consensus" position. "None of this," the author declares, "should be surprising to any Muslim who has studied his religion."²³

In reality, what this article proffers is a minority opinion, and one that runs counter to various explicit statements attributed to the Prophet and his followers.²⁴ (It is even more extreme than what is presented in al-Qaeda in the Arabian Peninsula's online magazine *Inspire*, which was launched in June 2010; there it is indicated that certain noncombatant men are not to be targeted.)²⁵ Not surprisingly, when the *Rumiyah* author mentions the views of famous scholars, they are presented in an incomplete or misleading manner. We read, for instance, that according to the teachings of the famous Islamic legal scholar Abu Hanifa (d. 767), there is no retaliation to be sought or blood money

---

²² *Rumiyah* 1 (September 2016), 34–36.

²³ *Rumiyah* 1 (September 2016), 36.

²⁴ See Peters (ed.), *Jihad in Classical and Modern Islam*, 34–35 (ibn Rushd's *al-Bidaya*), 49 (ibn Taymiyya's *al-Siyasa*).

²⁵ A 2011 issue of *Inspire*, for instance, features an article attributed to the Yemeni-American preacher Anwar al-Awlaki (d. 2011) entitled "Targeting the Populations of Countries That Are at War with the Muslims"; the article refers, seemingly with approval, to a hadith that prohibits the killing of the elderly (*Inspire* 8 [Fall 2011; released in May 2012], 42 [article runs from pages 40–47]). And in a 2016 issue of *Inspire*, in a piece called "Rulings of Lone Jihad," a certain Shaikh Hammed al-Tameemi is quoted as saying that those who may be targeted are "every single male, adult, *mindful and able to fight* but irrespective of whether he fought or not" (*Inspire* 16 [Nov. 2016], 31 [emphasis added; article runs from pages 28–32]).

to be paid for the killing of a non-Muslim who was not under Muslim rule or protected by a truce;[26] we do not read about Abu Hanifa's widely discussed opinion that divine law prohibits the killing of various categories of "unprotected" non-Muslim men (and, of course, women and children).[27] Interestingly, ibn Taymiyya is invoked in four separate articles in the same issue of *Rumiyah* (not to mention many other ISIS publications),[28] but he is nowhere to be found in "The Kafir's Blood" article. More than likely this is because his view on the topic at hand is "inconvenient": he maintained that, in addition to women and children, "monks, old people, the blind, handicapped and their likes … shall not be killed, unless they actually fight," which for ibn Taymiyya would include spying and generating threatening propaganda.[29] As it turns out, *Rumiyah* offers conflicting messages: in the May 2017 issue, in the context of justifying the killing of Egyptian Copts (Christian citizens of a Muslim-majority nation that ISIS considers illegitimate), an anonymous author selectively refers to ibn Taymiyya and states that, in addition to "secluded" monks, noncombatant "women, children, the elderly, and the infirm" may not be targeted in war, though they may be killed as collateral damage.[30]

The topic of collateral killings is specifically addressed in the January 2017 issue of *Rumiyah*, in an article entitled "Collateral Carnage." Here we read that although Muslims may not exclusively target nonthreatening non-Muslim women and children who are neither under Muslim rule nor protected by a truce, such innocents may be generally attacked nonetheless if they are not "distinctly isolated" or "easily distinguishable" from enemy non-Muslim men, all of whom, this article suggests, would be considered combatants. And as the author clarifies in a footnote, although such killings may be considered retaliation for the killing of Muslim women and children, even if non-Muslims "were to have never killed a single Muslim woman or child, it would still be permissible to target the kafir masses."[31]

To justify this view, the *Rumiyah* author points to two reported prophetic precedents. One is Muhammad permitting the use of mangonels (the author uses the broader term "catapults"), which the author claims were "common in siege warfare," "even during the life of the Prophet." In

---

[26] *Rumiyah* 1 (September 2016), 36.
[27] See, for instance, Peters (ed.), *Jihad in Classical and Modern Islam*, 33–34 (ibn Rushd's *al-Bidaya*); and Al-Dawoody, *The Islamic Law of War*, 114.
[28] See *Rumiyah* 1 (September 2016), 4–6, 19–20, 29, 33.
[29] Peters (ed.), *Jihad in Classical and Modern Islam*, 49 (ibn Taymiyya's *al-Siyasa*).
[30] *Rumiyah* 9 (May 2017), 7–10 (article runs from pages 4–10).
[31] *Rumiyah* 5 (January 2017), 6–7.

fact, as noted earlier, according to the biographical record, Muhammad only tried to use a mangonel once against the enemy Thaqif tribe in a brief, unsuccessful attempt to breach walls that were guarded by combatants.[32] The author also controversially compares mangonels to "most missiles and explosives of today,"[33] even though many Muslim scholars historically distinguished between attacking fortifications with mangonels and using fire.[34]

Another invoked precedent comes from the aforementioned hadith (recorded by al-Bukhari and Muslim) in which the Prophet is queried as to whether it would be permissible to attack an enemy force at night, and he responds in the affirmative, indicating that any noncombatants harmed collaterally "are of" the combatants. With this in mind, the *Rumiyah* author asserts,

The best practice when conducting raids is to start during the night or at the break of dawn, before the sun rises, while the enemy is asleep. At such a time, it is very likely to enter buildings where no light shines and an adult male is not easily distinguishable from women and children.[35]

The author attempts to buttress this claim that it is *best* to attack in the dark, while the enemy is sleeping, by pointing to the example of God Himself, for the Qur'an states that He destroyed "many towns" at night or while people were sleeping in the afternoon (7:4). This represents a remarkable conflation of the human with the divine. As for the normative example of Muhammad, the *Rumiyah* author makes no reference to

---

[32] Cf. the problematic claim ascribed to al-Jassas (d. 981) and quoted by al-Qaeda's Ayman al-Zawahiri that the Prophet launched catapults "knowing full well that women and children would be struck" (Ibrahim [ed.], *The Al Qaeda Reader*, 164–5 [al-Zawahiri's *Jihad, Martyrdom, and the Killing of Innocents*]). This claim is likely based on a hadith that Muslim scholars historically considered "weak" in authenticity, a hadith that seems especially suspect because it appears to combine the biographical account of the Prophet using a mangonel at Ta'if with the aforementioned "they are of them" hadith (which we shall soon revisit). In this case, when the Prophet orders the use of the mangonel at Ta'if, he is informed that there are women and children inside the fortress; he responds, "They are of their fathers" (see al-Qarafi, *al-Dhakhira*, 3:408, including note 5). The wording here is identical to that of a well-known variant of the "they are of them" hadith (recorded by the scholar named Muslim). That the *Rumiyah* author never bothers to quote the dubious mangonel hadith is telling. I should add that, aside from the Ta'if episode, the author's only other specific mention of mangonel use is a passing reference to the Prophet's companion Amr ibn al-As's reported employment of mangonels in his successful siege of the fortified city of Alexandria in 645, well over a decade after Muhammad had passed away.

[33] *Rumiyah* 5 (January 2017), 7.

[34] See, for instance, al-Qarafi, *al-Dhakhira*, 3:408–409; and Peters (ed.), *Jihad in Classical and Modern Islam*, 35–36 (ibn Rushd's *al-Bidaya*).

[35] *Rumiyah* 5 (January 2017), 7.

and demonstrates no awareness of the well-known hadith (recorded by al-Bukhari) that states that "whenever the Prophet reached a people by night, he never started an attack until it was morning."[36] Various hadiths (including reports recorded by al-Bukhari and Muslim) tell us that this is precisely what happened when Muhammad reached the Arabian city of Khaybar after nightfall: he did not enter the city until its inhabitants were awake. In any case, notice that the noncombatant killings the *Rumiyah* author attempts to justify are far more intentional than what is suggested in the "they are of them" hadith as commonly understood, as the author calls for the *targeting* of "kafir masses" using highly destructive technology and weaponry, including the "missiles and explosives of today."

After citing select statements of influential Muslim scholars on the legitimacy of collateral damage, the *Rumiyah* author brazenly proclaims, "one should not avoid targeting gatherings of the kuffar [unbelievers] – whether military or civilian – in which kafir women and children outnumber the kafir men."[37] According to Islamic legal scholars such as Ahmed Al-Dawoody, the analogy between what Muslim scholars have permitted historically with regard to collateral damage and contemporary terrorist attacks is fundamentally flawed: "the classical jurists were addressing a context of war between two armies."[38] And even then, various leading jurists imposed limitations and expressed reservations that are never even hinted at in the "Collateral Carnage" article. For instance, when discussing attacks on enemy fortifications, some scholars forbade the use of fire altogether, others discouraged it, and yet others legitimized it but clarified that this tactic would be impermissible if noncombatants were inside the fortifications.[39]

As with al-Qaeda, numerous Muslim scholars and clerics have strongly condemned ISIS's extreme methods of fighting, even while possibly sharing some or many of its political grievances. According to the Saudi grand mufti Abdulaziz al-Shaykh, for instance, ISIS and al-Qaeda are "enemy number one of Islam";[40] to the mind of the grand imam of al-Azhar, Ahmed El-Tayeb, ISIS militants are operating "under the guise of this holy religion," while exporting "their false Islam";[41] and

---

[36] This hadith is translated and discussed in Al-Dawoody, *The Islamic Law of War*, 119 (emphasis added).

[37] *Rumiyah* 5 (January 2017), 7.

[38] Al-Dawoody, *The Islamic Law of War*, 119.

[39] See al-Qarafi, *al-Dhakhira*, 3:408–409; and Al-Dawoody, *The Islamic Law of War*, 123–124.

[40] McDowall, "Saudi Arabia's Grand Mufti Denounces Islamic State Group as Un-Islamic."

[41] Al Arabiya, "Head of Egypt's al-Azhar Condemns ISIS 'Barbarity'."

nearly 70,000 Sunni scholars from the Indian Barelvi movement issued a joint fatwa in December 2015 that proclaimed that organizations such as ISIS, al-Qaeda, and the Taliban are "not Islamic organizations" and, remarkably, that their members are "not Muslims."[42] And then there is the "Open Letter to Al-Baghdadi." Posted online in the fall of 2014 and initially signed by more than 120 prominent Muslim scholars and leaders from around the world (with dozens of other signatories added later), the "Letter" offers concise (though somewhat shallow) point-by-point refutations of, among other things, ISIS's Islamic legal methodology, caliphate, jihad tactics, reestablishment of slavery, and treatment of minorities, women, and children.[43]

In the discourses and practices of ISIS, many Muslim scholars see the sloppy appropriation of medieval Islamic tradition – and not simply in ISIS's justifications for killing noncombatants. Consider, for instance, ISIS's abduction and enslavement of Yazidi women and children following their August 2014 conquest of the Iraqi city of Sinjar. In an October 2014 *Dabiq* article entitled "Revival of Slavery before the Hour," an anonymous author attempts to cast the practice in a positive light by, among other things, invoking a famous hadith (versions of which appear in the collections of al-Bukhari and Muslim) that indicates that one of the signs of Judgment Day is that "the slave girl will give birth to her master."[44] According to the *Dabiq* author, this hadith, taken literally, shows that slavery, which is officially illegal in all Muslim-majority nations and never explicitly mandated in the Qur'an, will be reinstituted before the end of this world. The devoted reader is thus led to believe that ISIS's reestablishment of slavery is a righteous undertaking. Here I should pause to note that reports by human rights organizations and the media suggest that, in the words of Islamic legal scholar Kecia Ali, ISIS's "soldiers'

[42] Agarwall, "70,000 Clerics Issue Fatwa Against Terrorism."
[43] See "Open Letter to Al-Baghdadi." For other popular condemnations of ISIS, see Al-Yaqoubi, *Refuting ISIS*; and Bridge Initiative Team, "Here Are the (Many) Muslim Condemnations of ISIS You've Been Looking For." See also McCants and Fadel, "Experts Weigh In (Part 4)," in which Islamic legal scholar Mohammad Fadel notes that ISIS's claim "to represent the only legitimate Islamic territory is ... contrary to the last millennium of Muslim legal thought on the nature of what an Islamic territory means."
[44] *Dabiq* 4 (Oct. 2014), 14–17; see McCants's related discussion in *The ISIS Apocalypse*, 111–113. The *Dabiq* author offers a slightly different translation of the relevant passage: "the slave girl gives birth to her master." Incidentally, in other versions of the hadith, "mistress" (*rabbataha*) takes the place of "master" (*rabbaha*).

patterns of sexual violation have more in common with wartime rape or sex trafficking than with classical-era practices of enslavement and slave-holding."[45]

In any case, to bolster his/her claim, the *Dabiq* author cites discussions of the Prophet's "slave girl" statement by the influential medieval authorities al-Nawawi (d. 1277) and ibn Rajab (d. 1393). Both are quoted in *Dabiq* as conveying the opinion that the hadith foretells the future expansion of slavery.[46] As Islamic studies scholar Younus Mirza observes, however, the *Dabiq* author tells his/her readers only part of the story: although neither al-Nawawi nor ibn Rajab ever advocated complete abolition (which would have been highly unusual in their respective contexts), both were of the view that the Prophet's statement about the "slave girl" could not be employed for legal purposes to *justify* the expansion of slavery, as some of their (seemingly much less influential) contemporaries had maintained. Such contemporaries had invoked the hadith to argue that a slave woman who had a child with her master – a "concubine mother" (*umm walad*) – should be considered a permanent slave and not, as most scholars believed, a free woman once her master passed away. For if a "slave girl" gives birth to her master, this means she would remain enslaved following the death of her original master. For al-Nawawi, however, the "slave girl" statement pertains strictly to eschatology, not law: the future expansion of slavery need not align with what is religiously permissible. As for ibn Rajab, although he described various interpretations of the hadith, including the expansionist one, the only interpretation he defended and presented as his own was that the "slave girl" statement cannot be used to justify the permanent enslavement of concubine mothers; to the contrary, he argued, the Prophet's statement shows that a concubine mother becomes emancipated through her child, for the latter is likened to a master: the child (by its mere existence) is capable of (effectively) freeing the mother (once her actual master passes away). Incidentally, the *Dabiq* author never mentions another view conveyed by ibn Rajab, namely that the Prophet's statement pertains not to slavery per se but to children who disobey their mothers – in one

---

[45] Ali, *Sexual Ethics and Islam*, 68. In his rejoinder to ISIS, Syrian scholar Mohammad Al-Yaqoubi argues that the enslavement of Yazidis is "one of the worst crimes committed by ISIS" because it reintroduced slavery without justification and "breached a social contract long established" between Yazidis and Muslims (Al-Yaqoubi, *Refuting ISIS*, 38–43).

[46] *Dabiq* 4 (Oct. 2014), 16.

variant of the hadith, "woman" (*al-mar'a*) takes the place of "slave girl" (*al-ama*).[47] To the *Dabiq* author's credit, however, he/she does note that another important medieval authority, ibn Hajar (d. 1449), interpreted the "slave girl" statement metaphorically: the weak will seize power.[48] But the author dismisses this, opting for a more literal reading.

Of course one must be careful not to read too much into this and other instances of ISIS members rejecting metaphorical interpretations. As Islamic legal scholar Sohaira Siddiqui observes, ISIS *often* abandons strict literalism. We have already seen instances of this. Siddiqui herself offers the example of ISIS's infamous January 2015 immolation of a Jordanian pilot who was taken as a prisoner of war (ISIS circulated footage of the immolation in February of that year). In this case, ISIS appealed to the principle of reciprocity (as expressed in the *beginning* of a familiar passage, Qur'an 16:126, "If you [believers] respond to an attack, make your response proportionate") but constructed a tendentious analogy "between the effects of an airstrike and the deliberate burning of an individual."[49] In its selective use of Islamic sources, ISIS also invoked reports of early Muslims burning others but downplayed well-known hadiths that, taken literally, prohibit immolation altogether.[50]

* * *

Not surprisingly, Muslims in various parts of the world have an overwhelmingly negative opinion of ISIS (as indicated, for instance, by a 2015 Pew Research Center survey).[51] And yet it has succeeded in attracting thousands of recruits. Although journalists offer mixed messages regarding just how "Islamic" or secular the membership of ISIS is,[52] we know that many recruits have been moved by ISIS's "messianic fervor": they believe that by joining they will play a special role in ushering in the apocalypse.[53]

---

47 Mirza, "'The Slave Girl Gives Birth to Her Master'." For the relevant medieval discussions, see al-Nawawi, *Sharh Sahih Muslim*, 1:274; ibn Rajab, *Jami' al-'ulum wa-l-hikam*, 1:140–141; and ibn Rajab, *Fath al-bari*, 1:217–219.

48 See ibn Hajar, *Fath al-bari*, 1:148–150.

49 McCants and Siddiqui, "Experts Weigh In (Part 2)."

50 These hadiths appear in various collections, including that of al-Bukhari. For ISIS's justification for the immolation of the Jordanian pilot, see *Dabiq* 7 (Feb. 2015), 5–8. See also Al-Yaqoubi's response in Al-Yaqoubi, *Refuting ISIS*, 26–28.

51 See Poushter, "In Nations with Significant Muslim Populations, Much Disdain for ISIS."

52 See, for instance, Graeme Wood's book *The Way of the Strangers* and its predecessor, the popular *Atlantic* article "What ISIS Really Wants," the latter of which declares that ISIS is "Islamic. *Very* Islamic"; Christoph Reuter's *Der Spiegel* article "The Terror Strategist," which casts light on the secular dimensions of ISIS; and Ishaan Tharoor's *Washington Post* article with the self-explanatory title "It turns out many ISIS recruits don't know much about Islam."

53 McCants, *The ISIS Apocalypse*, 3.

(Some Muslim critics of ISIS also see them playing a foretold role, though hardly a good one.)[54] Nevertheless, many of these same recruits have also been driven by their "caliph's" call for revenge. This is a call that resonates with some Sunnis living in the war-torn and fragile lands of Iraq and Syria – Sunnis who may view Westerners, Shi'ites, and even other Sunni factions with suspicion and contempt. And the warfare they experienced may have been a catalyst for the region's messianic fervor in the first place.[55] Consider, for instance, that sales of Sunni books on the apocalypse shot up following the 2003 United States invasion of Iraq.[56] And a 2012 Pew Research Center survey of Muslims in dozens of countries with significant Muslim populations found that belief in the imminent return of the eschatological figure known as the *mahdi* (who, according to the hadith corpus, is a righteous leader whose appearance presages the events leading to the end of this world) was most pronounced in the volatile nations of Afghanistan and Iraq (Syria was not included in the survey).[57] As for the foreign recruits of ISIS who might not have a strong attachment to Iraq and Syria, it is striking that many of them have come from "regions with varied histories of resisting the influence of state institutions." These regions include Qassim (Saudi Arabia), North Governorate/Tripoli (Lebanon), Derna (Libya), the Tunisian heartland, and Xinjiang (China) – places where citizens "have long been frustrated by relationships with their respective federal governments."[58] In the final analysis, ISIS represents the extremes of both religion and geopolitics. For New Atheists such as Sam Harris and Ayaan Hirsi Ali, however, the extremism of ISIS, al-Qaeda, and other radical Muslim organizations is primarily a manifestation of the extremism intrinsic to the foundations of Islam.

---

[54] The "Open Letter to Al-Baghdadi," for instance, concludes with a quotation attributed to the Prophet's cousin and fourth caliph Ali (d. 661) in which he warns of the coming of a people with "black flags," "free-flowing" hair, and a "state." Their "names will be parental attributions, and their aliases will be derived from towns." (If you consider the name "Abu Bakr al-Baghdadi," the first part, "Abu Bakr," literally means "Father of Bakr," and the second part, "al-Baghdadi," means "of Baghdad.") Furthermore, these people "will fulfill neither covenant nor agreement" and "will call to the truth, but ... will not be people of the truth." Eventually, they will come to "differ among themselves," and "God will bring forth the Truth through whomever He wills." Al-Yaqoubi links ISIS to the group described by this report and downplays the weakness in its chain of transmission (Al-Yaqoubi, *Refuting ISIS*, 76–78).

[55] See McCants, *The ISIS Apocalypse*, 145–147.

[56] See Jean-Pierre Filiu, *Apocalypse in Islam*, chapter 7.

[57] Pew Research Center, "The World's Muslims: Unity and Diversity."

[58] Rosenblatt, "Inside the ISIS Enlistment Files."

PART III

THE NEW ATHEISM

Beginning with the publication of Sam Harris's *The End of Faith* in 2004, the figures who have come to be widely known as the New Atheists have produced a series of bestselling books and films that have reached and deeply affected countless individuals and communities the world over. Having been galvanized by 9/11, some of the New Atheists' works devote special attention to the "problem" of Islam and, in particular, armed jihad. Among the most prominent New Atheist critics of Islam – and the writers featured in the next three chapters – are Harris, Ayaan Hirsi Ali, Richard Dawkins, Christopher Hitchens, and Daniel Dennett.

6

"We Are at War with Islam"

The Case of Sam Harris

Before he was a bestselling author, Sam (or Samuel) Harris was perhaps best known as the son of an extremely successful television producer. His mother Susan Harris created popular television shows such as *The Golden Girls*, *Empty Nest*, *Soap*, and *Benson*. From 1965 to 1969, she was married to Sam's father, an actor named Berkeley Harris (d. 1984). Sam was born in 1967 in Los Angeles and was raised primarily by Susan. Although her background is Jewish (and Berkeley's family was Quaker), Sam grew up in a secular household.

He began his collegiate studies at Stanford University in the mid-1980s, though after his second year, he chose to travel to India to study meditation with Buddhist and Hindu teachers. More than a decade later, he returned to Stanford to complete a degree in philosophy. Between his graduation in 2000 and the completion of his doctorate in cognitive neuroscience from the University of California, Los Angeles, in 2009, Harris produced his landmark book and *New York Times* bestseller *The End of Faith: Religion, Terror, and the Future of Reason* (2004) as well as a popular follow-up entitled *Letter to a Christian Nation* (2006). *The End of Faith* is widely considered the first book of the New Atheist era.[1] Harris has since become a widely recognized public figure and is known for his active promotion of science and secular values.

---

[1] At times, Harris has expressed reservations about using labels such as "New Atheist" and even "atheist" (see, for instance, Harris, "The Problem with Atheism"). Ultimately, however, he appears to accept these designations. See, for example, Harris's positive back cover blurb for Victor Stenger's book *The New Atheism: Taking a Stand for Science and Reason* (2009), a book that presents Harris as a leading representative of the New Atheism.

Harris's other books include *The Moral Landscape: How Science Can Determine Human Values* (2010), *Lying* (2011), *Free Will* (2012), *Waking Up: A Guide to Spirituality Without Religion* (2014), and, more recently, a relatively short book coauthored with British Muslim activist Maajid Nawaz entitled *Islam and the Future of Tolerance: A Dialogue* (2015). In what follows, we shall examine, in sequential order, the two works most relevant to our project, *The End of Faith* and *Islam and the Future of Tolerance*. Separated by more than a decade, both books convey Harris's views on, among many other topics, jihad and violent radicalism.

ISLAM AND OTHERNESS

In *The End of Faith*, Harris attempts to disabuse his readers of the notion that religious beliefs are sacrosanct and exempt from rational inquiry and critique – especially when those beliefs threaten the well-being of others. Though critical of all monotheistic traditions, Harris devotes much of his attention to "The Problem with Islam," the title of the book's fourth chapter. Indeed, from the very beginning of the book, Harris casts a light on this particular "problem."

Harris opens *The End of Faith* in dramatic fashion, depicting a scene in which a suicide bomber detonates himself in a crowded bus. Harris tells us that the bomber's parents are sad when they hear the news but also "feel tremendous pride" because they "know that he has gone to heaven" and has "sent his victims to hell for eternity. It is a double victory." Assuming we know nothing else about the bomber, such as his past, economic status, intelligence, educational background, or profession, Harris rhetorically asks, "Why is it so easy ... so trivially easy – you-could-almost-bet-your-life-on-it easy – to guess the young man's religion?"[2] Harris's point here is clear: religious beliefs – in this case Islamic ones – can be dangerous. (We shall return to the topic of suicide bombing shortly.)

For Harris, what allows for such animosity toward Others, in this case non-Muslims, is an exclusivist paradigm that Harris believes comes directly from scripture:

Insofar as a person is Muslim – that is, insofar as he believes that Islam constitutes the only viable path to God and that the Koran enunciates it perfectly – he will feel contempt for any man or woman who doubts the truth of his beliefs.

---

[2] Harris, *The End of Faith*, 11–12.

What is more, he will feel that the eternal happiness of his children is put in peril by the mere presence of such unbelievers in the world.[3]

He adds,

We live in an age in which most people believe that mere words – "Jesus," "Allah," "Ram" – can mean the difference between eternal torment and bliss everlasting. Considering the stakes here, it is not surprising that many of us occasionally find it necessary to murder other human beings for using the wrong magic words, or the right ones for the wrong reasons.[4]

Accordingly, Harris writes, some Muslims consider the unbelief of non-Muslims "to be a sin so grave that it merits death whenever it becomes an impediment to the spread of Islam."[5] Such radicals hate non-Muslims because they are non-Muslim and not because of hatred "in any ordinary sense." In fact, Harris controversially alleges, "most Muslim extremists" have "far fewer grievances with Western imperialism than is the norm around the globe."[6]

With this in mind, Harris offers the following assessment of 9/11: the tragedy, he tells us, "proves beyond any possibility of doubt that certain twenty-first-century Muslims actually believe the most dangerous and implausible tenets of their faith."[7] And "[i]f you believe anything like what the Koran says you must believe in order to escape the fires of hell, you will, at the very least, be sympathetic with the actions of Osama bin Laden."[8] (We shall soon revisit this statement.) What is more, Harris declares, those who read the Qur'an "with the eyes of faith" will come to see that "the people who died on September 11 were nothing more than fuel for the eternal fires of God's justice."[9]

To justify the latter claim, Harris cites sixty carefully chosen Qur'anic passages from the second to the sixth chapter – avoiding any discussion of their respective contexts – that, in his eyes, "convey the relentlessness with which unbelievers are vilified."[10] Here are the first five passages, as they appear in *The End of Faith*:

[3] Harris, *The End of Faith*, 32.
[4] Harris, *The End of Faith*, 35.
[5] Harris, *The End of Faith*, 30.
[6] Harris, *The End of Faith*, 30; 240, note 10.
[7] Harris, *The End of Faith*, 246, note 5.
[8] Harris, *The End of Faith*, 117.
[9] Harris, *The End of Faith*, 117.
[10] Harris, *The End of Faith*, 117. In a March 2011 article, Harris requotes these sixty Qur'anic passages in a rejoinder to Keith Ellison, the first Muslim elected to the United States Congress. Ellison had recently appeared on the popular cable television show *Real Time with Bill Maher*. When host Bill Maher mentioned Harris's claim about the hateful

"It is the same whether or not you forewarn them [the unbelievers], they will have no faith" (2:6). "God will mock them and keep them long in sin, blundering blindly along" (2:15). A fire "whose fuel is men and stones" awaits them (2:24). They will be "rewarded with disgrace in this world and with grievous punishment on the Day of Resurrection" (2:85). "God's curse be upon the infidels!" (2:89).[11]

After citing all sixty passages, Harris concludes,

I cannot judge the quality of the Arabic; perhaps it is sublime. But the book's contents are not. On almost every page, the Koran instructs observant Muslims to despise non-believers. On almost every page, it prepares the ground for religious conflict.[12]

Harris seems to think that any Qur'anic reference to damned "unbelievers" or "infidels" necessarily applies to *all* non-Muslims. And there are, of course, Muslims who believe precisely this. This, however, is not the predominant view among Muslim theologians. Consider that the Arabic term for "unbeliever," *kafir*, denotes "one who conceals the truth" or "is ungrateful." A mere absence of belief need not be accompanied by concealment of the truth and ingratitude. Thus, for most theologians, although Muhammad's revelation supersedes other divine messages (such as the Torah of Moses and the Gospel of Jesus), God may save at least some "sincere" non-Muslims and, ultimately, only the Almighty knows who specifically among Muslims and non-Muslims will be saved and who will be damned. One of the most contentious questions among the theologians, then, is determining which general type or types of non-Muslims could be considered "sincere." On one end of the spectrum, we find theologians who only make room for non-Muslims who never truly encountered Islam, that is, the "unreached" (and some further argue that these would have to be "true" monotheists). On the other end, we find theologians who include "reached" non-Muslims (even nonmonotheists) who, in their heart of hearts,

---

nature of the Qur'an, Ellison dismissed the claim as "absurd, ridiculous, and untrue," for it involved taking passages "out of context" ("Bill Maher to Muslim Rep. Keith Ellison: The Qur'an Is a 'Hate Filled Holy Book'"). In his rejoinder to Ellison, Harris reproduces the sixty Qur'anic quotations appearing in *The End of Faith* (once again, without discussing their respective contexts) and concludes that such quotations "can be fairly said to convey the *central* message of the Qur'an – and of Islam at nearly every moment in its history ... The result is a unified message of triumphalism, otherworldliness, and religious hatred that has become a problem for the entire world" (Harris, "My Response to Rep. Keith Ellison"). I shall revisit Harris's claim concerning the Qur'an's "central" message.

[11] Harris, *The End of Faith*, 117–118.
[12] Harris, *The End of Faith*, 123.

simply do not find Islam convincing or compelling. It is not entirely
clear where most theologians fall on this spectrum. But consider this:
it is difficult to think of a theologian more influential than al-Ghazali
(d. 1111), and although he was not especially "liberal" – he assumed
that to be considered "sincere," a non-Muslim would at least have
to investigate Islam actively (without necessarily converting) after
encountering it in its "true" form – he nonetheless envisioned a paradise populated with most of humanity, Muslims and non-Muslims.
And even ibn Taymiyya, who is often cited in the works of al-Qaeda
and ISIS, imagined a day in which *every single* inhabitant of hell
would be admitted into heaven to spend the rest of eternity.[13] (To
the best of my knowledge, the leadership of al-Qaeda and ISIS has
never promoted this universalist salvation doctrine.)[14] These visions
of salvation are partly predicated on the scriptural emphasis on
divine mercy (see, for instance, Qur'an 1:1). All things considered,
most Muslim theologians would likely balk at the claim that the
non-Muslims who died on 9/11 were all simply "fuel for the eternal
fires of God's justice."

And while the conviction that Islam constitutes the primary path to
paradise might indeed lead to feelings of, as Harris puts it, "contempt
for any man or woman who doubts the truth of his beliefs," the matter
is not so simple. Consider, for instance, the words of the Muslim scholar
and academic Yasir Qadhi: while admitting "that a nonpluralistic view
could very easily lead to prejudice and intolerance," he contends that "the
opposite can and often does occur, and this is a tangible reality that those
within the Muslim community witness on a daily basis." This is because
a "nonpluralist Muslim might actually treat a non-Muslim better than
he or she would a Muslim, possibly with the opportunistic intention of
showing the non-Muslim the beauty of Islam and eventually winning him
or her over to the faith." Whatever one makes of this manner of thinking, the reality is that mainstream Muslims have "often managed to live
cordially with people of all faiths."[15] But with Harris intently focused on
the threat of Muslim terrorism, he sees not cordiality but hostility toward
Others in the name of Islam, and not a limited conflict but a civilizational
"clash."

---

[13] See Khalil, *Islam and the Fate of Others*.
[14] Such radicals may be unaware of or uninterested in this doctrine, or perhaps they accept
the problematic modern claim that this was not ibn Taymiyya's true, final position. For a
response to this claim, see Khalil, *Islam and the Fate of Others*, 86–88.
[15] Qadhi, "The Path of Allah or the Pathos of Allah?," 118.

JIHAD AND THE "CLASH"

Remarkably, Harris affirms what bin Laden had asserted about the West: "We are at war with Islam. It may not serve our immediate foreign policy objectives for our political leaders to openly acknowledge this fact, but it is unambiguously so."[16] (In his later work *Islam and the Future of Tolerance*, Harris notes that he is "careful to say that we are not at war with all [or even most] Muslims"; his "problem" is with their religion.)[17] Along these lines, Harris defends Samuel Huntington's well-known "clash of civilizations" thesis.[18] And, partly owing to his own particular reading of Islamic sources, Harris places much of the blame for this clash on Islam itself:

It is not merely that we are at war with an otherwise peaceful religion that has been "hijacked" by extremists. We are at war with precisely the vision of life that is prescribed to all Muslims in the Koran, and further elaborated in the literature of the hadith, which recounts the sayings and actions of the Prophet.[19]

Without faith, most Muslim grievances against the West would be impossible even to formulate, much less avenge.[20]

Nothing explains the actions of Muslim extremists, and the widespread tolerance of their behavior in the Muslim world, better than the tenets of Islam.[21]

Islam, more than any other religion human beings have devised, has all the makings of a thoroughgoing cult of death.[22]

Particularly troubling to Harris is "the duty of jihad," which he describes as "an unambiguous call to world conquest."[23] In making this statement, Harris invokes Islamic studies scholar Bernard Lewis. "The presumption" in Islam, according to Lewis, "is that the duty of jihad will

---

[16] Harris, *The End of Faith*, 109. Harris often rails against political correctness, as in his April 2012 blog entry "In Defense of Profiling." Here he tackles the sensitive topic of profiling at American airports, proclaiming, "We should profile Muslims, or anyone who looks like he or she could conceivably be Muslim, and we should be honest about it."

[17] Harris and Nawaz, *Islam and the Future of Tolerance*, 113–114.

[18] Harris, *The End of Faith*, 130; see Huntington, *The Clash of Civilizations and the Remaking of World Order*.

[19] Harris, *The End of Faith*, 109–110. Harris goes on to cite several hadiths (of varying levels of authenticity, according to traditional Sunni standards) that glorify jihad, noting that "Islamists regularly invoke [such hadiths] as a justification for attacks upon infidels and apostates" (*The End of Faith*, 112).

[20] Harris, *The End of Faith*, 138.

[21] Harris, *The End of Faith*, 137.

[22] Harris, *The End of Faith*, 123.

[23] Harris, *The End of Faith*, 111.

continue, interrupted only by truces, until all the world either adopts the Muslim faith or submits to Muslim rule."[24]

As Harris explains it, "from the point of view of Islam," the world "is divided into the 'House of Islam' and the 'House of War' ... The only future devout Muslims can envisage – *as Muslims* – is one in which all infidels have been converted to Islam, subjugated, or killed." In other words, a permanent sharing of power with the "enemies of God" is simply out of the question.[25] Accordingly, not only do "devout Muslims" "disdain" Western culture, they view Western success as "a diabolical perversity, and this situation will always stand as an open invitation for jihad."[26]

Harris fails to account for the fact that the terms "House of Islam" (or "abode of Islam") and "House of War" (or "abode of war"), neither of which appears in Islamic scripture, are principally descriptive (rather than prescriptive) designations. And although many Muslim scholars did indeed conceptualize armed jihad as a means of expansion and conquest, Harris is not concerned with those (in premodern or modern times) who instead stressed the defensive purpose of warfare. Nor does he seem acquainted with modern Muslim scholarly arguments (whether those of controversial clerics such as Yusuf al-Qaradawi or academics such as Sherman A. Jackson) against the practice of aggressive jihad in a world in which countries have fixed borders and there exists an assumed state of peace and tolerance. Furthermore, Harris's depiction of the "devout Muslim" outlook on Western prosperity ignores the fact that many practicing Muslims in and of the West actively contribute to its success and even take pride in their Westernness.

As for the Western side of the "clash," Harris rejects Noam Chomsky's assertion that the United States "itself is a leading terrorist state."[27] While

---

[24] Lewis, *The Crisis of Islam*, 31–32 (cited and discussed in Harris, *The End of Faith*, 111).

[25] Harris, *The End of Faith*, 110. Sentiments such as the one Harris expresses here about the "only future devout Muslims can envisage" have led some critics to accuse him of Islamophobia and bigotry (see, for instance, Greenwald, "Sam Harris, the New Atheists, and Anti-Muslim Animus"). Harris dismisses these accusations in his April 2013 blog entry "Response to Controversy" (which was updated in June 2014) and asserts that the term "Islamophobia" is a propaganda tool used to stifle criticism of Islam. His condemnations, he writes, pertain to Islamic doctrines and their adherents, not to all Muslims. And, he avers, "in the case of Islam, the bad acts of the *worst* individuals – the jihadists, the murderers of apostates, and the men who treat their wives and daughters like chattel – are the *best* examples of the doctrine in practice."

[26] Harris, *The End of Faith*, 32.

[27] Chomsky, 9–11, 119 (cited and discussed in Harris, *The End of Faith*, 140).

conceding that America "has much to atone for,"[28] Harris suggests that we should distinguish "between intending to kill a child, because of the effect you hope to produce on its parents (we call this 'terrorism'), and inadvertently killing a child in an attempt to capture or kill an avowed child murderer (we call this 'collateral damage')."[29] (Whether the United States has consistently taken the necessary steps to prevent wars or minimize collateral damage is a separate discussion.) Ultimately, for Harris, America is, "in many respects," a "well-intentioned giant."[30] It has gone to great lengths to protect Muslims, as when it defended Kuwait and Saudi Arabia during the 1991 Gulf War. "And yet," Harris contends, "the Muslim worldview is such that this fact, if acknowledged at all, is generally counted as a further grievance against us; it is yet another source of Muslim 'humiliation'."[31] Harris explains the humiliation felt by Muslim extremists in particular: "while their civilization has foundered, they have watched a godless, sin-loving people become the masters of everything they touch ... They feel the outrage of a chosen people who have been subjugated by barbarians." And this feeling is "a product of their faith."[32]

Here Harris points to the example of bin Laden. His "only apparent concerns," Harris submits, "are the spread of Islam and the sanctity of Muslim holy sites."[33] They do not include

the equal distribution of wealth around the globe. Even his demand for Palestinian statehood seems an afterthought, stemming as much from his anti-Semitism as from any solidarity he feels with the Palestinians (needless to say, such anti-Semitism and solidarity are also products of his faith). He seems most exercised over the presence of unbelievers (American troops and Jews) in the Muslim holy land and over what he imagines to be the territorial ambitions of Zionists. These are purely theological grievances. It would be much better, for all concerned, if he merely hated us.[34]

But, although motivated by religion, bin Laden's grievances were by no means "purely theological," as Harris maintains. All indications

---

[28] Harris, *The End of Faith*, 140.
[29] Harris, *The End of Faith*, 146. Given that bin Laden himself claimed that one must never target innocents, Harris would have done well to acknowledge this and then demonstrate bin Laden's disingenuousness.
[30] Harris, *The End of Faith*, 142.
[31] Harris, *The End of Faith*, 240, note 10.
[32] Harris, *The End of Faith*, 30.
[33] Harris, *The End of Faith*, 260, note 2.
[34] Harris, *The End of Faith*, 30.

suggest that bin Laden genuinely believed that the United States had played a sinister role in various Muslim-majority countries by occupying their lands, supporting corrupt regimes, imposing unjust sanctions, and stealing their oil. (These are widespread perceptions. Not surprisingly, a 2004 report commissioned by the United States Department of Defense concluded that the many Muslims who despise America hate it primarily because of its policies rather than its freedoms.)[35] Bin Laden saw his war against America as one that could be justified on the basis of reason: "what is wrong with resisting those who attack you? All religious communities have such a principle, for example these Buddhists, both the North Koreans and Vietnamese who fought America."[36] And with regard to the American presence in his Saudi homeland, consider this reflection: "if God had not blessed us with Islam then our ancestors in the pagan age would not have let these people come either."[37] Leaving aside his one-dimensional view of American foreign policy, we have no reason to doubt that bin Laden saw the United States as a bona fide imperialist threat. As for Israel, recall that bin Laden's proclaimed inspiration for attacking the Twin Towers was the 1982 Israeli attacks in Lebanon – attacks that involved the destruction of "towers" and the deaths of many innocent civilians; and his objection to bin Baz's 1994 call for peace with Israel was largely predicated on the conviction that Israelis were occupying land originally belonging to Palestinians, "poor men, women, and children who have nowhere to go."[38]

---

[35] Defense Science Board Task Force, *Report of the Defense Science Board Task Force on Strategic Communication*, 40. Here I should note that in an August 2016 episode of his *Waking Up* podcast, "What Do Jihadists Really Want?," Harris discusses and reads the entirety of the aforementioned article in the ISIS online magazine *Dabiq* entitled "Why We Hate You & Why We Fight You" (*Dabiq* 15 [July 2016], 30–33). As this article presents a theological basis for ISIS members' hatred of and antagonism against non-Muslims, Harris maintains that this article "confirms, more or less, everything I have been saying about jihadism for the last fifteen years." According to Harris, the article shows that Muslim radicals really do "hate us for our freedom" and that it would be "simply wrong" to think that they hate us for some other reason, like "our foreign policy." And yet, as noted earlier, a careful analysis of the "Why We Hate You" article, especially in conjunction with other, more authoritative ISIS statements, shows that the foreign policies of Western nations (at least as they are perceived) are indeed a cause of hatred and ISIS's primary justification for its terrorist operations against Westerners.

[36] Bin Laden, *Messages to the World*, 73–76.

[37] Bin Laden, *Messages to the World*, 89–90.

[38] Bin Laden, *Messages to the World*, 9.

TERRORISM AND THE TEXT

In dismissing the popular claim that there exists "no direct link between the Muslim faith and 'terrorism'," Harris writes,

It is clear ... that Muslims hate the West in the very terms of their faith and that the Koran mandates such hatred. It is widely claimed by "moderate" Muslims that the Koran mandates nothing of the kind and that Islam is a "religion of peace." But one need only read the Koran itself to see that this is untrue.[39]

To support this statement, Harris, in keeping with his tendency in *The End of Faith*, quotes two Qur'anic verses without discussing their respective contexts. These verses, 9:73 and 9:123, read as follows:

Prophet, *strive* [or do jihad] against the unbelievers and the hypocrites and be tough with them. Hell is their final home – an evil destination! (9:73)

You who believe, fight the unbelievers near you and let them find you standing firm: be aware that God is with those who are mindful of Him. (9:123)

Harris does not account for any other passage from the Qur'an's ninth chapter; nor does he consider the implications of Qur'an 9:73 being explicitly addressed to the Prophet; nor does he demonstrate an awareness of the view among some Qur'anic commentators that Qur'an 9:123 refers specifically to the antagonistic Arabs "near" Muhammad's community; nor does he mention that these passages are widely believed to have been revealed during the perilous Medinan stage of the Prophet's mission, a time when he was confronting violent enemies from within ("hypocrites") and without ("unbelievers").[40]

In showing how Islamic scripture glorifies jihad and martyrdom, Harris cites Qur'an 4:95–101, a particular selection of verses that begins by proclaiming that the believers who "commit themselves and their possessions to *striving* [or doing jihad] in God's way" are superior to those who "stay at home"; it concludes by discussing emigration and prayer. Interestingly, Harris presents the final two verses as follows:

He that leaves his dwelling to fight for God and His apostle and is then overtaken by death, shall be rewarded by God ... The unbelievers are your inveterate enemies.[41]

---

[39] Harris, *The End of Faith*, 31.
[40] See Nasr (ed.), *The Study Quran*, 503, 526 (commentary on Qur'an 9:73), 540 (commentary on Qur'an 9:123).
[41] Harris, *The End of Faith*, 33.

In contrast, here are the two verses in their entirety as translated by Qur'anic studies scholar M. A. S. Abdel Haleem:

[A]nd if anyone leaves home as a migrant towards God and His Messenger and is then overtaken by death, his reward from God is sure. God is most forgiving and merciful. When you [believers] are travelling in the land, you will not be blamed for shortening your prayers, if you fear the disbelievers may harm you: they are your sworn enemies.[42]

Throughout *The End of Faith*, Harris utilizes N. J. Dawood's 1956 translation of the Qur'an. Needless to say, every translation has its shortcomings. But as Abdel Haleem notes, "from the beginning [Dawood's] translation was seen to take too many liberties with the text of the Qur'an and to contain many inaccuracies, as was immediately pointed out by reviewers."[43] In this case, the Dawood translation that Harris utilizes goes beyond the literal text in an obvious way: notice Dawood's insertion of "to fight." And Harris's decision to remove the section mentioning the potential harm caused by Muhammad's enemies and replace it with an ellipsis makes the passage seem more belligerent.

While we are on the topic of the problematic uses of ellipses, notice how Harris quotes Qur'an 4:74–77 (incorrectly cited as 4:74–78)[44] in an attempt to show how Islamic scripture might promote suicide terrorism:

Let those who would exchange the life of this world for the hereafter, fight for the cause of God; whoever fights for the cause of God, whether he dies or triumphs, We shall richly reward him ... The true believers fight for the cause of God, but the infidels fight for the devil. Fight then against the friends of Satan ... Say: "Trifling are the pleasures of this life. The hereafter is better for those who would keep from evil ..."[45]

Here is the same passage in its entirety as translated by Abdel Haleem (the missing sections from Harris's quotation appear in italics):

---

[42] Abdel Haleem, *The Qur'an*, 60.

[43] Abdel Haleem, *The Qur'an*, xxviii. In his 2007 book *god is not Great*, the New Atheist writer Christopher Hitchens draws attention to Muslim complaints of the Dawood translation and notes that he himself uses the translation of the British Muslim scholar Marmaduke Pickthall (d. 1936) (124).

[44] In an April 2016 episode of his *Waking Up* podcast, "The End of Faith Sessions 1," Harris reads and comments on the introductory chapter of *The End of Faith*. In this podcast reading, Harris again mentions verse 78, and he mistakenly refers to verses 74–78 (as well as verse 29 of the same chapter) as "suras" (a sura is a chapter of the Qur'an; the aforementioned verses appear in the fourth sura).

[45] Harris, *The End of Faith*, 33–34.

Let those of you who are willing to trade the life of this world for the life to come, fight in God's way. To anyone who fights in God's way, whether killed or victorious, We shall give a great reward. *Why should you not fight in God's cause and for those oppressed men, women, and children who cry out, "Lord, rescue us from this town whose people are oppressors! By Your grace, give us a protector and give us a helper!"?* The believers fight for God's cause, while those who reject faith fight for an unjust cause. Fight the allies of Satan: *Satan's strategies are truly weak.* [Prophet], *do you not see those who were told, "Restrain yourselves from fighting, perform the prayer, and pay the prescribed alms"? When fighting was ordained for them, some of them feared men as much as, or even more than, they feared God, saying, "Lord, why have You ordained fighting for us? If only You would give us just a little more time."* Say to them, "Little is the enjoyment in this world, the Hereafter is far better for those who are mindful of God: *you will not be wronged by as much as the fibre in a date stone."* [46]

Harris rightly notes that this passage glorifies martyrdom. [47] But in the context of arguing that it also promotes terrorism, his ellipses misleadingly conceal the strictly protective dimension of the passage. Furthermore, Harris never acknowledges that according to the majority of Muslim commentators, this passage, in its entirety, calls for a regulated protective war (following years of divinely mandated pacifism) against the oppressive Meccan polytheists. [48]

Now if some Muslims – in opposition to most commentators – also see in this passage an invitation to martyrdom through terroristic means (we have seen how terrorists present their aggressive attacks as protective in nature), then, according to Harris, we must hold the Qur'an itself accountable. The Qur'an (and Bible), he writes, "must be appreciated, and criticized, for any *possible* interpretations to which [it is] susceptible – and to which [it] will be subjected, with varying emphases and elisions, throughout the religious world." [49] Of course Harris's premise stands at odds with the prevailing Muslim scholarly belief that human interpretations, however popular or compelling, are generally fallible and more likely to be erroneous and blameworthy in the absence of careful study. By this logic, believers attempting to interpret God's infallible words are in some ways comparable to scientists attempting to interpret

[46] Abdel Haleem, *The Qur'an*, 57–58.
[47] Harris, *The End of Faith*, 34.
[48] See Nasr (ed.), *The Study Quran*, 224–226 (commentary on Qur'an 4:74–77).
[49] Harris, *The End of Faith*, 34.

a God-created universe: both may err on account of their own deficiencies and limitations.[50]

But Harris goes beyond simply arguing that we should blame the Qur'an for all dangerous readings of the text. As he would have it, what makes "Muslim extremists" extreme is "their devotion to the *literal* word of the Koran and the hadith."[51] Violent radicals, we are led to believe, are monsters precisely because of their close adherence to the letter of scripture.

Harris concedes "that there are a few lines in the Koran that seem to speak directly against indiscriminate violence. Those who wage jihad are enjoined not to attack first (Koran 2:190), since 'God does not love aggressors'." But, he continues, "this injunction restrains no one" – a rhetorical overstatement – because, considering the "long history of conflict between Islam and the West, almost any act of violence against infidels can now be plausibly construed as an action in defense of the faith."[52]

Notice here Harris's use of the passive verb "construed." When thinking about terrorism in the name of Islam, one must be careful to consider *who* is doing the construing. If violent radicals (in opposition to the overwhelming majority of Muslim clerics, scholars, and laypeople) construe their widely rejected acts of terrorism as part of a defensive jihad, in part because of their specific assessments of the facts on the ground, this would seem to tell us more about these particular radicals than it would Islamic scripture.

As for the Islamic rules for conducting warfare justly, Harris refers to Bernard Lewis, who acknowledges that women, children, and the elderly can only be fought in self-defense.[53] But, still in the same sentence, Harris notes that "a little casuistry on the notion of self-defense allows Muslim militants to elude this stricture as well."[54] This muddles Harris's analysis, however, for one would not expect such "casuistry" to be practiced by true literalists.

---

[50] One obvious exception to this comes from the mystical Sufi tradition: according to one popular Sufi belief, *all* interpretations – reflecting the diversity of human dispositions – are, in a sense, "true" because they ultimately come from God. Even so, according to this paradigm (one not typically associated with contemporary terrorism), only certain interpretations – those that best reflect God's essence – are considered righteous and beneficial (see, for instance, Chittick, *Imaginal Worlds*, chapter 9).

[51] Harris, *The End of Faith*, 29.

[52] Harris, *The End of Faith*, 112.

[53] Harris, *The End of Faith*, 112–113; see Lewis, *The Crisis of Islam*, 39. Lewis adds, "At no point do the basic texts of Islam enjoin terrorism and murder." I shall say more on Lewis in what follows.

[54] Harris, *The End of Faith*, 113.

THE SUICIDE TERRORISM PROBLEM

Inspired as he was by 9/11 to compose *The End of Faith*, Harris has much to say about the problem of Muslim suicide terrorism. As he presents it, it is Islamic ideology – and not, as political scientist Robert Pape maintains, specific nationalist goals[55] – that best explains this phenomenon. After all, organizations such as al-Qaeda "define themselves in *religious* terms."[56] Of course the same is true for many of al-Qaeda's staunchest Muslim opponents, a much larger group. For Harris, however, Muslim suicide terrorism is ultimately "inextricable from notions of martyrdom and jihad, predictable on their basis, and sanctified by their logic. It is no more secular an activity than prayer is."[57] And its desired eschatological outcome must be recognized: "Most Muslims who commit atrocities are explicit about their desire to get to paradise."[58] For martyrdom "is the only way that a Muslim can bypass the painful litigation that awaits us all on the Day of Judgment and proceed directly to paradise."[59] Thus, conflating suicide terrorism with Islamic martyrdom, Harris declares it "rational" according to Islamic thought "for Muslim women to encourage the suicides of their children, as long as they are fighting for the cause of God. Devout Muslims simply *know* that they are going to a better place."[60]

But were any group of Muslims to claim that they *know* they are going to heaven, they would likely be deemed presumptuous by most of their coreligionists, certainly theologians. Again, the predominant view in Islamic theology is that only God knows our individual fates. And even in the midst of a just, regulated war, it is possible for God to deem a Muslim's death inglorious. For example, as noted earlier, the Prophet reportedly condemned a Muslim warrior who killed himself after he was wounded in combat. Thus, while martyrdom is indeed celebrated in Islamic sources, Harris's claim that "devout Muslims" regard suicide attacks as guarantees of paradise is highly problematic.

For Harris, however, the exception often proves the rule. And in his efforts to cast Islamic doctrines of jihad and martyrdom as a sufficient

---

55 Pape, "The Strategic Logic of Suicide Terrorism."
56 Harris, *The End of Faith*, 260, note 2.
57 Harris, *The End of Faith*, 260, note 2.
58 Harris, *The End of Faith*, 31.
59 Harris, *The End of Faith*, 34.
60 Harris, *The End of Faith*, 136.

explanation for radical Muslim terrorism, he highlights the case of a "failed Palestinian suicide bomber" named Zaydan Zaydan. The latter

described being "pushed" to attack Israelis by "the love of martyrdom." He added, "*I didn't want revenge for anything. I just wanted to be a martyr.*" Mr. Zaydan, the would-be martyr, conceded that his Jewish captors were "better than many, many Arabs." With regard to the suffering that his death would have inflicted upon his family, he reminded his interviewer that a martyr gets to pick seventy people to join him in paradise. He would have been sure to invite his family along.[61]

That Harris thought Zaydan's story was revealing and representative of a broader phenomenon of faith leading directly to destruction is suggested by the fact that this quoted passage appears in the introductory chapter of *The End of Faith*. Harris does not tell us anything else about Zaydan. But there is, in fact, more to his story.

When discussing and quoting Zaydan, Harris cites a June 8, 2002, *New York Times* article. A close reading of this article reveals another side to the would-be suicide bomber: Zaydan, "a fifth-grade dropout" who "can read but not write,"

became a carpenter, then a peddler of newspapers and other products in Israel. When the latest conflict began in September 2000, he said he sought work fruitlessly in Jenin, settling for a couple of hours spent each day carrying boxes of vegetables in the market there.

The rest of the day he spent sleeping or hanging around a pool hall, smoking. Then he happened to watch a religious lesson on television that convinced him he was wasting his time. In what he called his life's turning point, he quit billiards and began going to the mosque regularly. Eventually, he stopped smoking.

He insisted that he was drawn to martyrdom by what he read in books, not by anything he heard from his imam, or priest.

After Israel first raided Jenin's refugee camp at the beginning of March, Mr. Zaydan said, he began to think seriously about becoming a suicide bomber.

With regard to his planned attack, he "insisted that he had sought to kill only soldiers, whom he described as overwhelming adversaries."

The author of this article, James Bennet, informs us that his two-plus-hour conversation with Zaydan, then eighteen years old, took place shortly after the failed attack, in an Israeli hospital, while Zaydan was "expecting to be prosecuted." "Guarded by two Israeli police officers" and "manacled by a wrist and an ankle to his bed," he

---

[61] Harris, *The End of Faith*, 31 (emphasis added).

said bitterly that he knew he would be jailed for life and remembered only as a terrorist.

"I feel sorry, because it was a mistake," he said. "But as a human being, I should live like others. The way there is an Israeli state, there are people living in this state, enjoying life, having someone protect them. I don't live in this situation. I don't feel I'm secure."

Soldiers could enter Jenin at any time, he said, and he constantly feared being arrested. "As long as life continues like this," he said, "you will have people who think like me." He insisted that he wanted peace, but said he saw little chance for it.[62]

Assuming Zaydan genuinely sought martyrdom, it is difficult to over-look the obvious political dimensions of his actions, his challenging life experiences, his limited education, and the circumstances of his conversation with Bennet, with Israeli officers nearby and a trial looming. Furthermore, Bennet himself calls into question Zaydan's trustworthiness: Zaydan, he writes, "insisted today that he had not detonated his bomb, but instead had been shot twice in the stomach by soldiers. That account was not supported by his wounds, according to the hospital." These are not just details.

Returning to the Qur'an, Harris identifies only a single statement – an "ambiguous line" – that could be invoked to prohibit suicide terrorism: "Do not destroy yourselves" (4:29).[63] This statement arguably prohibits suicide, not necessarily terrorism. As for other, more pertinent passages that indicate that only belligerents may be targeted (for example, "Fight in God's cause against those who fight you, but do not overstep the limits" [2:190]), recall that for Harris, such passages restrain "no one." Accordingly, Harris calls for a challenge to the veracity of the Qur'an:

The corrective to the worldview of Osama bin Laden is not to point out the single line in the Koran that condemns suicide, because this ambiguous statement is set in a thicket of other passages that can be read only as direct summons to war against the "friends of Satan." [Harris has in mind the aforementioned passage, Qur'an 4:74–77.] The appropriate response to the bin Ladens of the world is to correct everyone's reading of these texts by making the same evidentiary demands in religious matters that we make in all others.[64]

---

[62] Bennet, "In Israeli Hospital, Bomber Tells of Trying to Kill Israelis."
[63] Harris, *The End of Faith*, 117. Here I use the translation as Harris presents it; I prefer "Do not kill (*taqtulu*) yourselves."
[64] Harris, *The End of Faith*, 34–35. Cf. page 242, note 18, where Harris states that there "may even be some credible evidence for reincarnation."

Given what we have seen of Harris's approach to the Qur'an, there is unintended irony in this last sentence.

Harris's approach to Muslim scholarly discourse is similarly disconcerting. He writes,

Surely there are Muslim jurists who might say that suicide bombing is contrary to the tenets of Islam (where are these jurists, by the way?) and that suicide bombers are therefore not martyrs but fresh denizens of hell. Such a minority opinion, if it exists, cannot change the fact that suicide bombings have been rationalized by much of the Muslim world ... Indeed, such rationalization is remarkably easy, given the tenets of Islam.[65]

As noted earlier, there are, in fact, multitudes of prominent clerics and scholars – from the Fiqh Council of North America to the Saudi Wahhabi establishment – who have condemned suicide missions and terrorism more broadly. And yet, Harris writes,

we need only ask why so many Muslims are eager to turn themselves into bombs these days. The answer: because the Koran makes this activity seem like a career opportunity. Nothing in the history of Western colonialism explains this behavior (though we can certainly concede that this history offers us much to atone for). Subtract the Muslim belief in martyrdom and jihad, and the actions of suicide bombers become completely unintelligible, as does the spectacle of public jubilation that invariably follows their deaths; insert these peculiar beliefs, and one can only marvel that suicide bombing is not more widespread.[66]

Notice Harris's words here: "one can only marvel that suicide bombing is not more widespread." With his focus firmly on Muslim radicals, he neglects the broader and historical Islamic landscape. He is apparently unaware, for instance, that suicide attacks of any kind were historically uncommon in the Sunni tradition claimed by al-Qaeda. Interestingly, the very authority Harris relies on when discussing jihad, Bernard Lewis, who is hardly an apologist for Islam, writes (in a coauthored book published after Harris completed *The End of Faith*),

The emergence of the by now widespread terrorism practice of suicide bombing ... is a development of the 20th century. It has no antecedents in Islamic history, and no justification in terms of Islamic theology, law, or tradition. It is a pity that those who practice this form of terrorism are not better acquainted with their own religion, and with the culture that grew up under the auspices of that religion.[67]

---

[65] Harris, *The End of Faith*, 123.
[66] Harris, *The End of Faith*, 32–33.
[67] Lewis and Churchill, *Islam*, 153.

Recall that Harris opens *The End of Faith* by depicting a suicide bomber and then asking the reader why it is "so easy" to guess his religion. But if one could somehow transport a copy of *The End of Faith* to people living in the 1970s (including a young Harris), they would likely not find guessing that bomber's religion easy at all. Again, until the early 1980s, there was simply no such thing as a Muslim suicide bomber. And it is worth reflecting on the fact that even after then, the tactic of suicide bombing was never once employed in a conflict as intense as the Soviet–Afghan War.

Harris's concern over Muslim suicide attacks is, of course, understandable. Suicide bombings in the name of Islam have become terribly common in recent decades. And certain polling data suggests that there has been a disturbing level of support for such bombings. Harris draws attention to a 2002 Pew Research Center survey and its findings concerning Muslims in a dozen countries. The most alarming results came from Lebanon (a country that has witnessed numerous suicide bombings), where 73 percent said that "suicide bombing in defense of Islam" is justified, and 82 percent said it *could* be justified.[68]

Owing to specific political developments and popular propaganda, we have good reason to think that many (if not most) Lebanese supporters of this tactic defended it specifically in the context of the Arab–Israeli conflict. But as this conflict has evolved, and as suicide bombings have become more prevalent and more devastating worldwide, we find that people's views have changed significantly in recent years: in 2014, Pew found that 29 percent of Lebanese respondents held that "suicide bombings can be" either "often" (7 percent) or "sometimes" (22 percent) justified; 45 percent said that such bombings "can never," not even "rarely," be justified. And the same survey found that 96 percent of Lebanese respondents had an "unfavorable opinion of al-Qaeda."[69]

Although the aforementioned 2002 Pew survey did not specifically cover 9/11, Harris moves quickly from his discussion of the survey to his claim that "a significant percentage of the world's Muslims believe that the men who brought down the World Trade Center are now seated at the right hand of God."[70] And because of the aforementioned controversy surrounding suicide in Islam, Harris speculates that had Pew asked

---

[68] Harris, *The End of Faith*, 124–126; Pew Research Center, "What the World Thinks in 2002" (see "Topline" for all data).

[69] Pew Research Center, "Concerns about Islamic Extremism on the Rise in Middle East."

[70] Harris, *The End of Faith*, 127.

the same Muslims, "Is it ever justified to target civilians in defense of Islam[?]" – without getting into the topic of suicide bombing – we could have expected to see "even greater Muslim support for terrorism."[71]

But the matter is not nearly as straightforward as Harris presents it. Other surveys, including some published after Harris completed *The End of Faith*, challenge his portrayal of a specifically Muslim attitudinal problem. In a survey published by Gallup in 2008, for instance, Palestinians (who are overwhelmingly Muslim) and Israelis (who are overwhelmingly non-Muslim) were asked, "When is it justified for individuals or small groups to target and kill civilians?" Among the Palestinians, 84 percent said "never," as compared to 73 percent of Israelis; 14 percent of Palestinians said "sometimes/depends," as compared to 22 percent of Israelis. When the same group was asked, "When is it justified for the military to target and kill civilians?," 86 percent of Palestinians said "never," as compared to 44 percent of Israelis; 12 percent of Palestinians said "sometimes/depends," as compared to 52 percent of Israelis.[72]

And according to another survey published by Gallup in 2011, 21 percent of residents in the United States and Canada said that it is "sometimes justified" for "an individual person or a small group of persons to target and kill civilians," as compared to 9 percent of residents in the Middle East and North Africa; 77 percent of Americans and Canadians said it is "never justified," as compared to 85 percent of Middle Easterners and North Africans. Furthermore, 47 percent of Americans and Canadians said that it is "sometimes justified" for the military "to target and kill civilians," as compared to 13 percent of Middle Easterners and North Africans; 50 percent of Americans and Canadians said it is "never justified," as compared to 79 percent of Middle Easterners and North Africans.[73] All this data leaves us with a hazy, colorful picture, as opposed to the fairly sharp black-and-white image presented in *The End of Faith*.

CELEBRATIONS OR CONDEMNATIONS?

Harris also draws attention to a February 2002 CNN poll that showed that 61 percent of Muslims in nine Muslim-majority nations did "not believe that Arabs were responsible" for the 9/11 attacks. This surely

---

[71] Harris, *The End of Faith*, 125.
[72] Saad, "Palestinians and Israelis Favor Nonviolent Solutions."
[73] Gallup, "Views of Violence."

reveals a problem of denial, and one that suggests both the scapegoating of others and the foreignness of bin Laden's tactics (I have heard more than a few Muslims say that their coreligionists "could not have done something like this"). In any case, Harris remarks, "No doubt the 39 percent who thought otherwise represent millions who wish the Arab world would take credit for a job well done."[74]

Here Harris oversteps his limitations. As noted earlier, in a different 2008 Gallup survey – one of the most extensive surveys of Muslim opinion to date – the overwhelming majority of respondents found the 9/11 attacks to be objectionable to varying degrees; a disturbing yet relatively small percentage (7 percent) thought they were "completely justified."[75] But even before Gallup published these findings, there was good reason to think that most Muslims had rejected bin Laden's tactics.

Although it was published nearly three years after 9/11, *The End of Faith* gives no clear indication that numerous well-known Muslim figures – including many strongly opposed to American foreign policy – explicitly and publicly condemned the attacks in September 2001 on religious grounds. As Harris would have it, "If you believe anything like what the Koran says you must believe in order to escape the fires of hell, you will, at the very least, be sympathetic with the actions of Osama bin Laden."[76] He also writes, "we must acknowledge that Muslims have not found anything of substance to say against the actions of the September 11 hijackers." This is an unfortunate myth. (It is ironic that Harris would proceed to ridicule certain Muslims for propagating myths of their own, including the absurd idea that the 9/11 hijackers "were really Jews.")[77] The reality is that the targeting of innocents was a recurring theme in the September 2001 condemnations issued by scholars, clerics, and the leadership of, among many other institutions, the fifty-seven-nation Organization of the Islamic Conference, al-Azhar in Egypt, the Muslim Brotherhood in Egypt, Jamaat-e-Islami in both Pakistan and Bangladesh, the Nahda Renaissance Movement in Tunisia, the Pan-Malaysian Islamic Party (Parti Islam SeMalaysia), and even Hamas.[78]

If Harris had picked up an issue of the *San Jose Mercury News* five days after the attacks, he would have come across an interview with a

[74] Harris, *The End of Faith*, 264, note 30.
[75] Esposito and Mogahed, *Who Speaks for Islam?*, chapter 3.
[76] Harris, *The End of Faith*, 117.
[77] Harris, *The End of Faith*, 134.
[78] Kurzman (ed.), "Islamic Statements Against Terrorism."

fellow Californian named Hamza Yusuf (né Mark Hanson), an extremely influential Muslim scholar who offered something "of substance to say against the actions of the September 11 hijackers." In the interview, Yusuf – a staunch critic of American foreign policy – declared that if the 9/11 perpetrators were indeed Muslims,

they're obviously very sick people and I can't even look at it in religious terms … It's like some misguided Irish using Catholicism as an excuse for blowing up English people.

They're not martyrs, it's as simple as that.

… You can't kill innocent people. There's no Islamic declaration of war against the United States …

In Islam, the only wars that are permitted are between armies and they should engage on battlefields and engage nobly. The Prophet Muhammad said, "Do not kill women or children or non-combatants and do not kill old people or religious people," and he mentioned priests, nuns and rabbis …

The fact that there are any Muslims – no matter how statistically insignificant their numbers – who consider these acts to be religious acts is in and of itself shocking. And therefore we as Muslims have to ask the question, "How is it that our religious leadership has failed to reach these people with the true message of Islam?" …

… One of the worst crimes in Islam is brigandry – highway robbery, or today we'd say armed robbery – because it disrupts the sense of well-being and security among civilians.

… There is no vigilantism in Islam. Muslims believe in the authority of government. Imam Malik [d. 795], an early Islamic legal authority, said that 60 years of oppression under an unjust ruler is better than one hour of anarchy.

… The perpetrators of this and, really, all acts of terror are people who hate too much. There's a verse in the Koran [5:8] that says do not let the hatred of a people prevent you from being just. Being just is closer to piety …

When asked about some of the "Palestinians and others celebrating the attacks in the streets," Yusuf responded,

When you see ignorant people in the streets, rejoicing – the Prophet condemned it. It's rejoicing at the calamities of your enemies, and Islam prohibits that.

They do have a lot of anger toward America, because America produces much of Israel's military hardware and so many American tax dollars go to support Israel. You have a lot of animosity in the Arab world. But the vast majority of Arabs are horrified by what's happened.

After stating that both suicide and the killing of civilians are strictly prohibited in Islam, he concluded with the following words about martyrdom:

The Prophet said that a martyr who dies doesn't have a reckoning on the Day of Judgment. It's an act through which he is forgiven. But the Prophet also said that there are people who kill in the name of Islam and go to hell. And when he was asked why, he said, "Because they weren't fighting truly for the sake of God."

If there are any martyrs in this affair it would certainly be those brave firefighters and police that went in there to save human lives and in that process lost their own.[79]

Weeks after 9/11, the denunciations continued. In an October 8, 2001, article published in *The New York Times*, for instance, we find the well-known Muslim leader and Islamic studies scholar Ingrid Mattson (then a professor at Hartford Seminary) disavowing al-Qaeda's tactics, proclaiming, "Even in a legitimate war – even if Osama bin Laden were a legitimate head of state, which he's not – you're not permitted to indiscriminately kill civilians, just to create terror in the general population."[80] And in another piece published in *The New York Times*, this one on January 27, 2002, we read that despite bin Laden's appeal as an anti-imperialist icon, "many Muslim scholars criticize him." For example, Safir Akhtar of the Islamic University in Islamabad, warns, "Don't make the mistake of thinking that Osama bin Laden is the true face of a billion Muslims, or the true voice of the Koran." What is more, the article's author John Burns tells us, "many of Islam's most militant theologians now rebuke Mr. bin Laden." Burns goes on to quote the so-called "spiritual leader of Hezbollah," the Lebanese Grand Ayatollah Muhammad Hussain Fadlallah (d. 2010), who condemned the attacks, "accused Mr. bin Laden of having ignored Koranic texts," and held that "the perpetrators were not martyrs as Mr. bin Laden has claimed, but 'merely suicides,' because they killed innocent civilians, and in a distant land, America."[81]

Closer to home, and a couple of days before the one-year anniversary of 9/11, numerous leaders representing North American Islamic organizations (including what is widely considered the largest of them all, the Islamic Society of North America) and influential Western scholars (including Khaled Abou El Fadl, Asma Afsaruddin, Tariq Ramadan, Abdulaziz Sachedina, Zaid Shakir, and Muzammil Siddiqi) issued a statement (for many, a "restatement") in which they condemned bin Laden by name. They declared "unequivocally that neither the al-Qaeda organization nor Usama bin Laden represents Islam or reflects Muslim beliefs

---

[79] Scheinin, "Expert Says Islam Prohibits Violence Against Innocents" (this article was posted online on the evening of September 15, 2001, and distributed in print the next day).

[80] Steinberg, "Experts Say bin Laden Is Distorting Islamic Law."

[81] Burns, "A Nation Challenged."

and practices" and that "bin Laden and al-Qaeda's actions are criminal, misguided and counter to the true teachings of Islam."[82]

Harris's apparent unfamiliarity with this abundance of Muslim scholarly and clerical denunciations may be explained by his overreliance on a limited array of sources. For instance, in discussing contemporary Muslim terrorism, Harris leans on *New York Times* columnist Thomas Friedman, whom Harris describes as "a tireless surveyor of the world's discontents."[83] Although Friedman is indeed an accomplished journalist, in the days and years following 9/11, he wrote a great deal about Muslim terrorism but seemed not to notice Muslim scholarly and clerical condemnations of said terrorism. Two days after 9/11, for instance, he wondered why "not a single Muslim leader" would say that Islam "is being distorted when it is treated as a guidebook for suicide bombing."[84] Three months later, Friedman quoted an "unidentified Saudi sheik" who appeared in a then recently released video with bin Laden celebrating 9/11; in it the "sheik" assured the al-Qaeda leader that "in the mosques in Saudi Arabia the reaction to the terror acts had been 'very positive'." Friedman did not mention the Saudi clerical criticisms of 9/11, though he did offer the vague observation that "some" Muslims – the only examples he provided were an Arab journalist and a Pakistani-American reader who sent him an email affirming her and other Muslims' desire for an "Islamic enlightenment" – were "eager" to "delegitimize" bin Laden's ideas and "reform Islam."[85] Years later, on July 8, 2005 (after the publication of *The End of Faith*), Friedman proclaimed without clarification or equivocation, "To this day – to this day – no major Muslim cleric or religious body has ever issued a fatwa condemning Osama bin Laden."[86] And years after that, on December 15, 2009, Friedman wrote, "How many fatwas – religious edicts – have been issued by the leading bodies of Islam against Osama bin Laden and Al Qaeda? Very few."[87]

---

[82] "American Muslims and Scholars Denounce Terrorism"; Kurzman (ed.), "Islamic Statements Against Terrorism." The signatories of this statement include non-Muslim scholars of Islam and Muslims residing in countries such as Algeria, Egypt, Iran, Jordan, Lebanon, Malaysia, the Maldives, Morocco, Pakistan, the Philippines, South Africa, and Turkey.

[83] Harris, *The End of Faith*, 131.

[84] Friedman, "Foreign Affairs; World War III."

[85] Friedman, "Spiritual Missile Shield."

[86] Friedman, "If It's a Muslim Problem, It Needs a Muslim Solution."

[87] Friedman, "www.jihad.com." By the time of bin Laden's death, Harris had become more critical of Friedman. In Harris's eyes, Friedman had "grown so manic as to imagine that bin Laden was never very popular among Muslims in the first place." Whereas Friedman saw bin Laden's support as having been initially "passive" and then almost nonexistent,

The fact of the matter is that even before 9/11, various prominent Muslims had expressly rejected suicide terrorism. One example is the Saudi grand mufti Abdulaziz al-Shaykh, whose condemnatory statement, issued several months before the attacks, may not have received media attention in the West but was at least acknowledged by American policy experts.[88] And before the one-year anniversary of 9/11, the clear majority of leading clerics, scholars, and religious bodies had strongly denounced the culprits of the attacks, some condemning bin Laden and al-Qaeda by name, others choosing to avoid mentioning specific individuals until the perpetrators could be found guilty in a court of law. Friedman's readers simply could not have known this without examining other sources. And yet, interestingly, they would not have needed to look far: the condemnations of bin Laden and 9/11 appeared in other sections of *The New York Times*, such as the October 2001 and January 2002 articles mentioned earlier and in a full-page ad printed in the October 17, 2001, issue that was paid for by the Becket Fund for Religious Liberty and included statements by various Muslim clerics and leaders.[89]

HARRIS ON ISLAM

Harris asserts that "nobody suffers the consequences of Islam more than [Muslims] do." One reason for this is that wherever Muslim terrorist "events occur, we will find Muslims tending to side with other Muslims, no matter how sociopathic their behavior. This is the malignant solidarity that religion breeds."[90] Along these lines, Harris opines, "it seems all but certain that if the West underwent a massive conversion to Islam – and,

---

Harris viewed it as having been initially – "passive or otherwise" – "shockingly high" and then smaller but "still appalling" (Harris, "Further Thoughts on the Death of Osama bin Laden").

[88] See Paz, "The Saudi Fatwa Against Suicide Terrorism." This is a policy paper published in May 2001 by the Washington Institute for Near East Policy. The paper's author, Reuven Paz (d. 2015), acknowledges the general nature of al-Shaykh's condemnation but suggests that he might have been "thinking more about Osama bin Laden than recent Palestinian actions." In fact, al-Shaykh has consistently rejected suicide terrorism altogether (see, for instance, "Saudi Mufti"; and Kurzman [ed.], "Islamic Statements Against Terrorism").

[89] See Esposito, *The Future of Islam*, 31.

[90] Harris, *The End of Faith*, 234 (from the afterword to the 2005 paperback edition). A similar point is made in Harris's September 2014 blog entry "Sleepwalking Toward Armageddon."

perforce, repudiated all Jewish interests in the Holy Land – the basis for Muslim 'hatred' would simply disappear."[91]

While there can be no denying that "in-group loyalty" and "out-group hostility" is indeed often a grave problem, we now have good reason to think that Harris overestimates this phenomenon among Muslims. Furthermore, it is critical to stress that "Muslim 'hatred'," wherever it may exist, is often the product of multiple factors, ideological affiliation being but one. Indeed, adherence to Islam has not prevented countless cases of intra-Sunni and intra-Shi'ite violence, to say nothing of conflicts between Sunnis and Shi'ites. Nor has it dissuaded many scholars, clerics, and leaders from condemning radicals of their own sect or denomination. And their condemnations often invoke the Qur'an itself, including the injunction, "You who believe, uphold justice and bear witness to God, even if it is against yourselves, your parents, or your close relatives" (4:135).[92] If some manifestations of religion breed "malignant solidarity," others directly combat it.

Looking to the future, Harris warns that if Muslims do not learn "to ignore most of their canon" as "most Christians have learned to do," then "Islam and the West" will "stand on the brink of mutual annihilation."[93] "Islam," he goes on to proclaim, "must find some way to revise itself, peacefully or otherwise," and "the West must either win the argument or win the war. All else will be bondage."[94] But what is one to make of this ignore-or-revise proposal when Harris's own conception of Islam is, at times, inaccurate and incomplete? When, as Islamic studies scholar Rory Dickson observes, "Harris's depiction of Islam betrays a profound

---

[91] Harris, *The End of Faith*, 30–31.

[92] See, for example, Khan, "Islam Condemns Extremism"; and "Muslim Statements Condemning Terrorism."

[93] Harris, *The End of Faith*, 110.

[94] Harris, *The End of Faith*, 131. Cf. page 31, where Harris suggests that Islam offers "no valid mechanism by which [its] core beliefs can be tested and revised." While wishing for a long-term Islamic "revision," Harris advances a short-term proposal that is imperialist in nature: "It appears that one of the most urgent tasks we now face in the developed world is to find some way of facilitating the emergence of civil societies everywhere else ... It seems all but certain that some form of benign dictatorship will generally be necessary to bridge the gap. But benignity is the key – and if it cannot emerge from within a state, it must be imposed from without. The means of such imposition are necessarily crude: they amount to economic isolation, military intervention (whether open or covert), or some combination of both. While this may seem an exceedingly arrogant doctrine to espouse, it appears we have no alternatives. We cannot wait for weapons of mass destruction to dribble out of the former Soviet Union – to pick only one horrible possibility – and into the hands of fanatics" (Harris, *The End of Faith*, 150–151).

ignorance of Islamic history and a critical lack of knowledge concerning key elements of the Islamic tradition."[95]

Now I should pause to underline the fact that Harris is not a pacifist. And yet he twice contrasts Islam with the pacifist Jain religion. First, he states that there is a reason "we must now confront Muslim, rather than Jain terrorists, in every corner of the world."[96] For Harris, the reason is simply the nature of the Islamic tradition. (To place his statement in perspective, the entire Jain population amounts to no more than one half of one percent of the worldwide Muslim population and is mostly concentrated in India.) Second, he asserts that, in contrast with Islamic fundamentalism, a "rise of Jain fundamentalism would endanger no one" because "observant Jains generally will not kill anything, including insects."[97] Nevertheless, just a few pages earlier, and in the context of defending the use of military technology, he describes pacifism as "a deeply immoral position that comes to us swaddled in the dogma of highest moralism"; it allows a "variety of monsters currently loose in the world" to threaten "the rest of us."[98] Then, shortly after defending the limited use of torture when dealing with terrorists, he elaborates on "the false choice of pacifism" and explains why "we must accept the fact that violence (or its threat) is often an ethical necessity."[99] Thus, Harris's conception of legitimate violence actually overlaps, to a large extent, with that of many Muslims. And we certainly have no good reason to think that it is more tempered than that of, say, the aforementioned Islamic legal scholar Muhammad Afifi al-Akiti.[100]

---

[95] Dickson, "Religion as Phantasmagoria," 39.

[96] Harris, *The End of Faith*, 108.

[97] Harris, *The End of Faith*, 148. See Harris and Nawaz, *Islam and the Future of Tolerance*, 68, in which Harris states that, unlike with Jainism, no one can "say that the central message of Islam is pacifism."

[98] Harris, *The End of Faith*, 142–143. See page 129, where Harris states that in the case of an Islamist regime acquiring nuclear weapons, "the only thing likely to ensure our survival may be a nuclear first strike of our own." Although "this would be an unthinkable crime – as it would kill tens of millions of innocent civilians in a single day," Harris maintains that this "unconscionable act of self-defense" may "be the only course of action available to us, given what the Islamists believe." Harris warns his readers that "a catastrophe of this sort seems increasingly likely" and that "time is not on our side." Elsewhere Harris rebukes critics for, ironically, taking his words out of context and claiming that he *advocates* "a nuclear first-strike against the Muslim world" (Harris, "Response to Controversy").

[99] Harris, *The End of Faith*, 199 (see pages 199–203).

[100] See al-Akiti, *Defending the Transgressed*.

In Harris and Maajid Nawaz's 2015 dialogue-turned-book *Islam and the Future of Tolerance*, we encounter a more mature Harris, one willing to challenge and rethink some of his own views. His dialogue partner, Nawaz, is a British Muslim activist, writer, and politician of Pakistani heritage. He was once a member of the controversial Islamist organization Hizb ut-Tahrir and was imprisoned in Egypt from the end of 2001 to 2006. He eventually abandoned Islamism altogether but remained Muslim (he describes himself as a "non-devout Muslim")[101] and became a founder and the chairman of Quilliam, a "counterextremism" organization based in London.

Harris opens this book by recounting his first conversation with Nawaz. This was a seemingly uncomfortable exchange that took place at a dinner following an October 2010 Intelligence Squared debate, which had pitted Nawaz and American Muslim writer Zeba Khan against Ayaan Hirsi Ali and the British neoconservative writer Douglas Murray. At the dinner, Ali asked Harris, who was attending the debate as a guest, if he had anything to say. Addressing Nawaz, Harris recalls himself saying,

Maajid, I have a question for you. It seems to me that you have a nearly impossible task and yet much depends on your being able to accomplish it. You want to convince the world – especially the Muslim world – that Islam is a religion of peace that has been hijacked by extremists. But the problem is that Islam *isn't* a religion of peace, and the so-called "extremists" are seeking to implement what is arguably the most honest reading of the faith's actual doctrine. So your maneuvers on the stage tonight – the claims you made about interpretations of scripture and the historical context in which certain passages in the Qur'an must be understood – appear disingenuous.

Everyone in this room recognizes that you have the hardest job in the world, and everyone is grateful that you're doing it. Someone has to try to reform Islam from within, and it's obviously not going to be an apostate like Ayaan, or infidels like Douglas [Murray] and me. But the path of reform appears to be one of pretense. You seem obliged to *pretend* that the doctrine is something other than it is – for instance, you must pretend that jihad is just an inner spiritual struggle, whereas it's primarily a doctrine of holy war. I'd like to know whether this is, in fact, the situation as you see it. Is the path forward a matter of pretending certain things are true long enough and hard enough so as to *make* them true?[102]

---

[101] Dubuis and Mann, "Maajid Nawaz Sent Death Threats by ISIS."
[102] Harris and Nawaz, *Islam and the Future of Tolerance*, 2–3.

Harris proceeded to ask Nawaz, "It's understandable in the public context, but here in this room can't you just be honest with us?"[103]

In reflecting on this conversation, Nawaz says,

"Can't you just be honest with us in here?" implied that I hadn't been honest out there. My honest view is that Islam is not a religion of war *or* of peace – it's a religion. Its sacred scripture, like those of other religions, contains passages that many people would consider extremely problematic. Likewise, all scriptures contain passages that are innocuous. Religion doesn't inherently speak for itself; no scripture, no book, no piece of writing has its own voice ... At Intelligence Squared, being under the unnatural constraints of a debate motion, I asserted that Islam is a religion of peace simply because the vast majority of Muslims today do not subscribe to its being a religion of war. If it holds that Islam is only what its adherents interpret it to be, then it is currently a religion of peace ... [T]he motion forced me to take a side: war or peace. I chose peace.[104]

Throughout this dialogue, we find the two sides agreeing on some things and disagreeing on others, in what appears to be an amicable exchange.[105] (As my focus here is on Harris, I shall not dwell on Nawaz's views.) In the final analysis, however, much of what Harris proffers is echoes and rearticulations of *The End of Faith*:

[T]here certainly seem to be many cases in which people have no intelligible grievance apart from a theological one and become "radicalized" by the idea of sacrificing everything for their faith. I'm thinking of the Westerners who have joined groups like al-Qaeda and [ISIS], for instance. Sometimes religious ideology appears to be not merely necessary but *sufficient* to motivate a person to do this ... The truth is that some people appear to be almost entirely motivated by their religious beliefs.[106]

[Religion] creates in-group loyalty and out-group hostility, even when members of one's own group are acting in abhorrent ways ... [This] is especially a problem among Muslims in the twenty-first century.[107]

[S]cripture, read in anything but the most acrobatic, reformist way, seems to be on the side of the barbarians ... [G]roups like [ISIS] and al-Qaeda are enacting very literal (and therefore plausible) interpretations of Islamic doctrine.[108]

However I squint my eyes or cock my head, a hatred and fear of infidels seems central to the Qur'an. Muslims are told to have no friends among them and

---

103 Harris and Nawaz, *Islam and the Future of Tolerance*, 5.
104 Harris and Nawaz, *Islam and the Future of Tolerance*, 5–7.
105 As of this writing, Harris and Nawaz are completing a documentary based on *Islam and the Future of Tolerance* (Williams, "Maajid Nawaz's Radical Ambition").
106 Harris and Nawaz, *Islam and the Future of Tolerance*, 45–46.
107 Harris and Nawaz, *Islam and the Future of Tolerance*, 60. Harris makes a similar observation earlier in the book (11).
108 Harris and Nawaz, *Islam and the Future of Tolerance*, 114–115.

are assured that Allah will mock, curse, shame, and destroy them on the Day of Judgment ... [T]hey will burn for eternity in hellfire. There's simply no question that, under Islam, being an infidel is considered the worst possible deviation from the good life ... [T]his idea isn't foreign to other religions – Judaism and Christianity both have a version of it. The difference is in emphasis. The evil of unbelief is spelled out in the Qur'an on almost every page, and one finds only a few stray lines – for example, "There is no compulsion in religion" (2:256) – with which to offset the general message of intolerance. There is also the doctrine of "abrogation," under which later – generally less tolerant – verses are believed to supersede earlier ones.[109]

Harris goes on to say that, according to his understanding, Qur'an 2:256 was "nullified" by abrogation. This, however, represents the opinion of only a segment of Muslim scholars (who nonetheless generally affirm limited notions of freedom of belief for non-Muslims living under Muslim rule or protected by a truce).[110] And considering Harris's focus on scriptural literalism, I must stress the obvious: the often debated specifics of the doctrine of abrogation (for example, that Qur'an 2:256 was nullified) are predicated on contested interpretations, not the letter of scripture.

Without reiterating my previous critiques, I would like to draw attention to Harris's claim that "a hatred and fear of infidels seems central to the Qur'an." Harris makes similar claims elsewhere, including a September 2014 blog entry posted on his website *SamHarris.org* entitled "Sleepwalking Toward Armageddon." In the blog entry, Harris responds to then American president Barack Obama's position that ISIS is not representative of Islam. In contending that it is, Harris avers that "hatred of infidels is arguably the *central* theme of the Koran."[111] Remarkably, Harris overlooks a much more pronounced theme: the consequential worship of and obedience to the one God. Furthermore, it is difficult to see "hatred of infidels" in Qur'anic chapters such as 93, 94, 97, and 112, none of which make any kind of reference to unbelievers; and passages such as 5:5, which permits some forms of interreligious marriage, and 60:7–8:

God may still bring about affection between you and your [present enemies] – God is all powerful, God is most forgiving and merciful – and He does not forbid you to deal kindly and equitably with anyone who has not fought you for your faith or driven you out of your homes: God loves those who act equitably.

[109] Harris and Nawaz, *Islam and the Future of Tolerance*, 83–84.
[110] See Crone, "'No Compulsion in Religion'" (for the exegetical dimension); and Al-Dawoody, *The Islamic Law of War*, 78, 81 (for the jurisprudential dimension).
[111] Harris, "Sleepwalking Toward Armageddon." Harris makes a comparable assertion about the Qur'an in his aforementioned March 2011 *Huffington Post* article "My Response to Rep. Keith Ellison."

According to various Qur'anic commentators, the latter half of this Medinan passage (that is, Qur'an 60:8) was revealed after a Muslim named Asma (a daughter of Abu Bakr) had refused to meet her visiting mother, a Meccan polytheist; following this revelation, Asma received her mother in her home.[112]

Harris also presents violent radicals as occupying a central position among Islam's adherents. When discussing with Nawaz how he imagines "public opinion" to be divided in Muslim communities, he presents a schema that perfectly illustrates his problematic privileging of violent radicalism:

I picture several concentric circles: At the center are groups like [ISIS], al-Qaeda, [al-Shabaab], Boko Haram, and so on. Their members apparently wake each morning yearning to kill infidels and apostates. Many of them also seem eager to be martyred in the process. Most of us refer to these people as "jihadists." Then there is a larger circle of Islamists who are more politically motivated and appear less eager to kill and be killed. Beyond that is a wider circle of Muslims who probably support jihad and Islamism – financially, morally, or philosophically – but are not inclined to get their hands dirty. Finally, one hopes, there is a much larger circle of so-called moderate Muslims, whether they would label themselves that way or not, who want to live by more modern values. Although they may not be quite secular, they don't think that groups like [ISIS] represent their faith. Perhaps there are also millions of truly secular Muslims who just don't have a voice.[113]

As in *The End of Faith*, Harris promotes an ignore-or-revise solution to the "problem" of Islam; however, here his doubts about the prospect

---

[112] See, for instance, al-Tabari, *Tafsir al-Tabari*, 22:572–574, in which al-Tabari provides commentary on Qur'an 60:8, discusses the context of its revelation, and asserts that it was never abrogated and that its application is not restricted to non-Muslim relatives; and Nasr (ed.), *The Study Quran*, 1361 (commentary on Qur'an 60:8). Here I should note that some Muslims themselves all too easily downplay the significance of Qur'an 60:8. For instance, the aforementioned February 2002 open letter popularly attributed to bin Laden (and addressed to Saudi leaders) claims, in passing and without supporting evidence, that this verse applies only to relatives and that, according to the scholars of Islam, it was abrogated by the "sword verse" (Ibrahim [ed.], *The Al Qaeda Reader*, 43–44 [February 2002 open letter]). Yet in her thorough study of Qur'anic commentaries and their discussions of war and peace, Islamic studies scholar Asma Afsaruddin finds that a "majority of the exegetes surveyed affirm that Qur'an 60:7–9 remain unabrogated, and their injunctions to treat peaceful non-Muslims justly and kindly remain valid for all times" (Afsaruddin, *Striving in the Path of God*, 279; see pages 82–87).

[113] Harris and Nawaz, *Islam and the Future of Tolerance*, 16–17. Harris estimates that Islamists account for "about 20 percent" of the worldwide Muslim population (22). Incidentally, in the book's first footnote, which is attached to Nawaz's comments, we read that a 2013 Pew study found that "support for suicide bombing against civilians in defense of Islam" – though still alarmingly high – "has declined in recent years" (6, note 1; see Pew Research Center, "The World's Muslims: Religion, Politics and Society").

of a true revision are more apparent. Approximately halfway into their conversation, he tells Nawaz,

The problem is that moderates of all faiths are committed to reinterpreting, or ignoring outright, the most dangerous and absurd parts of their scripture – and this commitment is precisely what makes them moderates. But it also requires some degree of intellectual dishonesty, because moderates can't acknowledge that their moderation comes from *outside* the faith …

… I want to be clear that when I used terms such as "pretense" and "intellectual dishonesty" when we first met, I wasn't casting judgment on you personally. Simply living with the moderate's dilemma may be the only way forward, because the alternative would be to radically edit these books. I'm not such an idealist as to imagine that will happen … [T]his problem confronts religious moderates everywhere, but it's an excruciating problem for Muslims.[114]

Whatever one makes of Harris's description of "moderates" and their "dilemma," this statement and others quoted earlier imply that, unlike "moderation," the radicalism manifested in the thoughts and actions of terrorists such as bin Laden "comes from [*inside*] the faith." Yet a careful consideration of the al-Qaeda leader's statements suggests otherwise. Recall, once again, his disturbing explanation for the 9/11 attacks:

God knows that the plan of striking the towers had not occurred to us, but the idea came to me when things went just too far with the American–Israeli alliance's oppression and atrocities against our people in Palestine and Lebanon.

The events that made a direct impression on me were during and after 1982, when America allowed the Israelis to invade Lebanon … They started bombing, killing, and wounding many, while others fled in terror. I still remember those distressing scenes … The whole world heard and saw what happened, but did nothing. In those critical moments, many ideas raged inside me, ideas difficult to describe, but they unleashed a powerful urge to reject injustice and a strong determination to punish the oppressors.

As I looked at those destroyed towers in Lebanon, it occurred to me to punish the oppressor in kind by destroying towers in America, so that it would have a taste of its own medicine and would be prevented from killing our women and children. On that day I became sure that the oppression and intentional murder of innocent women and children is a deliberate American policy. It seemed then that "freedom" and "democracy" are actually just terror, just as resistance is labelled "terrorism" and "reaction" …

… For if you could avoid perpetrating these injustices, you Americans would be on the right path towards the security you enjoyed before September 11.[115]

---

[114] Harris and Nawaz, *Islam and the Future of Tolerance*, 65–69. In his closing remarks, Harris declares that "the only hope of moving beyond the current religious chaos, through pluralism and secularism, and finally to a convergence on liberal values, is to modify the beliefs of millions of people through honest conversation" (126).

[115] Bin Laden, *Messages to the World*, 239–240.

Recall also bin Laden's very modern and unusual claim that all tax-paying citizens living in a democracy qualify as combatants[116] as well as his aberrant conception of reciprocity, which he justified by erroneously invoking medieval authorities such as al-Qurtubi.[117] If Harris insists that "moderation" is fostered by factors external to scripture, however faithful "moderates" might be, then he must concede that the same is true for violent radicalism, however faithful radicals might be.

Before leaving Harris, I must say a word about his portrayal of his actual and would-be critics among Western liberals. He tells Nawaz,

> In the West, there is now a large industry of apology and obfuscation designed, it would seem, to protect Muslims from having to grapple with the kinds of facts we've been talking about. The humanities and social science departments of every university are filled with scholars and pseudo-scholars – deemed to be experts in terrorism, religion, Islamic jurisprudence, anthropology, political science, and other fields – who claim that Muslim extremism is never what it seems. These experts insist that we can never take Islamists and jihadists at their word and that none of their declarations about God, paradise, martyrdom, and the evils of apostasy have anything to do with their real motivations.

> When one asks what the motivations of Islamists and jihadists actually are, one encounters a tsunami of liberal delusion. Needless to say, the West is to blame for all the mayhem we see in Muslim societies. After all, how would *we* feel if outside powers and their mapmakers had divided our lands and stolen our oil? These beleaguered people just want what everyone else wants out of life ... Liberals imagine that jihadists and Islamists are acting as anyone else would given a similar history of unhappy encounters with the West. And they totally discount the role that religious beliefs play in inspiring a group like [ISIS] – to the point where it would be impossible for a jihadist to prove that he was doing *anything* for religious reasons.[118]

He adds, "We have extremists playing both sides of the board in a clash of civilizations, and liberals won't speak sensibly about what's happening."[119]

Harris's depiction of his actual and would-be critics in Western academia is a straw-man caricature. (And we must demand a definition of

---

[116] Bin Laden, *Messages to the World*, 140–141.

[117] Bin Laden, *Messages to the World*, 118–119; cf. al-Qurtubi, *al-Jami' li-ahkam al-Qur'an*, 7:372 (commentary on Qur'an 5:8).

[118] Harris and Nawaz, *Islam and the Future of Tolerance*, 46–47. Harris makes similar claims in his September 2014 blog entry "Sleepwalking Toward Armageddon" and his October 2014 entry "Can Liberalism Be Saved From Itself?"

[119] Harris and Nawaz, *Islam and the Future of Tolerance*, 54.

who qualifies as a "pseudo-scholar.") Nevertheless, Harris is right to call out those scholars who completely discount the religious motivations of Muslim radicals, however idiosyncratic they might be. But until Harris presents a deeper and more nuanced understanding of Islamic scripture and thought, the burden is on him to show that Muslim radicals stand at the center of Islam. The same, in fact, could be said about another well-known New Atheist, Ayaan Hirsi Ali, whose works we shall now examine.

7

"It *Is* about Islam"

The Case of Ayaan Hirsi Ali

Ayaan Hirsi Ali (née Ayaan Hirsi Magan) was born into a Muslim family in Somalia in 1969. The daughter of a once-imprisoned Somali politician, Hirsi Magan Isse (d. 2008), her family relocated to Saudi Arabia, then to Ethiopia, then to Kenya before she received asylum in the Netherlands as a young adult. There she worked at various institutions as a translator for Somali refugees, including abused Somali women. Her growing interest in political science ultimately led her to pursue a master's degree in the field at Leiden University; she completed the degree in 2000.

By her own admission, the September 11 tragedy and the recorded statements of Osama bin Laden played a critical role in her move away from Islam toward atheism.[1] And this move was hardly discreet, as she publicly criticized Islam in various writings, including the screenplay of her 2004 short film *Submission* – a film whose producer, Theo van Gogh, was brutally murdered shortly after its release by a member of the Muslim terrorist cell known as the Hofstad Group as an act of reprisal. Such threats did not paralyze Ali, who by this time was serving in the Dutch Parliament, after having won a seat there the year prior.

In 2006, after the validity of her Dutch citizenship was publicly called into question,[2] she relocated to the United States (she became

---

[1] Ali, *The Caged Virgin*, 76; Ali, *Infidel*, 268–274; Ali, *Nomad*, xii. See Ali, *Heretic*, 44, in which Ali indicates that although "the more profound cause" of her "crisis of faith" was her exposure to "the foundations of Western thought," 9/11 was "the catalyst" that led her to question her "faith as a Muslim."

[2] Ali's asylum application served as the focal point of a 2006 government and media debate over the legitimacy of her Dutch citizenship, which she still retains as of this writing. She acknowledged that she offered false and misleading information to Dutch

an American citizen in 2013) and served as a fellow at the American Enterprise Institute in Washington, DC. As founder of the Ayaan Hirsi Ali (AHA) Foundation – a charitable organization that aims "to help protect and defend the rights of women in the West"[3] – and a fellow at Harvard University's John F. Kennedy School of Government, she remains an influential figure, particularly in the West.

As an author, Ali made her first big splash in the English-speaking world in 2006, with the publication of *The Caged Virgin: An Emancipation Proclamation for Women and Islam*.[4] This was followed by two popular autobiographical works, *Infidel: My Life* (2007) and *Nomad: From Islam to America* (2010). Her more recent publication, *Heretic: Why Islam Needs a Reformation Now* (2015), offers her most serious critique of Islam to date. In what follows, I shall examine her earlier books before turning to *Heretic*.

THE 9/11 TURNING POINT

The tragedy of 9/11 compelled many Muslims to reassess their religion. In the case of Ali, she came to believe that "the aggression, the hatred" the world witnessed that day was "inherent in Islam itself."[5] She describes how she arrived at this conclusion:

Videotapes of old interviews with Osama Bin Laden began running on CNN and Al-Jazeera. They were filled with justification for total war on America, which, together with the Jews, he perceived as leading a new Crusade on Islam. Sitting in a dainty house in picture-perfect Leiden, I thought it sounded far-fetched, like the ravings of a madman, but Bin Laden's quotes from the Quran resonated in my brain: "When you meet the unbelievers, strike them in the neck" [Qur'an 47:4]. "If you do not go out and fight, God will punish you severely and put others in your place" [Qur'an 9:39]. "Wherever you find the polytheists, kill them, seize them, besiege them, ambush them" [Qur'an 9:5]. "You who believe, do not take

---

authorities when applying for asylum: she stated that she had come directly from war-torn Somalia (to improve her chances of receiving asylum) and that she was born in 1967; she also used a different last name, Ali instead of Magan. In a conversation with Sam Harris, Ali explained that she did all this so that her family – particularly her father and a man she "had been married off to" – would not find her (Harris, "Lifting the Veil of 'Islamophobia'").

[3] Ali, *Nomad*, 275.

[4] This book was published in 2004 in Dutch under the title *De maagdenkooi*. This was her second Dutch book, her first being the 2002 work *De zoontjesfabriek: over vrouwen, Islam en integratie* (The Son Factory: On Women, Islam, and Integration).

[5] Ali, *The Caged Virgin*, ix.

the Jews and Christians as friends; they are allies only to each other. Anyone who takes them as an ally becomes one of them" [Qur'an 5:51].[6]

Ali has more to say in *Heretic* about most of these Qur'anic passages, so I shall comment on her reading of scripture later.

Ali continues,

I didn't want to do it, but I had to: I picked up the Quran and the *hadith* and started looking through them, to check. I hated to do it, because I knew that I would find Bin Laden's quotations in there, and I didn't want to question God's word. But I needed to ask: Did the 9/11 attacks stem from true belief in true Islam? And if so, what did *I* think about Islam?[7]

Ali recounts a conversation she had with Ruud Koole, a politician and her former teacher, the morning after the attacks:

He said, "It's so weird, isn't it, all these people saying this has to do with Islam?" I couldn't help myself ... I blurted out, "But it *is* about Islam. This is based in belief. This is Islam."[8]

Addressing the reader, Ali elaborates,

It was not a lunatic fringe who felt this way about America and the West. I knew that a vast mass of Muslims would see the attacks as justified retaliation against the infidel enemies of Islam. War had been declared in the name of Islam, my religion, and now I had to make a choice. Which side was I on? I found I couldn't avoid the question. Was this really Islam? Did Islam permit, even call for, this kind of slaughter? Did I, as a Muslim, approve of the attack? And if I didn't, where did I stand on Islam?

... Mohamed Atta, the hijackers' leader, had instructed them on how to "die as a good Muslim." He used the prayer every Muslim utters when he is dying: he asks Allah to stand by him as he comes to Him. I read it and I recognized it. Everything about the tone and substance of [Atta's] letter [to the other hijackers] was familiar to me. This was not just Islam, this was the core of Islam. Mohamed Atta believed that he was giving his life for Allah.

... Every devout Muslim who aspired to practice genuine Islam – the Muslim Brotherhood Islam, the Islam of the Medina Quran schools – even if they didn't actively support the attacks, they must at least have approved of them. This ... had nothing to do with frustration. It was about belief.[9]

---

[6] Ali, *Infidel*, 271. Here Ali also cites the aforementioned hadith that foretells a future Muslim–Jewish battle that presages Judgment Day – a hadith bin Laden mentioned in the process of dismissing the utopian illusion of everlasting peace in this world (bin Laden, *Messages to the World*, 125–126; cf. Suleiman et al., "The Myth of an Antisemitic Genocide in Muslim Scripture").

[7] Ali, *Infidel*, 271.

[8] Ali, *Infidel*, 268.

[9] Ali, *Infidel*, 269–270. For an English translation of Atta's letter, see "Last Words of a Terrorist." One noteworthy feature of this letter is Atta's brief references to the women

Like Ali, countless Muslims would have recognized at least some of the prayers made and religious sentiments expressed by bin Laden and the hijackers. But what does this really tell us? In an American Protestant context, for instance, the Reverend Martin Luther King Jr. (d. 1968) was certainly familiar with many of the biblical sentiments expressed by members of the Ku Klux Klan, a terrorist organization vehemently opposed to his civil rights mission. Their overlapping attributes did not negate their fundamental differences. In the case of Islam, we have no good reason to think that "every" or even most devout Muslims "must at least have approved" of 9/11. There is no reliable polling data to support Ali's claim; in fact, the data and condemnations discussed earlier strongly suggest the opposite.

It is curious that Ali singled out only two rather different traditions, "Muslim Brotherhood Islam" (one form of Islamism) and "the Islam of the Medina Quran schools" (one form of Salafism), as being representative of "genuine Islam." Yet even representatives of these traditions came out strongly against 9/11. Indeed, in September 2001, the leadership of the Muslim Brotherhood stated that it was "horrified" by 9/11, "strongly" condemned it, and asserted that the operation was "against all human and Islamic norms"; the Saudi grand mufti Abdulaziz al-Shaykh proclaimed that the attacks "constitute a form of injustice that cannot be tolerated by Islam, which views them as gross crimes and sinful acts"; and in a televised statement, the Chairman of the Supreme Judicial Council of Saudi Arabia, Saleh Al-Luheidan, stressed that "these acts are from the depths of depravity and the worst of evils." Years later, in an August 2005 lecture on the "evils of terrorism," Muhammad al-Aqeel, a professor of creed (*aqida*) at the Islamic University of Medina, denounced "riotous killing," presented its growing prevalence as a sign of "the end of time," and declared that "the ugliest face of terrorism is that which is established in the name of religion" – and "all of the religions from the Prophets (peace be upon them) are free from such terrorism."[10]

---

of paradise who will be awaiting the "martyrs." Since 9/11, there has been much popular discussion about the notion that every Muslim martyr will be rewarded with seventy-two virgins in the afterlife. Although the Qur'an speaks in general terms of the beautiful companions of paradise (see, for example, 44:54), as Islamic studies scholar Jonathan A. C. Brown notes, "the promise of seventy-two huris, or 'dark-eyed heavenly beauties,' for each martyr is actually found in a problematic and unreliable Hadith of exhortation" (Brown, *Misquoting Muhammad*, 238).

[10] Kurzman (ed.), "Islamic Statements Against Terrorism."

Now Ali was aware of the fact that at least some Muslim scholars and imams had condemned 9/11 shortly after the attacks.[11] (Presumably she would say that such Muslims were not aspiring to practice "genuine Islam.") But in response to such Muslims, and in an attempt to draw a connection between Islam and terrorism, Ali offers the following observations:

- Muslims were responsible for most (eleven "and possibly twelve" of sixteen) of the "major international terrorist acts committed between 1983 and 2000" (Ali provides no reference here);
- Most of the states and organizations that "support terrorists" according to the United States State Department are "Muslim countries" and "Muslim organizations";
- Although only one-fifth of the world's population is Muslim, "Muslims were involved in two-thirds of the thirty-two armed conflicts in the year 2000" according to the International Institute of Strategic Studies in London.[12]

This data is indeed disturbing, but it is also extremely selective: Ali's time frame starts in 1983. Yet even if one chooses to focus on recent decades only, the fact remains that, however genuinely alarming Muslim terrorism may be, it remains a phenomenon of a relatively small minority. One could just as easily highlight the deeds of the minority of Muslims who have assumed remarkable conciliatory roles in times of conflict, from Nobel Peace Prize laureates to largely unrecognized citizens in contexts such as mid-1990s Rwanda. In either case, one could hardly draw general conclusions about Islam or its foundations from such limited data. For Ali, however, Muslim terrorism is a revelation of the religion's inherent bellicosity. Speaking as a secular Muslim, Ali asserts, "we Muslims have refused to acknowledge that a once peaceful, powerful, and robust religion carried within it elements of fanaticism and violence."[13] The reader is left to wonder, then, how these elements could have remained latent during the bygone era alluded to by Ali.

SCRIPTURE AND OTHERNESS

The 9/11 operation, Ali maintains, "was about religious belief, a one-way ticket to Heaven," and "not frustration, poverty, colonialism, or Israel."[14]

---

[11] See Ali, *The Caged Virgin*, 10–11.
[12] Ali, *The Caged Virgin*, 11.
[13] Ali, *The Caged Virgin*, 12. See Ali, *Nomad*, 201, in which Ali states that Islam "is not just a belief; it is a way of life, a violent way of life."
[14] Ali, *Infidel*, 270.

She traces the attacks back to Islamic scripture. The Qur'an, she writes, "spreads a culture that is brutal, bigoted, ... and harsh in war."[15] (Keep in mind this is the same scripture of a "once peaceful, powerful, and robust religion.")

Ali recalls a conversation she had with a young Somali imam shortly after the attacks: Ali told the imam,

All these statements that Bin Laden and his people quote from the Quran to jus-tify the attacks – I looked them up; they are there. If the Quran is timeless, then it applies to every Muslim today. This is how Muslims may behave if they are at war with infidels. It isn't just about the battles of Uhud and Badr in the seventh century.[16]

The imam expressed his own confusion on this matter. Ali continued, "those verses about peace in the Quran apply only to life among the Muslims. The Prophet also said 'Wage war on the unbelievers'. Who are the unbelievers, and who gives the signal to wage war?"

The imam replied, "It's certainly not Bin Laden who's the author-ity." He added, "We can't wage war against a whole hemisphere where Muslims aren't in control."

Ali interjected, "[I]f we say the Quran is not timeless, then it's not holy, is it?" To this the imam was unable to offer Ali an adequate response.[17]

As should be evident by now, many Muslims, scholars and laypeople, would reject the idea that the "verses of peace" apply only to Muslims. So, too, would they object to the notion that because the Qur'an is the final divine message for all of humanity, its specific injunctions to the Prophet and his community (some calling for war and others calling for peace) must apply to all Muslims at all times. The very existence and widespread acceptance of centuries-old Islamic legal institutions attests to the ubiquity of the conviction that one cannot rightfully adhere to God's message without an interpretive methodology, specifically one that accounts for context. It is precisely this conviction that allows certain modern scholars to accept the idea of aggressive jihad in the context of a borderless, United Nations-less world but reject it in the present day, when there exists an assumed state of peace. This methodological spirit is captured in a statement we encountered earlier, from the thirteenth-century Egyptian cleric al-Qarafi: "Holding to rulings that have been deduced on the basis of custom, even after this custom has changed, is a

[15] Ali, *Infidel*, 272.
[16] Ali, *Infidel*, 273.
[17] Ali, *Infidel*, 273.

violation of Unanimous Consensus and an open display of ignorance of the religion."[18]

Ali recognizes the "systematic" dimensions of the Islamic tradition but, much like Harris, privileges radical interpretations: "True Islam, as a rigid belief system and a moral framework, leads to cruelty. The inhuman act of those nineteen hijackers was the logical outcome of this detailed system for regulating human behavior." "Their world," she continues, "is divided between 'Us' and 'Them' – if you don't accept Islam you should perish."[19]

If by "accept Islam" Ali means "become Muslim" (which the "Us" and "Them" binary suggests), the fact of the matter is that, technically, not even bin Laden or the leadership of ISIS would say that *all* non-Muslims should "perish" – unless perhaps by "perish" Ali has in mind punishment in the afterlife. Ali informs us that she herself was raised to believe that non-Muslims who are exposed to Islam yet remain non-Muslim are "immoral" and "blind" and that God will punish these "unfaithful" Others "most atrociously in the hereafter." In fact, as Ali would have it, the feeling among Muslims "that God has granted them special salvation goes further" than what one finds among Christians and Jews.[20]

But from a historical standpoint, Christians and Christian theologians, for instance, have not generally affirmed an evidently more inclusive conception of salvation than their Muslim counterparts. Thus, Ali's statement concerning Muslims seems more reasonable if one focuses on specific contexts in which exclusionary ideologies and tendencies are especially pronounced. With this in mind, Ali's characterization of her own Islamic upbringing is revealing: "Muslim children all over the world are taught *the way I was*: taught with violence, taught to perpetrate violence, taught to wish for violence against the infidel, the Jew, the American Satan."[21]

---

[18] Al-Qarafi, *Kitab al-ihkam*, 231 (translated and discussed in Jackson, "Jihad and the Modern World," 9; see page 8).

[19] Ali, *Infidel*, 272.

[20] Ali, *The Caged Virgin*, x.

[21] Ali, *Nomad*, 201 (emphasis added). Elsewhere Ali writes, "Many madrassas [Islamic schools] imbue their pupils with an irrational hatred of Jews and an aversion to nonbelievers, a message that is also frequently repeated in the mosques ... I myself experienced how insidious the effects of years of this indoctrination can be: the first time I saw a Jew with my own eyes, I was surprised to find a human being of flesh and blood" (Ali, *The Caged Virgin*, 38).

(Ali does not offer any supporting evidence to justify her claim about the education of Muslim children worldwide.)

All this helps to explain why, from Ali's vantage point, it is *ignorance* of scripture that allows many Muslims to champion inclusion and peace (despite what is taught in many Muslim schools): "Most Muslims never delve into theology, and we rarely read the Quran; we are taught it in Arabic, which most Muslims can't speak." Accordingly, "most people *think* that Islam is about peace. It is from these people, honest and kind, that the fallacy has arisen that Islam is peaceful and tolerant."[22]

The Prophet and the "Clash"

Although Ali concedes that Muhammad "did teach us a lot of good things,"[23] as she sees it, the potentially "embarrassing, and even painful" reality for "moderate Muslims" is the "historical fact" that Muhammad "built the House of Islam using military tactics."[24] His policies gave his religion "a strongly expansionist character," as "much importance is attributed to the conquest and conversion of those who do not believe in Allah."[25] (I shall return to this topic shortly.) Furthermore, privileging terrorist propaganda and its appropriation of the Prophet, Ali stresses the fact that terrorists often quote Muhammad "to justify their actions and to call on other Muslims to support their cause."[26] As such, Ali criticizes the analysts who were fixated on bin Laden rather than Muhammad in the aftermath of 9/11: "Most articles analyzing Bin Laden and his movement were scrutinizing a symptom, a little like analyzing Lenin and Stalin without looking at the works of Karl Marx."[27]

In the context of discussing Muslim terrorism, Ali alleges that most Muslims are "caught in a mental cramp of cognitive dissonance" because they "know that Muhammad calls for slaughter of infidels; they know that the open society rightly condemns the slaughter of innocents." It is, therefore, "up to the West to support the reformists in trying to ease them out of that painful contradiction."[28] This claim of a "contradiction" is problematic, however, because it suggests that the generality of Muslims

[22] Ali, *Infidel*, 272.
[23] Ali, *Infidel*, 272.
[24] Ali, *The Caged Virgin*, 173.
[25] Ali, *The Caged Virgin*, 49.
[26] Ali, *The Caged Virgin*, 173.
[27] Ali, *Infidel*, 271.
[28] Ali, *The Caged Virgin*, 176.

believe that the Prophet called for the "slaughter of innocents," and simply on account of their unbelief (Ali does not qualify the term "infidels").
Again, strictly speaking, not even bin Laden or the leadership of ISIS
would issue an open-ended call for the "slaughter of infidels" (as even
radicals know not to target certain noncombatants, to say nothing of
non-Muslims living under Muslim rule or protected by a truce).

Not surprisingly, Ali fully embraces a "clash of civilizations" worldview. Recall her words: "I had to make a choice. Which side was I on?"
To her mind, "reason" was not to be found on the Islamic "side":

Osama Bin Laden said, "Either you are with the Crusade, or you are with Islam,"
and I felt that Islam all over the world was now in a truly terrible crisis. Surely,
no Muslim could continue to ignore the clash between reason and our religion?
For centuries we had been behaving as though all knowledge was in the Quran,
refusing to question anything, refusing to progress. We had been hiding from reason for so long because we were incapable of facing up to the need to integrate
it into our beliefs. And this was not working; it was leading to hideous pain and
monstrous behavior.[29]

To be sure, Ali's characterization of the relationship between Muslims
and reason is one dimensional and ignores countless counter-examples.
It also stands in sharp contrast with the opinion held by many of bin
Laden's critics, namely that his horrific methods were precisely the result
of his "reason" and departure from Muhammad's example.

With regard to those sympathetic to bin Laden, Ali proffers that he
"appeals to the colorful fantasies and dreams of Muslims who do not
want to take responsibility for their own state and for their own deeds."
These are people "who shift blame for their country's and their own
problems onto outside 'authorities' – onto the West, onto the United
States."[30] Ali also draws attention to the fact that many Muslims scape-
goat Jews, buying into "the conspiracy theory that claims they control
the world."[31]

Regardless of whether Ali is too dismissive of Muslim grievances, her
"conspiracy theory" criticism is worthy of serious consideration. And
I imagine many Muslims would likely agree with her on this and indeed
on the broader point that they should not blame others for their own
shortcomings and failings. Perhaps some would even invoke the Qur'an
in support of this idea: "God does not change the condition of a people

---

[29] Ali, *Infidel*, 271.
[30] Ali, *The Caged Virgin*, 38.
[31] Ali, *Nomad*, 200.

unless they change what is in themselves" (13:11). Even bin Laden, for all his sharp denunciations of America and Israel, affirmed, at least verbally, a paradigm of Muslim self-accountability;[32] and yet his can-do-no-wrong attitude suggests the opposite: a lack of introspection.

So how does Ali envision the way forward? In her 2006 book *The Caged Virgin* she argues that because "[m]any Muslims lack the necessary willingness and courage to address" the need for reform, the "West needs to help Muslims help themselves." Thus, "both Muslims and non-Muslims" must "face the malicious extremism manifest in the attacks of September 11," recognize that "fear of that kind of Islam is valid" and that "fanaticism in Islam is a reality," and "stand together" in rejecting such fanaticism "instead of blaming each other and cultivating mutual distrust. That solves nothing, and the fanatics may benefit from it."[33] She goes on to declare that 9/11 "was the beginning of the end of Islam as we know it."[34]

Despite her atheistic worldview, in her 2010 book *Nomad*, Ali goes a step further and encourages churches to "win" the "battle" against Islam "for the souls of humans in search of a compassionate God, who now find that a fierce Allah is closer to hand."[35] She has since backed away from this call for a Christian solution – a call that would serve to foster the very "mutual distrust" she cautioned against in *The Caged Virgin*. This takes us to her 2015 book *Heretic*.

A "HERETICAL" STANCE

In *Heretic*, Ali elaborates on most of her previous assessments of Islam and jihad. She remarks that since 9/11, she has "been making a simple argument in response" to Muslim terrorism:

[I]t is foolish to insist, as our leaders habitually do, that the violent acts of radical Islamists can be divorced from the religious ideals that inspire them. Instead we must acknowledge that they are driven by a political ideology, an ideology embedded in Islam itself, in the holy book of the Qur'an as well as the life and teachings of the Prophet Muhammad contained in the hadith.[36]

---

[32] As Michael Scheuer would have it, "Bin Laden's was a long way from the argument of Bernard Lewis and others who claimed Muslims blamed others for their failings" (Scheuer, *Osama Bin Laden*, 77; cf. Bernard Lewis, *What Went Wrong?*).

[33] Ali, *The Caged Virgin*, 13.

[34] Ali, *The Caged Virgin*, 84.

[35] Ali, *Nomad*, 251.

[36] Ali, *Heretic*, 2–3. One example Ali provides to illustrate this is "the bloody battles of jihad playing out across Syria and Iraq. Many of today's Sunni and Shiite fighters believe

Thus, those who maintain that Muslim terrorism is actually "a problem of poverty, insufficient education, or any other social precondition" are offering "facile explanations." This is because the "imperative for jihad" – "a type of religious warfare to spread the land ruled by Allah's laws" – "is embedded in Islam itself. It is a religious obligation."[37] "The root problem of the violence that is plaguing our world today," therefore, is not a mis-interpretation of Islam but "the doctrine of Islam itself."[38] This a point Ali stresses and reiterates: "Islamic violence is rooted not in social, economic, or political conditions – or even in theological error – but rather in the foundational texts of Islam itself." In short, *Islam is not a religion of peace.*"[39]

By merely expressing this idea, Ali writes, "I have been deemed to be a heretic, not just by Muslims – for whom I am already an apostate – but by some Western liberals as well, whose multicultural sensibilities are offended by such 'insensitive' pronouncements." For "in the present atmosphere, anything that makes Muslims feel uncomfortable is branded as 'hate'."[40] And since her understanding of Islam is based on her "know-ledge and experience of being a Muslim, of living in Muslim societies – including Mecca itself, the very center of Islamic belief" – and on her "years of study of Islam as a practitioner, student and teacher," the "real" reason her critics would like to silence her, she declares, "is because they cannot actually refute what I am saying."[41]

---

they are participating in battles foretold in seventh-century prophecies – the accounts in the hadith that refer to the confrontation of two massive armies in Syria" (*Heretic*, 102).

[37] Ali, *Heretic*, 176–178. Ali approvingly cites Islamic studies scholar David Cook's prob-lematic assertion that, as Islam evolved, "the armed struggle – aggressive conquest – came first, and then additional meanings became attached to the term [*jihad*]" (Cook, *Understanding Jihad*, 42, cited in Ali, *Heretic*, 102; cf. Afsaruddin, *Striving in the Path of God*, 304, note 54). Ali holds that jihad was, in essence, a sanctified permutation of tribal raiding (*Heretic*, 85).

[38] Ali, *Heretic*, 190.

[39] Ali, *Heretic*, 3.

[40] Ali, *Heretic*, 3.

[41] Ali, *Heretic*, 8. Ali provides an example of her being "silenced." She describes being invited (in the fall of 2013) to receive an honorary degree at Brandeis University in the spring of 2014; however, the invitation was revoked following objections from Brandeis faculty members and an online petition initially organized by the Council on American–Islamic Relations (CAIR) to protest the decision by Brandeis administrators. Ali notes that faculty members had expressed their "shock and dismay" at her statements that were, ironically, taken out of context (Ali, *Heretic*, 4–8). Incidentally, Ali maintains that her words were also twisted by the Norwegian far-right terrorist Anders Breivik, whose infamous manifesto cites Ali. "No one quoted by Breivik," she insists, "is responsible for him" (as quoted in Harris, "Lifting the Veil of 'Islamophobia'").

But in blaming Islam's foundational texts for contemporary terrorism and its attendant political ideology, while downplaying other factors, Ali presents an explanation that is just as "facile" as those of the apologists she criticizes. When considering bin Laden, for instance, Ali's analysis fails to explain why the al-Qaeda leader's justifications for 9/11 were rejected by the overwhelming majority of the world's leading Muslims, including many vehemently opposed to American foreign policy. Ali's analysis also does not clarify why bin Laden was hostile toward, for example, the United Kingdom and the Saudi kingdom but not the Swedish kingdom.[42] And what is one to make of his apparently consequential misreading of Islamic sources? After all, he invoked the Qur'anic commentator al-Qurtubi (d. 1273) to suggest that Muslims may intentionally kill women and children if the enemy does the same – a position rejected by al-Qurtubi himself![43]

Nevertheless, from Ali's vantage point, Muslim terrorism begins with the Qur'an, for it "explicitly urges pitilessness." She writes that we cannot be "wholly surprised" when fundamentalists kill "infidels," for the Qur'an commands, "slay them wherever ye catch them" (2:191); or when they decapitate "infidels," for the Qur'an states, "when ye meet the Unbelievers [in fight], smite at their necks; At length, when ye have thoroughly subdued them, bind a bond firmly [on them]" (47:4).[44] Yet

---

[42] See bin Laden, *Messages to the World*, 238. As we saw earlier, in his 2004 statement to the "people of America," bin Laden noted that he had not attacked Sweden since he deemed the country nonthreatening. Even if we assume he later changed his mind on Sweden – it is not clear if in 2004 he was aware of the fact that some Swedish troops had been deployed in Afghanistan with the NATO-led International Security Assistance Force (ISAF) – it would appear that he never plotted or sponsored any attack on Swedish targets. The Stockholm bombings of December 11, 2010, which injured two individuals and killed only the suicide bomber, may have been inspired by al-Qaeda, but we have no reliable evidence of bin Laden's involvement in the operation. Incidentally, ten minutes prior to the explosions, email threats were sent to a Swedish news organization and police; the messages made reference to the Swedish military presence in Afghanistan (at that time, Sweden had approximately 500 soldiers in Afghanistan with ISAF) and a Swedish cartoonist, Lars Vilks, who depicted Muhammad as part-dog (Nyberg, "Explosions in Stockholm Believed to Be Failed Terrorist Attack"; Stavrou, "The Debate over Swedish Troops in Afghanistan").

[43] Bin Laden, *Messages to the World*, 118–119; al-Qurtubi, *al-Jami' li-ahkam al-Qur'an*, 7:372 (commentary on Qur'an 5:8).

[44] Ali, *Heretic*, 188. If Ali's focus were strictly the command to "smite at the necks," it is curious that she went on to quote the order to "bind a bond firmly [on them]" but not the continuation of the verse: "thereafter [is the time for] either generosity or ransom ..."

perhaps we should be more than a little surprised by such acts. The passages Ali quotes here come from the translation of the Muslim scholar Abdullah Yusuf Ali (d. 1953). But whereas Yusuf Ali provides background information on these passages (in the commentary accompanying his translation),[45] Hirsi Ali presents them in isolation. She thus neglects to note that the violent passages she quotes are widely understood to be in reference to specific repressive, bellicose foes, not innocent civilians.[46] If her argument is that, whatever the background information, the letter of the Qur'an itself inspires terrorism, it is significant that she makes no reference to surrounding verses, such as 2:190, which describes those who are to be fought as "those who fight you"; and verses 1, 32, and 34 of the forty-seventh chapter (Muhammad), which indicate that the "unbelievers" mentioned in this wartime chapter (there is an explicit reference to "war" in a section of verse 4 not quoted by Ali) are those who "bar others from God's path,"[47] and not simply non-Muslims more generally.

In her attempt to draw connections between scripture and the jihad paradigm of violent radicals, Ali cites the following "key verses" from the Qur'an – words that "have lost none of their appeal":[48]

- the aforementioned "sword verse," 9:5;
- 8:60, which commands Muslims to prepare "whatever forces [they] can muster" in order to "frighten off" – or, as Ali (and Yusuf Ali) has it, "strike terror into (the hearts of)" – their enemies;
- 8:39, which commands believers to "fight" the unbelievers "until there is no more persecution, and all worship[49] is devoted to God alone";

---

45 See, for example, Ali, *The Holy Qur'an*, 76, note 205; 1377.

46 See Nasr (ed.), *The Study Quran*, 83–85 (commentary on Qur'an 2:190–194), 1236–1237 (commentary on Qur'an 47:1, 4).

47 An alternative interpretation of the expression translated here as "bar others from" (*saddu 'an*) is simply "turn from." Some scholars assume both understandings, thus taking Qur'an 47:1, 32, and 34 to be referring to those who both turn away and bar others from God's path (see Nasr [ed.], *The Study Quran*, 1236 [commentary on Qur'an 47:1]). In any case, what I present here ("bar others from God's path") is a prevailing interpretation, one congruous with that of the Yusuf Ali translation used by Hirsi Ali.

48 Ali, *Heretic*, 178–179.

49 According to M. A. S. Abdel Haleem, "worship" here refers to worship at "the Sacred House" in Mecca (Abdel Haleem, *The Qur'an*, 112, note b; see Qur'an 2:191–193 and

- 8:65, which urges "the believers to fight," adding that twenty "stead-fast" believers "will overcome two hundred" enemies.

Ali does not discuss the contexts of these passages or the surrounding verses we encountered earlier, such as 9:4 and 6–13, which suggest that the "sword verse" refers to threatening enemies; and 8:61: "But if they incline toward peace, you [Prophet] must also incline toward it ..." Instead, she remarks that, "[b]eguilingly presented by modern theorists of jihad," the "key verses" cited here "can readily inspire young men to try to replicate the achievements of Muhammad's warriors in battle."[50] (Here Ali is apparently using the term "beguilingly" to suggest not that "jihad theorists" are twisting the meaning of the Qur'an to entice potential recruits and inspire violence but rather that they are using scripture *as it is* to do these things.)

Remarkably, Ali asserts that the Qur'anic verses revealed late in Muhammad's life command Muslims "to fight *all* non-Muslims, whether they are the aggressors or not."[51] And in an attempt to link the prevailing Sunni interpretations of the Qur'an to the actions of ISIS, Ali invokes an Egyptian author and a self-described former radical named Tawfik Hamid. Ali quotes Hamid's claim that, according to "the four main schools" of Sunni thought, the Qur'an (specifically 9:29, which we encountered earlier) teaches "that Muslims must fight non-Muslims and offer them the following choices: Convert to Islam, pay a humiliating tax called [*jizya*] or be killed."[52] Of course this statement, as it appears in *Heretic*, does not adequately capture the views of most Sunni scholars, past or present, for it does not specify which Muslims must fight and which non-Muslims are to be fought, it offers no sense of context, and it conceals Sunni debates over the purpose of armed jihad.

As a further attempt to show that Islam is inherently oppressive, Ali asserts that according to "[m]ainstream Islamic jurisprudence," the Qur'anic principle "There is no compulsion in religion" (2:256) has been

---

217). This parallels the reading of prominent medieval commentators such as al-Razi (d. 1209) (al-Razi, *Tafsir al-Fakhr al-Razi*, 15:169 [commentary on Qur'an 8:39]).

[50] Ali, *Heretic*, 179.

[51] Ali, *Heretic*, 98 (emphasis added); cf. Al-Dawoody, *The Islamic Law of War*, 78 (see pages 78–82).

[52] Hamid, "Does Moderate Islam Exist?" (cited and discussed in Ali, *Heretic*, 94). Incidentally, at the end of Hamid's article, we find an "important note" indicating that he has authored a work that offers "the ONLY available peaceful interpretation" of Qur'an 9:29.

abrogated.[53] Yet as indicated earlier, this is the view of only a segment of Muslim scholars (who nonetheless generally affirm limited freedoms for non-Muslims living under Muslim rule or protected by a truce). Continuing on the theme of intolerance, Ali points to the example of the early Muslims. She maintains that during the period of Muhammad's successors' "extremely brutal" conquests, "most" of the conquered peoples felt compelled to convert to Islam (as opposed to dying or accepting second-class status) "and were incorporated wholesale into the growing Muslim supertribe."[54] In making this claim, Ali does not make reference to any historical studies on conversion patterns. Perhaps the most well-known of these studies is Richard Bulliet's *Conversion to Islam in the Medieval Period*. This dated but important work suggests that conversion to Islam in Muslim-controlled lands was actually generally gradual and spanned centuries.[55]

Ali maintains that "there was always a strain of 'eliminationism' in Islam." She cites as evidence for this Muhammad's reported intention to allow only Muslims to reside in the "Arabian Peninsula."[56] Ali does not discuss the historical understanding of the "peninsula of the Arabs," namely that it roughly corresponds to the sensitive Hijaz region rather than the entire peninsula.[57] More importantly, she does not account for the fact that when Muhammad's companions conquered Jerusalem, a third holy city (after Mecca and Medina), they reportedly not only permitted Christians

---

[53] Ali, *Heretic*, 98. Here Ali cites Raymond Ibrahim's 2014 online article "Ten Ways Islam and the Mafia Are Similar." She also quotes political scientist David Bukay, who states that the "verse of the sword" (Qur'an 9:5) "abrogated, canceled, and replaced 124 verses that called for tolerance, compassion, and peace" (Bukay, "Peace or Jihad?"). As support for this claim, Ali, invoking Bukay, asserts that the eleventh-century Muslim scholar ibn Salama (d. 1019) was of the view that Qur'an 9:5 "abrogated some 124 of the more peaceful Meccan verses" (Ali, *Heretic*, 98). However, this is a problematic citation: Bukay presents various Medinan verses as also having been reportedly abrogated and tells us that ibn Salama "mentioned only 114" verses abrogated by Qur'an 9:5 (Bukay, "Peace or Jihad?"; see note 58). In any case, as Islamic studies scholar Khalid Y. Blankinship notes, the doctrine of abrogation "reached its zenith" with ibn Salama and ibn Hazm (d. 1064) (Blankinship, "Sword Verses").

[54] Ali, *Heretic*, 83. Sam Harris makes a comparable observation: "Islam was spread primarily by conquest, not conversation" (Harris and Nawaz, *Islam and the Future of Tolerance*, 99).

[55] On the significance and limitations of Bulliet's study, see Wasserstein, "Conversion and the *ahl al-dhimma*," 189–192.

[56] Ali, *Heretic*, 191.

[57] See Brown, *Misquoting Muhammad*, 127.

to live there, they reintroduced Jewish families who had been previously expelled from the city.[58]

As further evidence of Islamic "eliminationism," Ali mentions the injunction in Qur'an 5:51 not to take Jews and Christians as "friends and protectors." In the very next sentence, Ali notes that Qur'an 5:5 permits Muslim men to marry Jewish and Christian women but forbids Muslim women to marry non-Muslim men "because under Islamic law the religious identity of children is passed through the father."[59] (Although the prevailing view among Muslim scholars is indeed that Muslim women may not marry non-Muslim men, Qur'an 5:5 does not explicitly address this.)

Ali does not acknowledge the apparent contradiction in her claim. As she portrays it, the same Qur'anic chapter – the fifth chapter, al-Ma'ida (The Feast) – both prohibits friendship with Jews and Christians and permits marriage – a relationship of "love and kindness" (Qur'an 30:21) – to at least some of them. This incongruity stems from Ali's (and many others') understanding of Qur'an 5:51. In Ali's earlier work *Infidel*, she states that she became convinced that bin Laden's terrorism was tied to Islam by picking up the Qur'an and locating the verses he had quoted, such as "do not take the Jews and Christians as *friends [awliya']* [Qur'an 5:51]."[60] In place of "friends," Ali in *Heretic* opts for "friends and protectors," the translation of Yusuf Ali.[61] In the context of arguing that Islam contains "a strain of 'eliminationism'," this translation is potentially misleading, in part because the word "friends" can be understood very broadly. However one translates the Arabic term in question, *awliya'* – here I prefer "patrons" – it is important to recognize that various scholars regard Qur'an 5:51 as a specific warning to Muhammad's followers not to take as patrons the Jewish and Christian clans opposed to the Prophet, those who are but "patrons of one another" (Qur'an 5:51).[62] Such a reading allows for the possibility of harmonious relationships with non-Muslims, including the marriages permitted earlier in the same Qur'anic chapter.

---

[58] Gil, "The Jewish Community," 167.

[59] Ali, *Heretic*, 191.

[60] Ali, *Infidel*, 271 (emphasis added).

[61] Ali, *The Holy Qur'an*, 259 (Qur'an 5:51 is numbered as 5:54).

[62] See Nasr (ed.), *The Study Quran*, 302–303 (commentary on Qur'an 5:51); and Brown, *Misquoting Muhammad*, 210. Also see al-Akiti, *Defending the Transgressed*, 32, in which Muhammad Afifi al-Akiti mentions the "well known rule" in Islamic law "that a Muslim authority could seek help from a non-Muslim with certain conditions, including for example that the non-Muslim allies are of goodwill towards the Muslims."

"ACTIVATION"

Ali insists that she is not saying "that Islamic belief makes Muslims naturally violent," for "there are many millions of peaceful Muslims in the world." Yet she contends that "Islam is not a religion of peace" because "the call to violence and the justification for it are explicitly stated in the sacred texts of Islam" (recall her comment that most Muslims "rarely read the Qur'an" or understand it). Furthermore, "this theologically sanctioned violence is there to be activated by any number of offenses, including ... something as vague as threats ... to the honor of Islam itself." Thus, as she sees it, there is an "unavoidable connection" between Islam and organizations such as al-Qaeda and ISIS.[63] Needless to say, for many Muslim critics of such organizations, an act of terrorism committed in the name of Islam would not be an "activation" of the Qur'an itself but rather a transgression, an "activation" of a "twisted" interpretation.

In any case, the theme of perilous "activation" is pronounced in *Heretic*. It appears, for instance, in Ali's description of the brutal murder of her film collaborator Theo van Gogh: after shooting and attempting to decapitate van Gogh, the murderer used a knife to attach a disturbing note to his victim's body. The note contained Qur'anic verses and a threat to Ali. Whereas some Dutch academics claimed that the murderer's "real motivation in wanting to kill [Ali] was socioeconomic deprivation or postmodern alienation," an unintimidated Ali asserts that "when a murderer quotes the Qur'an in justification of his crime, we should at least discuss the possibility that he means what he says."[64] While this is certainly a reasonable assertion, Ali's project obviously goes much further than this and indeed greatly overlaps with that of Sam Harris.

Harris, incidentally, shows up in *Heretic* to offer additional scenarios, hypothetical and actual, of perilous "activation." Ali provides a second-hand account of a private conversation he had with actor Ben Affleck and *New York Times* columnist Nicholas Kristof immediately after their October 2014 appearance on the popular cable television show *Real Time with Bill Maher*. Following a heated exchange – both Affleck and Kristof were critical of Harris's assessment of Islam and Muslims – Harris asked them,

"What do you think would happen if we had burned a copy of the Qur'an on tonight's show?" Sam then answered his own question, "There would be riots in

[63] Ali, *Heretic*, 7.
[64] Ali, *Heretic*, 5–7.

scores of countries. Embassies would fall. In response to our mistreating *a book*, millions of Muslims would take to the streets, and we would spend the rest of our lives fending off credible threats of murder. But when [ISIS] crucifies people, buries children alive, and rapes and tortures women by the thousands – *all in the name of Islam* – the response is a few small demonstrations in Europe and a hashtag [#NotInOurName]."[65]

While Harris's point is worthy of serious contemplation – even if he sidesteps the fact that many Muslims have been and are still engaged in *combat* against ISIS – it is problematic to assume that riots and other extreme responses are useful indicators of worldwide Muslim sentiments. Most Muslims, it would be safe to say, do not take to the streets to riot (and certainly do not murder others); and among those who do riot, many likely choose to express their anti-Western sentiments visibly because of a perception that Muslims are under siege by much stronger Western forces. This, of course, does not discount the fact that many devout Muslims find insults to their holy book genuinely hurtful; however, I suspect that many of these same Muslims are more profoundly offended by the brutal acts of ISIS, an organization that claims to represent their religion yet has killed and harmed thousands of people, mostly fellow Muslims.

Be that as it may, sounding much like Harris, Ali declares that because the "killers" in radical organizations such as ISIS and Boko Haram "cite the same religious texts that every other Muslim in the world considers sacrosanct," it "simply will not do for Muslims to claim that their religion has been 'hijacked' by extremists." "We in the West," she proclaims, "need to challenge and debate the very substance of Islamic thought and practice," instead of letting Muslims "off the hook with bland clichés about Islam as a religion of peace." "We need to hold Islam accountable for the acts of its most violent adherents and demand that it reform or disavow the key beliefs that are used to justify those acts."[66]

A "HERETICAL" REFORMATION

Although Ali suggests that the violence committed by Muslim radicals is hardly "the work of a lunatic fringe of extremists,"[67] she stresses that

---

[65] Ali, *Heretic*, 214.

[66] Ali, *Heretic*, 12.

[67] Ali, *Heretic*, 11. See Ali, *Heretic*, 15–16, in which Ali cites author Ed Husain's estimate that "3 percent of the world's Muslims understand Islam in ... militant terms." Ali goes on to say that on the basis of "survey data on attitudes toward sharia in Muslim

"the clear majority throughout the Muslim world ... are not inclined to practice violence." They "focus on religious observances." Their "problem," according to Ali, is that "their religious beliefs exist in an uneasy tension with ... [t]he rational, secular, and individualistic values of modernity." Ali refers to these believers as "Mecca Muslims."[68] Recall that Muhammad migrated from Mecca, where his position was that of a pacifist prophet, to Medina, where he was a commander and a political leader as well as a religious figure. Accordingly, Ali conceptualizes "Mecca Muslims" as being out of line with the Prophet's final teachings, including his teachings on warfare. But considering that Muhammad's Medinan teachings actually encompass most religious observances (from the congregational prayer to the fast of Ramadan) and nearly every aspect of Islamic law (pertaining to, among other things, marriage, divorce, inheritance, commerce, and diet), Ali's "Mecca Muslim" label seems odd.

In any case, Ali's "Mecca Muslims" are to be distinguished from, on the one hand, "Modifying Muslims" (these may be devout or secular), who, like Ali, seek to reform Islam, and, on the other hand, "Medina Muslims," who are fundamentalists and violent radicals (including members of al-Qaeda and ISIS) who supposedly aim to "live by the strict letter" of the Islamic creed. The latter is most disconcerting to Ali, for they

argue for an Islam largely or completely unchanged from its original seventh-century version ...

... They aim not just to obey Muhammad's teaching, but also to emulate his warlike conduct after his move to Medina. Even if they do not themselves engage in violence, they do not hesitate to condone it ...

... It is Medina Muslims who prescribe beheading for the crime of "nonbelief" in Islam ...

Medina Muslims believe that the murder of an infidel is an imperative if he refuses to convert voluntarily to Islam."[69]

countries" – here she cites a 2013 Pew study entitled "The World's Muslims: Religion, Politics and Society" – "I would put the proportion significantly higher; I also believe it is rising." The Pew survey, which involved tens of thousands of face-to-face interviews in dozens of Muslim-majority countries, found, among other things, that "roughly three-quarters or more Muslims reject suicide bombing and other forms of violence against civilians"; however, as Ali observes (20), a "quarter of Bangladeshis and one in eight Pakistanis think that suicide bombings in defense of Islam are often or sometimes justified." Incidentally, the survey also found "no consistent link between support for enshrining sharia as official law and attitudes toward religiously motivated violence."

[68] Ali, *Heretic*, 16.
[69] Ali, *Heretic*, 14–18.

As Ali does not qualify these statements, I must repeat a familiar refrain: *not even bin Laden or the leadership of ISIS* would call for the murder of *all* non-Muslims.

However imprecise Ali's characterization of "Medina Muslims" might be, she submits what she considers to be "the only viable strategy that can hope to contain" the threat they pose to others, namely "to side with the dissidents and reformists and to help them a) identify and repudiate those parts of Muhammad's moral legacy that stem from Medina and b) persuade the Mecca Muslims to accept this change and reject the Medina Muslims' summons to intolerance and war."[70]

Along these lines, Ali identifies five "inherently harmful" things that Muslims must either reform or discard:

1. Muhammad's semi-divine and infallible status along with the literal reading of the Qur'an, particularly those parts that were revealed in Medina;
2. The investment in life after death instead of life before death;
3. Sharia, the body of legislation derived from the Qur'an, the hadith, and the rest of Islamic jurisprudence;
4. The practice of empowering individuals to enforce Islamic law ...;
5. The imperative to wage jihad, or holy war.[71]

Leaving aside her questionable word choice (for instance, countless Muslims would object to any attribution of "semi-divinity" to Muhammad), Ali is in effect calling for a truly radical reformation of the Islamic tradition. But behind her call is a conception of Islam and Islamic law marked by, among other things, excessive bellicosity. Given that Ali conceives of jihad as "pitiless" in nature and a catalyst for terrorism, one can understand why she would call for its termination:

The only way the arms race ended was with the ideological and political collapse of Soviet communism, after which there was a large-scale (though not complete) decommissioning of nuclear weapons. In much the same way, we need to recognize that this is an ideological conflict that will not be won until the concept of jihad has itself been decommissioned. We also have to acknowledge that, far from being un-Islamic, the central tenets of the jihadists are supported by centuries-old Islamic doctrine.[72]

[70] Ali, *Heretic*, 20–21.
[71] Ali, *Heretic*, 24.
[72] Ali, *Heretic*, 205.

She continues,

It is obviously next to impossible to redefine the word "jihad" as if its call to arms is purely metaphorical (in the style of the hymn "Onward Christian Soldiers"). There is too much conflicting scripture, and too many examples from the Qur'an and hadith that the jihadists can cite to bolster their case.

Therefore I believe the best option would be to take it off the table. If clerics and imams and scholars and national leaders around the world declared jihad "*haram*," forbidden, then there would be a clear dividing line ...

And if that is too much to expect – if Muslims simply refuse to renounce jihad completely – then the next best thing would be to call their bluff about Islam being a religion of peace. If a tradition truly exists within Islam that interprets jihad as a purely spiritual activity, as Sufi Muslims tend to do, let us challenge other Muslims to embrace it. Christianity was itself once a crusading faith, as we have seen, but over time it abandoned its militancy. If Islam really is a religion of peace, then what is preventing Muslims from doing the same?[73]

To be clear, like Harris, Ali is not a pacifist. While she states that she is "arguing for peaceful reform" and "not advocating a war,"[74] she also maintains that the ideology of "Medina Muslims" cannot be fought "*solely* with air strikes and drones or even boots on the ground."[75] Given her openness to the use of force, one is left to wonder why her reform project would not invoke Muslim scholarly arguments against aggressive jihad – a stance that affirms only the defensive form of armed jihad – and the rules of war according to scholars such as Muhammad Afifi al-Akiti. After all, such approaches would be considerably less controversial among Muslims and therefore potentially much more practically effective than Ali's proposal to purge jihad altogether.

In fact, Ali does not seem particularly interested in any potentially promising "internal" solutions that affirm armed jihad in any way. This comes out in her discussion of the work of her then Harvard Kennedy School colleague Jessica Stern, specifically Stern's research on Saudi deradicalization programs that were initiated in 2004 and have reportedly

---

73 Ali, *Heretic*, 206.
74 Ali, *Heretic*, 234.
75 Ali, *Heretic*, 219 (emphasis added). In a 2007 interview with *Reason* magazine, Ali notoriously declared that "we are at war with Islam" – not radical Islam, she clarified, but Islam itself. She said that it must be "defeated" and that the "enemy" must be "crush[ed]." When asked if she meant "militarily," she responded, "in all forms" (van Bakel, "'The Trouble Is the West'"). In his defense of Ali, journalist Jeffrey Tayler maintains that, in the context of the interview, Ali was not proposing an all-out war against all Muslims; at least domestically, he writes, she had in mind "a struggle (obviously non-military) against the imposition of the faith in the public sphere" (Tayler, "Free Speech and Islam").

"rehabilitated" thousands of militants. The programs offer various forms of support, including housing, counseling, and religious instruction. Ali is "deeply skeptical" of these programs for two reasons: (1) over the past three decades, Saudis and individuals from other Gulf states have been greatly responsible for funding the "global jihadist network"; and (2) the clerics affiliated with the "rehabilitation program" teach militants traditional Islamic rules. These teachings drive home the point that only "legitimate rulers" – not radicals like Osama bin Laden – are authorized to declare jihad and that one must not take Qur'anic verses out of context. (In the words of one participant, "Now I understand that I cannot make decisions by reading a single verse. I have to read the whole chapter.") Ali writes, "No matter how well intentioned this approach may be, it leaves the core concept of jihad intact."[76] Ultimately, however, one would need a more compelling reason to cast doubt on the program's success, especially given that Ali's skepticism of the program stems from a guilt-by-association outlook and her own particular understanding of jihad.

As of this writing, the effectiveness of Saudi deradicalization efforts remains a topic of debate. "Saudi officials say recidivism is low," though "independent assessments are rare."[77] According to a 2015 Middle East Institute report, it would seem that although the rehabilitation programs have not been particularly effective in transforming "hard-core militants," who make up roughly 10 percent of all participants, they have been successful in rehabilitating many "minor offenders" and "jihadist supporters and sympathizers who may already be looking for a way out

---

[76] Ali, *Heretic*, 204; Stern, "Mind over Martyr."

[77] Hubbard, "Inside Saudi Arabia's Re-education Prison for Jihadists." A widely circulated November 28, 2016, *New York Post* report quoted a Saudi al-Qaeda operative detained at Guantanamo Bay, Ghassan al-Sharbi, as claiming at a parole hearing that the Saudi program was actually "a hidden *radicalization* program" (Sperry, "Gitmo Prisoner Reveals that Saudi 'Terrorist Rehab' Center Is a Scam" [emphasis added]). It is not clear, however, how al-Sharbi, who has been detained since 2002, would have known this (the Saudi program described by Stern was initiated in 2004). Indeed, the parole hearing transcript cited by the *New York Post* offers no concrete evidence to support his claim. It does reveal, however, al-Sharbi's insistence that he not be released to Saudi Arabia, in particular, and his desire to live in the United States. In the end, he was denied parole ("Unclassified: The Detainee Session for ISN 682," 4–11 [this document was available online on January 4, 2017, but no longer available as of April 18, 2017]). I should add that his "Guantanamo Detainee Profile" indicates that he "has been mostly non-compliant and hostile with the guards" and "has made conflicting statements during his detention about the extent of his affiliation with al-Qaʻida and the training he received" ("Unclassified: Guantanamo Detainee Profile"). In short, he is by no means a "reliable witness."

of jihadism, having been disillusioned by the circumstances leading to their capture." All in all, the report continues, the efficacy of Saudi deradicalization efforts "in undermining jihadist groups is demonstrated by the attempts of hardened radicals to subvert" it; some, for instance, "warn users of jihadist sites against talking to clerics" involved in deradicalization, as they regard such clerics "as an effective threat to their level of support." Interestingly, many former radicals have gone on to work for deradicalization programs.[78] All this suggests that such programs are at least partially successful.

Before leaving Ali, I must say a word about her identification of the Muslim "investment in life after death instead of life before death" as one of the "inherently harmful" things that Muslims must either reform or discard. Ali writes,

Until Islam stops fixating on the afterlife, until it is liberated from the seductive story of life after death, until it actively chooses life on earth and stops valuing death, Muslims themselves cannot get on with the business of living in *this* world.[79]

Ali links this fixation on the hereafter to terrorism: Muslims find all the motivation they need to participate in jihad in the scriptural promise of a reward for martyrs. The early Muslims "not only welcomed war, they welcomed death in war because it elevated their status in paradise."[80] What is more, she writes, "Islam teaches that there is nothing so glorious as taking an infidel's life – and so much the better if the act of murder costs you your own life."[81] In this light, 9/11 was "the most spectacular martyrdom operation ever undertaken."[82]

---

[78] Casptack, "Deradicalization Programs in Saudi Arabia." For a 2010 RAND survey of deradicalization efforts in various Muslim-majority and other countries, see Rabasa et al., *Deradicalizing Islamist Extremists*. According to the authors of this report, although there is "not enough reliable data to reach definitive conclusions about the short-term, let alone the long-term, effectiveness of most existing deradicalization programs," such programs "may be necessary to permanently defuse the threat posed" by militants. "Moreover, there may be a tipping point. When enough militants renounce radical Islamism, the ideology and the organizations that adhere to it are fatally discredited. Even short of this tipping point, as greater numbers of militants renounce extremism, radical Islamist organizations will experience greater hurdles in attracting adherents and sympathizers within the Muslim community" (xiv–xvi).

[79] Ali, *Heretic*, 127.

[80] Ali, *Heretic*, 111.

[81] Ali, *Heretic*, 117.

[82] Ali, *Heretic*, 119.

With all this in mind, consider her critique of the aforementioned "Open Letter to Al-Baghdadi":

the letter does not question the overall concept of martyrdom or challenge the primacy of the afterlife. Predictably, it has had a very limited impact. There are no [ISIS] fighters laying down their arms as a result of it; no would-be Western jihadists have been persuaded by it to abandon the search for martyrdom in Syria.[83]

I am not aware of any studies that have measured the effects of the "Open Letter" on radicals and would-be radicals; however, it is difficult to imagine that revising it in the manner Ali suggests would improve matters in any concrete way. Rather, by challenging the "primacy of the afterlife" and discrediting a fundamental Islamic tenet, Muslim scholars would likely undermine their efforts. Furthermore, although Islamic scripture does indeed stress life after death, it certainly does not discount the significance of this life, as one can see, for instance, in the widely recited Qur'anic invocation, "Our Lord, give us good *in this world* and in the Hereafter, and protect us from the torment of the Fire" [2:201].

In point of fact, Muslims' belief in the "primacy of the afterlife," accompanied by their rejection of the killing of civilians, offers an alternative consideration: if Muslims believe that slaying innocents is strictly prohibited and therefore may have dreadful consequences in the next world, that is, hell rather than paradise, then this would likely serve as an effective deterrent in the minds of many believers. The Saudi grand mufti Abdulaziz al-Shaykh is one example, among many, of a prominent Muslim cleric using precisely the threat of hell to discourage suicide bombers.[84] Of course this logic might not appeal to New Atheists, who, to borrow from John Lennon, "imagine there's no heaven" and "no hell below us" in the first place.

---

[83] Ali, *Heretic*, 126–127 (the "Open Letter" was completed and signed in the fall of 2014, not, as Ali has it, 2013).
[84] See, for instance, "Saudi Mufti."

8

"Imagine a World with No Religion"

A Word on Richard Dawkins, Christopher Hitchens, and Daniel Dennett

Moving beyond the writings of Sam Harris and Ayaan Hirsi Ali, we encounter some familiar themes in the works and statements of three other prominent New Atheists: Richard Dawkins, Christopher Hitchens, and Daniel Dennett. We begin with Dawkins, one of the most widely recognized New Atheists. Born in 1941 in British Kenya, he is a renowned English evolutionary biologist and longtime faculty member at the University of Oxford (currently an emeritus fellow). Beginning with his 1976 classic *The Selfish Gene* (which, among other things, gave us the term *meme*), Dawkins has authored numerous books on science.

Of course not all of his books are strictly scientific. For our purposes, his 2006 *New York Times* bestseller *The God Delusion* is most relevant. On the first page of the book, he sets the tone: "Imagine, with John Lennon, a world with no religion. Imagine no suicide bombers, no 9/11, no 7/7, no Crusades, ... no Indian partition, no Israeli/Palestinian wars, no Serb/Croat/Muslim massacres ..."[1] Religion, we are encouraged to believe, is the best explanation for these horrors.

Reflecting on 7/7, the July 7, 2005, London suicide bombings that we know now were at least loosely linked to al-Qaeda and that claimed the lives of more than fifty civilians, Dawkins proclaims, "Only religious faith is a strong enough force to motivate such utter madness in otherwise sane and decent people." The four bombers, Dawkins tells us, "were British citizens, cricket-loving, well-mannered, just the sort of young men whose company one might have enjoyed." And unlike some other terrorists in other countries, these men

[1] Dawkins, *The God Delusion*, 1.

had no expectation that their bereaved families would be lionized, looked after or supported on martyrs' pensions. On the contrary, their relatives in some cases had to go into hiding. One of the men wantonly widowed his pregnant wife and orphaned his toddler. The action of these four young men has been nothing short of a disaster not just for themselves and their victims, but for their families and for the whole Muslim community in Britain, which now faces a backlash.[2]

Again, for Dawkins, "only religious faith" can "motivate such madness." But aside from a passing comment that "London had been braced for just such an event ever since [then British prime minister Tony] Blair volunteered us as unwilling side-kicks in Bush's invasion of Iraq," Dawkins does not discuss the political grievances of the "cricket-loving young men."[3] Such grievances were not irrelevant: in September 2005, Al Jazeera posthumously released a video message by one of the bombers, Mohammad Sidique Khan. In it Khan affirmed his faith in Islam and desire for paradise; but he also stated,

Your democratically elected governments continuously perpetuate atrocities against my people all over the world.

And your support of them makes you directly responsible, just as I am directly responsible for protecting and avenging my Muslim brothers and sisters.

Until we feel security, you will be our targets. And until you stop the bombing, gassing, imprisonment and torture of my people we will not stop this fight.

We are at war and I am a soldier. Now you too will taste the reality of this situation.

Khan went on to pray that God would raise him among "the prophets, the messengers, the martyrs and today's heroes like our beloved Sheikh Osama Bin Laden" and his associates "and all the other brothers and sisters that are fighting" in the way "of this cause."[4] In a second video message that Al Jazeera aired posthumously on July 6, 2006 (presumably after Dawkins had finished writing *The God Delusion*, which was published in October of that year), another bomber, Shehzad Tanweer, warned that more attacks would follow "until you pull your forces out of Afghanistan and Iraq."[5]

---

[2] Dawkins, *The God Delusion*, 303.

[3] Dawkins, *The God Delusion*, 303.

[4] BBC, "London Bomber." Cf. Dawkins, *The God Delusion*, 303, in which Dawkins declares that bin Laden "had nothing to do with the London bombings." According to a 2011 statement by United States national security officials, however, bin Laden likely did play a role in planning the attacks (see "July 7 Bombings Were Last Successful al-Qaeda Attack Osama bin Laden Played a Role in, US Claims").

[5] BBC, "Video of 7 July Bomber Released."

When downplaying the political grievances of Muslim radicals and focusing on their religious motivations, Dawkins leans on Sam Harris and *The End of Faith*. He makes reference to Harris's aforementioned (incomplete) treatment of the "failed Palestinian suicide bomber" Zaydan Zaydan and the latter's claim that he was driven to kill Israelis by "the love of martyrdom," not "revenge."[6] Dawkins also cites a fairly long passage from a November 19, 2001, *New Yorker* article that quotes another young Palestinian, a "failed suicide bomber" who expressed a strong desire for martyrdom.[7] Dawkins does not refer to the part of the article that outlines the political grievances of this "failed bomber" and others like him: "Over and over, I heard them say, 'The Israelis humiliate us. They occupy our land, and deny our history' ... 'The Israelis kill our children and our women. This is war, and innocent people get hurt'."[8]

Dawkins's tendency to understate political motivations also appears in his discussion of 9/11. In response to the question, "Why would anyone want to destroy the World Trade Center and everybody in it?," Dawkins quotes from Harris's *The End of Faith*:

The answer to this question is obvious – if only because it has been patiently articulated ad nauseum by bin Laden himself. The answer is that men like bin Laden *actually* believe what they say they believe. They believe in the literal truth

---

[6] Harris, *The End of Faith*, 31 (cited in Dawkins, *The God Delusion*, 304–305).

[7] Dawkins, *The God Delusion*, 305.

[8] Hassan, "An Arsenal of Believers." A similar example of selective quotations comes from Ali A. Rizvi's book *The Atheist Muslim* (2016). When discussing the brutal murder of British soldier Lee Rigby in 2013, Rizvi states that "one of his murderers, Michael Adebolajo, referenced the holy book to justify his actions." Adebolajo is quoted as saying, "We are forced by the Qur'an in ... *Surah Al-Tawbah* [the ninth chapter] and many, many other *ayahs* [verses], which state we must fight them as they fight us." Rizvi proceeds to refer to Qur'an 9:29–30 to suggest that Adebolajo was inspired by "the command to fight Christians and Jews until they either convert or pay the [*jizya*] tax." Thus, Rizvi draws a connection between specific scriptural dictates and the brutal murder of Rigby (Rizvi, *The Atheist Muslim*, 31). Rizvi chooses not to discuss other dimensions of the attack. In the very source he cites – a partial transcript of Adebolajo's postmurder rant – the latter is also quoted as saying, "The only reason we've killed this man today is because Muslims are dying daily by British soldiers ... [W]e will never stop fighting you until you leave us alone ... Tell them [your politicians] to bring our troops back so you can all live in peace. Leave our lands and you will live in peace" (Bond, "Video"). To Rizvi's credit, elsewhere in *The Atheist Muslim*, he indicates that although he sees Islam as a "key driver" of "radical jihadism," he recognizes the involvement of other factors (Rizvi, *The Atheist Muslim*, 44–45). Incidentally, in his postmurder rant, Adebolajo seemed to refer not to Qur'an 9:29–30, as Rizvi assumes, but rather to the principle of reciprocity expressed in passages such as Qur'an 9:36. The latter verse commands Muhammad's followers to fight their enemies – in this case, "the polytheists" – "all together as they fight you all together."

of the Koran. Why did nineteen well-educated middle-class men trade their lives in this world for the privilege of killing thousands of our neighbors? Because they believed that they would go straight to paradise for doing so. It is rare to find the behavior of human beings so fully and satisfactorily explained. Why have we been reluctant to accept this explanation?[9]

To Dawkins's mind, the "take-home message is that we should blame religion itself, not religious *extremism* – as though that were some kind of terrible perversion of real, decent religion." Dawkins concedes that "[p]atriotic love of country or ethnic group" can also lead to a "version of extremism," as with the Japanese kamikazes in the 1940s (whose suicide attacks numbered in the thousands) and the Sri Lankan Tamil Tigers in recent decades (whose suicide attacks numbered in the hundreds). But, Dawkins insists, "religious faith is an especially potent silencer of rational calculation."[10] Yet given that, as noted earlier, before the 1980s, suicide attacks were historically unusual among Sunni Muslims, who account for hundreds of millions more people than the combined populations of Japan and Sri Lanka, one would have to concede that modern terrorism by Sunni Muslims (whose suicide attacks now number in the thousands) represents at least a historical deviation, if not a "terrible perversion." This is not to deny the critical role of religious faith in terrorism by Sunni Muslims; rather, it is to say that the faith of these terrorists is idiosyncratic in critical ways and hardly their only motivating factor.

Dawkins suspects that "moderate" religion leads to irrationality and extremism "mostly ... because of the easy and beguiling promise that death is not the end, and that a martyr's heaven is especially glorious" – Dawkins does not consider the alternative possibility, namely that the threat of damnation (and indeed the prospect of paradise) might discourage certain believers from causing harm. "But," Dawkins continues, "it is

---

[9] Harris, *The End of Faith*, 29 (cited with minor modifications in Dawkins, *The God Delusion*, 303–304). Accordingly, Dawkins bemoans the fact that Western politicians "avoid mentioning the R word (religion), and instead characterize their battle as a war against 'terror', as though terror were a kind of spirit or force, with a will and a mind of its own. Or they characterize terrorists as motivated by pure 'evil'. But they are not motivated by evil. However misguided we may think them, they are motivated, like the Christian murderers of abortion doctors, by what they perceive to be righteousness, faithfully pursuing what their religion tells them. They are not psychotic; they are religious idealists who, by their own lights, are rational. They perceive their acts to be good, not because of some warped personal idiosyncrasy, and not because they have been possessed by Satan, but because they have been brought up, from the cradle, to have total and unquestioning *faith*" (Dawkins, *The God Delusion*, 304).

[10] Dawkins, *The God Delusion*, 306. Cf. Harris, *The End of Faith*, 233, in which Harris states that Buddhism inspired "suicidal violence" in World War II Japan.

also partly because [religious faith] discourages questioning, by its very nature."[11] A more precise assessment, however, would be that a *particular approach* to religious faith discourages questioning. And one is certainly right to express concern about unquestioning approaches, whether in religious or secular contexts.

Returning to the 7/7 bombers, Dawkins quotes – seemingly with approval – the controversial Christian writer Patrick Sookhdeo:

> For today's radical Muslims – just as for the mediaeval jurists who developed classical Islam – it would be truer to say "Islam is war" … Could it be that the young men who committed suicide [in the 7/7 bombings] were neither on the fringes of Muslim society in Britain, nor following an eccentric and extremist interpretation of their faith, but rather that they came from the very core of the Muslim community and were motivated by a mainstream interpretation of Islam?[12]

Dawkins ends the quotation here without addressing Sookhdeo's question, leaving it to appear rhetorical. In fact, the question of whether the 7/7 bombers were truly inspired by a "mainstream interpretation of Islam" is to some extent immaterial to Dawkins. As he would have it, "how can there be a perversion of faith, if faith, lacking objective justification, doesn't have any demonstrable standard to pervert?"[13]

There is indeed no "objective justification" for matters of faith. Of course the same is arguably true for morality. But in the absence of objectivity, can one still speak of a "standard" of some sort? In the case of morality, at least, Dawkins seems to think so. In responding to the question, "How … do we decide what is right and what is wrong?," Dawkins writes, "No matter how we answer that question, there is a consensus about what we do as a matter of fact consider right and wrong: a consensus that prevails surprisingly widely." It has "no obvious connection with religion," he argues, but it "extends … to most religious people."[14] This "mysterious consensus … changes over the decades."[15] Yet, Dawkins

---

[11] Dawkins, *The God Delusion*, 306. Dawkins offers a comparable critique of religion in his January 2006 Channel 4 (United Kingdom) television documentary *The Root of All Evil?* (which was retitled *The God Delusion* when it was aired on the More4 channel in August 2010).

[12] Sookhdeo, "The Myth of Moderate Islam" (cited in Dawkins, *The God Delusion*, 307). As Sookhdeo would have it, "Those who deny the validity of [Islamic] terrorists' interpretation are usually very liberal Muslims, whose own interpretations of Islam are unacceptable to the majority" (Sookhdeo, *Understanding Islamist Terrorism*, 12).

[13] Dawkins, *The God Delusion*, 306.

[14] Dawkins, *The God Delusion*, 262. On Dawkins's views on the "roots of morality," see chapter 6 of *The God Delusion*.

[15] Dawkins, *The God Delusion*, 265.

states, the "onus is not on me" to explain where the "concerted and steady changes in social consciousness come from."[16] Using a comparable line of reasoning when thinking about Islam within a religious framework, one could indeed speak of a "standard," one predicated on, to borrow Dawkins's wording, an evolving "mysterious consensus" that "prevails surprisingly widely." And the reality is that, throughout the world, one finds Muslim scholars and laypeople of different backgrounds, sects, schools of thought, and political persuasions generally agreeing that 9/11, 7/7, and other terrorist operations reflect perversions of their religion.

Needless to say, Dawkins views their religion very differently. As with Harris and Ayaan Hirsi Ali, Dawkins makes use of an inadequate selection of sources, thereby sacrificing critical nuance at the altar of convenience. At one point in *The God Delusion*, he invokes the authority of Ibn Warraq, whom Dawkins considers "a deeply knowledgeable scholar of Islam." (When claiming that Islam has no "standard to pervert," he notes that Ibn Warraq "made a similar point.")[17] A former Muslim who was born in India, raised in Pakistan, and educated in Britain (he studied Arabic and philosophy as an undergraduate), Ibn Warraq has written a series of polemical books on Islam. The works themselves use a limited array of sources and have been sharply criticized by a variety of Western scholars, including Fred Donner, who takes Ibn Warraq to task for his "inconsistent handling of Arabic materials," his "thoroughly one-sided" approach, and his "agenda, which is not scholarship, but anti-Islamic polemic."[18] To get a sense of his monolithic portrayal of the religion, here is a passage from what Dawkins refers to as "his excellent book,"[19] *Why I Am Not a Muslim*:

The totalitarian nature of Islam is nowhere more apparent than in the concept of jihad, the holy war, whose ultimate aim is to conquer the entire world and submit

---

[16] Dawkins, *The God Delusion*, 270.

[17] Dawkins, *The God Delusion*, 306–307.

[18] Donner, "*The Quest for the Historical Muhammad* by Ibn Warraq," 75. Another scholar, Herbert Berg, says Ibn Warraq "is somewhat polemic and inconsistent" and faults him for "not present[ing] counterarguments" (Berg, "*The Origins of the Koran: Classic Essays on Islam's Holy Book* by Ibn Warraq," 558). In contrast, David Cook writes, "As a scholar of Islam myself, I find Ibn Warraq's attitude to be very refreshing, and his scholarship for the most part to be accurate and devastating in pinpointing weaknesses in Muslim orthodoxy" (Cook, "Ibn Warraq's *Virgins? What Virgins? and Other Essays*," 235). I would hazard that this represents a minority opinion among Western scholars of Islam.

[19] Dawkins, *The God Delusion*, 307.

it to the one true faith, to the law of Allah. To Islam alone has been granted the truth: there is no possibility of salvation outside it.[20]

Reading this, one would think that all "sincere" Muslim clerics must be conquest-driven exclusivists.

In *The God Delusion*, Dawkins does not exactly go quite as far as Ibn Warraq does: he states that, unlike Judaism and Christianity, Islam added "a powerful ideology of military conquest to spread the faith."[21] In the world of social media, however, we encounter a less reserved Dawkins. In February 2013, for instance, he posted the following message on *Twitter*: "I think Islam is the greatest force for evil in the world today. I've said so often and loudly ..."[22] Shortly thereafter, he posted, "Haven't read Koran so couldn't quote chapter & verse like I can for Bible. But often say Islam greatest force for evil today [*sic*]."[23] He later added, "Of course you can have an opinion about Islam without having read Qur'an. You don't have to read Mein Kampf to have an opinion about nazism [*sic*]."[24] The obvious flaw in this analogy is that the face of Nazism was also the author of *Mein Kampf*, and it would be absurd to claim that Hitler misinterpreted his own book.

We now turn our attention to another well-known English author, Christopher Hitchens. Born in 1949 in the United Kingdom, Hitchens became one of the world's most prominent journalists; he died in 2011 in his adopted American homeland. Aside from his contributions to, among other periodicals, the *New Statesman*, *The Nation*, *The Atlantic*, and *Vanity Fair*, Hitchens authored numerous popular books. Relevant for

---

[20] Ibn Warraq, *Why I Am Not a Muslim*, 217.

[21] Dawkins, *The God Delusion*, 37.

[22] Dawkins (@RichardDawkins), *Twitter*, 9:48 p.m., 28 Feb. 2013.

[23] Dawkins (@RichardDawkins), *Twitter*, 10:01 p.m., 28 Feb. 2013. Along these lines, following the January 2015 *Charlie Hebdo* shooting in Paris (in which Muslim gunmen affiliated with al-Qaeda in the Arabian Peninsula shot and killed satirical cartoonists and others), Dawkins posted the following message on *Twitter*: "No, all religions are NOT equally violent. Some have never been violent, some gave it up centuries ago. One religion conspicuously didn't" (Dawkins [@RichardDawkins], *Twitter*, 7:08 a.m., 7 Jan. 2015; Dawkins offers a more measured response to the 2006 Danish cartoon controversy in *The God Delusion*, 24–27). When he appeared on television a few days later, he was asked whether Islam is a "religion of peace." Dawkins responded that while many Muslims are peaceful, "in its history [Islam] has never been a religion of peace ... [T]he ideology itself is founded in war, it was spread by war" (BBC, "Religion and Violence"). For some examples of Muslim scholarly and other condemnations of the *Charlie Hebdo* shooting, see Black, "Charlie Hebdo killings condemned by Arab states"; and Shaikh, "Muslim Scholars on Charlie Hebdo."

[24] Dawkins (@RichardDawkins), *Twitter*, 1:18 a.m., 25 Mar. 2013.

our purposes is his celebrated 2007 *New York Times* bestseller *god is not Great: How Religion Poisons Everything.*

In this work, Hitchens calls into question the messenger of Islam and his message: Although Muslim sources generally portray Muhammad as having lived an austere life, Hitchens submits that "we may flinch a little" at "the keen interest" the Prophet took in the "division of the spoils after his many battles and numerous massacres."[25] And with regard to the Qur'an, Hitchens bemoans the fact that Saudi Wahhabi translations of the Islamic holy book had recently been circulating among American prisoners, for such translations "went *even further* than the original in recommending holy war against *all* Christians and Jews and secularists."[26]

Hitchens once described Ibn Warraq's *Why I Am Not a Muslim* as his "favorite book on Islam."[27] Perhaps it is not surprising that he, too, presents Islam in a monolithic manner, as an exclusivist, conquest-driven faith: "Not only did Islam begin by condemning all doubters to eternal fire, but it still claims the right to do so in almost all of its dominions, and still preaches that these same dominions can and must be extended by war."[28]

Hitchens's characterization of 9/11 is especially provocative:

The nineteen suicide murderers of New York and Washington and Pennsylvania were beyond any doubt the most sincere believers on those planes. Perhaps we can hear a little less about how "people of faith" possess moral advantages that others can only envy. And what is to be learned from the jubilation and the ecstatic propaganda with which this great feat of fidelity has been greeted in the Islamic world?[29]

Thus, much like other New Atheists, Hitchens suggests that Muslim terrorists are *more Muslim* than others and offers a highly selective account of the Muslim responses to 9/11.

Hitchens had more to say about Islam at public events. In a 2010 debate with Rabbi David Wolpe on the existence of God, Hitchens described Islam as "the most toxic form religion takes," at least "at the moment."[30] Nevertheless, at a later event that same year, a debate with

---

[25] Hitchens, *god is not Great*, 135.

[26] Hitchens, *god is not Great*, 33 (emphasis added).

[27] Hitchens, "Holy Writ."

[28] Hitchens, *god is not Great*, 125.

[29] Hitchens, *god is not Great*, 32.

[30] "Christopher Hitchens – Don't waste my time with Islam [2010]." Reaffirming his conception of Islam as an exclusivist faith, Hitchens in this debate remarked, "Islam rather dangerously says ours is the last and final [revelation] ... That's straightaway a temptation to violence and intolerance."

Muslim scholar Tariq Ramadan on whether Islam is a "religion of peace," Hitchens agreed with Ramadan that when it comes to Muslim violence and intolerance, "the problem is not the book, but the reader." Yet he went on to say that he did not "like the idea of a paradise reward for martyrs."[31] (He was not particularly fond of hell either.)[32]

Last but not least in our brief survey is Daniel C. Dennett, an eminent cognitive scientist and philosopher and a longtime professor at Tufts University. Born in 1942 in Boston, he was just five years old when his father (also Daniel C. Dennett), a scholar of Islamic history, died in a tragic plane crash. Unlike his father, Dennett does not write a great deal about Islam, and what he does say betrays his unfamiliarity with the religion.

In his popular 2006 book *Breaking the Spell: Religion as a Natural Phenomenon*, for instance, Dennett asserts that the Qur'an "undeniably" says that "all infidels and especially kafirs (apostates from Islam) deserve death."[33] In the same sentence, Dennett refers to Qur'an 5:44 to justify this claim. In the subsequent electronic and paperback editions of the book, he refers to 4:89.

Dennett's assertion is problematic for two reasons: First, scholars of Islamic studies typically translate the Arabic term *kafir* as "unbeliever"; some use the term "infidel." An "apostate," or *murtadd* in Arabic, is someone who renounces his or her religion. Dennett presumably means to say that, according to the Qur'an, "all infidels and especially murtadds (apostates from Islam) deserve death."[34] Second, Dennett's Qur'anic references do not justify his assertion. We can assume his reference to 5:44 in the original edition of his book was a mistake, for it reads,

We revealed the Torah with guidance and light, and the prophets, who had submitted to God, judged according to it for the Jews. So did the rabbis and the scholars in accordance with that part of God's Scripture which they were entrusted to preserve, and to which they were witnesses. So [rabbis and scholars] do not fear people, fear Me; do not barter away My messages for a small

---

[31] "Christopher Hitchens and Tariq Ramadan Debate."
[32] See, for instance, Hitchens, *god is not Great*, 5, 219.
[33] Dennett, *Breaking the Spell*, 289.
[34] Along these lines, in an article published in *The Chronicle of Higher Education*, Dennett states in passing that it is "unknown how many Muslims truly believe that all infidels deserve death, which is what the Koran undeniably says." Here Dennett does not cite any Qur'anic verses. He continues, "Most Muslims, I would guess, are sincere in their insistence that the injunction that apostates be killed is to be disregarded" (Dennett, "Common-Sense Religion").

price; those who do not judge according to what God has sent down are rejecting [God's teachings]. (5:44)

This takes us to Qur'an 4:89, which reads,

[The hypocrites] would dearly like you to reject faith, as they themselves have done, to be like them. So do not take them as patrons until they migrate [to Medina] for God's cause. If they turn,[35] then seize and kill them wherever you encounter them. Take none of them as a patron or supporter. (4:89)

In this case, however, the following verses offer a critical qualification:

But as for those who reach people with whom you have a treaty, or who come over to you because their hearts shrink from fighting against you or against their own people, God could have given them power over you, and they would have fought you. So if they withdraw and do not fight you, and offer you peace, then God gives you no way against them. You will find others who wish to be safe from you, and from their own people, but whenever they are back in a situation where they are tempted [to hostility], they succumb to it. So if they neither withdraw, nor offer you peace, nor restrain themselves from fighting you, seize and kill them wherever you encounter them: We give you clear authority against such people. (4:90–91)

Thus, far from indicating that "all infidels" deserve death, Qur'an 4:89 speaks of "hypocrites" who posed a threat to Muhammad's community.[36] And although many Muslim scholars – with many others opposing them – advocate the punishment, even execution, of apostates who refuse to repent, the fact remains that the Qur'an does not prescribe a penalty for an apostate's "unbelief by itself."[37] Perhaps Dennett had in mind the Qur'anic statement we encountered earlier, "If they do fight you, kill them – *this is what such unbelievers deserve*" (2:191); however, even here one can see that those unbelievers who "deserve" death are those who initiate hostilities and seek to kill. To be sure, there is nothing "undeniable" about Dennett's characterization of the Qur'an.

---

35 See Chapter 1, note 10.

36 On the range of popular interpretations of this passage, see Nasr (ed.), *The Study Quran*, 231–233 (commentary on Qur'an 4:88–90).

37 Griffel, "Apostasy." Scholars who hold that apostates should be punished (by people, in this life) typically invoke select statements from the hadith corpus. According to clerics such as the former Egyptian grand mufti Ali Gomaa, these prophetic reports condemn not apostasy per se (indeed there are other reports of Muhammad pardoning apostates) but "a betrayal of the Muslim state and polity," essentially "high treason" (Brown, *Misquoting Muhammad*, 188; see Gomaa, *al-Bayan li-ma yashghalu al-adhhan*, 81–84). There is, in fact, no reliable evidence that Muhammad ever killed anyone for apostasy (see Brown, "The Issue of Apostasy in Islam").

Conclusion

I opened this book by quoting an exchange between Sam Harris and journalist Fareed Zakaria on the topic of jihad. Harris asserted that Osama bin Laden's "interpretation of Islam is very straightforward and honest and you really have to split hairs and do some interpretive acrobatics in order to get it ... to look non-canonical."[1] But consider some of the "interpretive acrobatics" bin Laden performed in his generally unsuccessful attempt to convince Muslim clerics and Islamists – including many who already held anti-American sentiments – that the September 11 attacks could be justified:

(1) Recognizing that he was neither a state authority nor a certified scholar, and seeking to enlist "all Muslims" in a war that would employ extreme tactics, bin Laden attempted to demonstrate that his manifestly aggressive attacks were, in fact, part of a defensive jihad. (According to the centuries-old Islamic legal tradition of aggressive jihad, he lacked the requisite authority to launch and manage a war, and his tactics would have been even more difficult to justify.)

(2) In making the case for a defensive jihad, bin Laden went to great lengths to present the United States as a bona fide threat to Muslims worldwide; he pointed to various American actions and sanctions while oversimplifying and misrepresenting some of the facts on the ground.

[1] CNN, "Zakaria, Harris Debate Extremism in Islam."

(3) Recognizing the Prophet's explicit prohibition against the killing of noncombatants, most notably women and children, bin Laden argued that al-Qaeda's tactics against the United States were necessary and served the common good (notwithstanding indications to the contrary). And although the 9/11 attacks were directed mostly at civilians (many busy at work), he asserted that he was not targeting innocents but rather "the symbol" of a threatening enemy and that collateral casualties were therefore acceptable (an assertion widely regarded as disingenuous). For good measure, however, he also attempted to make an obviously modern argument that American adult civilians could be treated as combatants because both the taxes they paid (as required by law) and the decisions made by their government officials (who were neither unanimously elected nor unanimously supported) helped shape America's foreign policy. And, finally, notwithstanding his (superficial) claim that he was not targeting innocents, he endeavored to advance and defend an aberrant, expansive conception of retaliation in order to justify the intentional killing of American noncombatants – a conception not supported and, in at least one case, explicitly rejected by the very scholarly sources he invoked to justify it.

A true literalist he was not. Of course the same could be said about Muslims in general. And yet it is critical to recognize that the attempts of al-Qaeda and ISIS to justify terrorism on Islamic grounds typically *require* the abandonment of *both* strict literalism and the historically prevailing interpretations of Islamic thought. The interpretations of such radicals are hardly "straightforward." They are their own thing.

Yet we cannot simply leave it at that. We must ask, What motivated "nineteen post-secondary students" to kill thousands of innocent American civilians and themselves on a tragic Tuesday morning? What inspired the "cricket-loving young men" to kill dozens of Londoners and themselves nearly four years later? How can we explain the many brutal acts of ISIS, which considers itself the world's lone "Islamic state"? And why does it seem like Muslim – not Christian, Hindu, or atheist, but Muslim – suicide killers are almost always on the news these days?

Beginning with Harris, we have seen how various prominent New Atheist authors explain such phenomena by pointing to Islam – not idiosyncratic interpretations of the religion but the core of the religion itself – and downplaying other factors. While the worldwide Muslim scholarly and clerical condemnations of 9/11 show that al-Qaeda "is on the fringes of the jihad tradition,"[2] Harris places al-Qaeda, along with ISIS and other radicals, firmly in the center; and Ayaan Hirsi Ali suggests that such radicals are *not*, in fact, "a lunatic fringe of extremists."[3] As Richard Dawkins sees it, the matter is fairly simple: "Suicide bombers do what they do because they really believe what they were taught in their religious schools: that duty to God exceeds all other priorities, and that martyrdom in his service will be rewarded in the gardens of Paradise."[4]

Now compare such assessments with the more incisive analysis offered by terrorism specialist Jessica Stern, the aforementioned former Harvard colleague of Ali's who studied deradicalization efforts in Saudi Arabia: Stern maintains that terrorists are typically motivated by multiple factors and that "[t]errorist movements often arise in reaction to an injustice, real or imagined, that they feel must be corrected." Furthermore, she writes,

terrorists who claim to be driven by religious ideology are often ignorant about Islam. Our hosts in Riyadh told us that the vast majority of the deradicalization program's "beneficiaries," as its administrators call participants, had received little formal education and had only a limited understanding of Islam. In the Netherlands and elsewhere in Europe, second- and third-generation Muslim youth are rebelling against the kind of "soft" Islam practiced by their parents and promoted in local mosques. They favor what they think is the "purer" Islam, uncorrupted by Western culture, which is touted on some Web sites and by self-appointed imams from the Middle East who are barely educated themselves. For example, the Netherlands-based terrorist cell known as the Hofstad Group designed what one police officer described as a "do-it-yourself" version of Islam based on interpretations of *takfiri* ideology (*takfir* is the practice of accusing other Muslims of apostasy) culled from the Internet and the teachings of a drug dealer turned cleric.

… Terrorism spreads, in part, through bad ideas. The most dangerous and seductive bad idea spreading around the globe today is a distorted and destructive interpretation of Islam, which asserts that killing innocents is a way to worship God. Part of the solution must come from within Islam and from Islamic scholars, who can refute this ideology with arguments based on theology and ethics. But bad ideas are only part of the problem. Terrorists prey on vulnerable populations – people who feel humiliated and victimized or who find their identities by joining extremist movements. Governments' arsenals against terrorism must include tools to strengthen the resilience of vulnerable populations. These tools should look more like anti-gang programs and public diplomacy than war.[5]

---

[2] Hashmi, "9/11 and the Jihad Tradition," 150.
[3] Ali, *Heretic*, 11.
[4] Dawkins, *The God Delusion*, 308.
[5] Stern, "Mind over Martyr."

There can be little doubt that religious faith is indeed a critical motivating factor for many Muslim terrorists, from the wealthy bin Laden to any number of middle-class ISIS operatives.[6] But, as we have seen, their Islam is distinct in important ways from the broader Islamic tradition and is often shaped and guided by particular, often crude readings of the facts on the ground. Even if one insists that the Qur'an itself inspires terrorism, then one would also have to concede that this same scripture – a scripture that existed long before the radicalization of bin Laden, and one not going anywhere – provides an especially potent antidote. There is a reason Muslim scholarly condemnations of terrorist acts regularly invoke statements from the Qur'an and hadith corpus. There is a reason the multifaceted Saudi deradicalization efforts described by Stern – which appear to be at least partially effective – involve an engagement with the Islamic tradition. There is a reason, as noted earlier, when Gallup interviewed Muslims in Indonesia, they found that those who condemned 9/11 – unlike those who defended it – often invoked religion. And all this, of course, is besides the fact that countless "everyday" Muslims derive from Islamic sources motivation for constructive actions.

The New Atheist authors examined here reserve some of their strongest criticisms of religion for Islam in particular. Yet despite the impressive academic backgrounds that some of them boast (outside Islamic studies), they describe Islam and jihad in ways that are often inaccurate and incomplete. This is at least partly due to their methodologies, as they rely heavily on sources that fail to provide a representative spectrum of views. This might explain why their suggestions for solving the very real problem of Muslim terrorism – from Harris's ignore-or-revise proposal to Ali's "heretical" reformation – are rather unrealistic. They seem to be generally unaware

---

[6] Here it is not my intention to determine the *precise* extent to which religious faith and ideology motivates Muslim terrorists. And the available evidence does not permit me to confirm or deny Sterns's claim that ideology is rarely the *most* important factor in an individual's decision to become a terrorist (see Stern, "Mind over Martyr"). But all indications suggest that ideology is at least a very important factor for many violent radicals. In any case, it is instructive to consider anthropologist Scott Atran's finding that many Muslim terrorists (or "jihadis") "are 'born again' and come to religion [relatively] late in life, and only very seldom through mosques or madrassahs" (Atran, "Beyond Belief"). In at least the case of "homegrown" European Muslim terrorists, political scientist Olivier Roy maintains that many such individuals are "violent nihilists who adopt Islam, rather than religious fundamentalists who turn to violence" (Roy, "Who Are the New Jihadis?"; see Roy, *Jihad and Death*; cf. Kepel, *Terror in France*).

of the nuances of modern Islamic thought and therefore overlook other, potentially more effective avenues for action and reform.

* * *

Less than a month before his interview with Fareed Zakaria, Harris had appeared on *Real Time with Bill Maher*. (This was the October 2014 episode I mentioned earlier.) In the midst of a heated exchange with actor Ben Affleck on the subject of Islam, Harris, having stated that he was "actually well-educated on" the topic, proclaimed, "We have to be able to criticize bad ideas, and Islam is the mother lode of bad ideas." He proceeded to explain his problematic "concentric circles" schema, in which would-be suicide bombers occupy the center of the Muslim community. He added, "We're misled to think that the fundamentalists are the fringe," to which host Bill Maher chimed in, "That's the key point."[7]

The Islam that Harris portrays in his writings does indeed appear to be a "mother lode of bad ideas." But it is an Islam that the vast majority of Muslims, whether scholars or laypeople, would likely not recognize – a "mother lode" of bad analysis. It is even more extreme in some ways than bin Laden's Islam. After all, Harris draws a nearly straight line from the Islamic tradition to 9/11: he erroneously downplays the significance of nonreligious factors when assessing the al-Qaeda leader, asserting that bin Laden's grievances were "purely theological"[8] and that his "*only* apparent concerns [were] the spread of Islam and the sanctity of Muslim holy sites."[9] Bin Laden's Islam, however, was not that simple: his views on jihad were formed through convoluted reasoning and guided by a warped perception of geopolitical reality. (Notwithstanding their differences, the same is generally true for the leadership of ISIS.) As such, Zakaria missed the mark when he told Harris, "The problem is you and Osama bin Laden agree ... after all, you're saying ... his interpretation of Islam is correct."[10] Although bin Laden and Harris both envisioned a civilizational clash, Harris's interpretation of Islam is so aberrant that it cannot even be ascribed to the man behind 9/11.

---

[7] "Real Time with Bill Maher."
[8] Harris, *The End of Faith*, 30.
[9] Harris, *The End of Faith*, 260, note 2 (emphasis added).
[10] CNN, "Zakaria, Harris Debate Extremism in Islam."

Bibliography

Abdel Haleem, M. A. S. *The Qur'an: A New Translation*. Oxford: Oxford University Press, 2010.

Abou El Fadl, Khaled. "The Rules of Killing at War: An Inquiry into Classical Sources." *The Muslim World* 89 (1999): 144–157.

Abu Id, Arif. *Al-'Alaqat al-kharijiyya fi dawlat al-khilafa*. Kuwait: Dar al-Arqam, 1983.

Afsaruddin, Asma. *The First Muslims: History and Memory*. Oxford: Oneworld Publications, 2008.

Striving in the Path of God: Jihad and Martyrdom in Islamic Thought. New York: Oxford University Press, 2013.

Agarwall, Priyangi. "70,000 Clerics Issue Fatwa Against Terrorism, 15 Lakh Muslims Support It." *The Times of India*, Dec. 9, 2015, http://timesofindia .indiatimes.com/india/70000–clerics-issue-fatwa-against-terrorism-15–lakh-Muslims-support-it/articleshow/50100656.cms (last accessed April 4, 2017).

Ahmad, Ahmad Atif. *Islam, Modernity, Violence, and Everyday Life*. New York: Palgrave Macmillan, 2009.

Ahmad, Barakat. *Muhammad and the Jews: A Re-Examination*. New Delhi: Vikas, 1979.

al-Akiti, Muhammad Afifi. *Defending the Transgressed by Censuring the Reckless Against the Killing of Civilians*. Birmingham: Aqsa Press, 2005.

Al Arabiya English. "Head of Egypt's al-Azhar Condemns ISIS 'Barbarity'," Dec. 3, 2014, http://english.alarabiya.net/en/News/middle-east/2014/12/03/Head-of-Egypt-s-al-Azhar-condemns-ISIS-barbarity-.html (last accessed April 4, 2017).

Al-Dawoody, Ahmed. *The Islamic Law of War: Justifications and Regulations*. New York: Palgrave Macmillan, 2011.

Ali, A. Yusuf. *The Holy Qur'an: Text, Translation and Commentary*. Brentwood, MD: Amana, 1983.

Ali, Ayaan Hirsi. *The Caged Virgin: An Emancipation Proclamation for Women and Islam*. New York: Free Press, 2006.

De zoontjesfabriek: over vrouwen, Islam en integratie. Amsterdam: Augustus, 2002.

Heretic. New York: Harper, 2015.

Infidel. New York: Free Press, 2007.

Nomad: A Personal Journey through the Clash of Civilizations. New York: Free Press, 2010.

Ali, Kecia. *Sexual Ethics and Islam: Feminist Reflections on Qur'an, Hadith, and Jurisprudence*. Expanded and Revised Edition. London: Oneworld Publications, 2016.

Al-Yaqoubi, Muhammad. *Refuting ISIS*. Second Edition. Herndon, VA: Sacred Knowledge, 2016.

"American Muslims and Scholars Denounce Terrorism." Center for the Study of Islam and Democracy, Sept. 9, 2002, http://web.archive.org/web/20020916085653/www.islam-democracy.org/terrorism_statement.asp (last accessed April 4, 2017).

Amin, ElSayed. *Reclaiming Jihad: A Qur'anic Critique of Terrorism*. Markfield, UK: Islamic Foundation, 2014.

Arafat, W. N. "New Light on the Story of Banu Qurayza and the Jews of Medina." *Journal of the Royal Asiatic Society of Great Britain and Ireland* 2 (1976): 100–107.

Aslan, Reza. "Reza Aslan: Sam Harris and 'New Atheists' Aren't New, Aren't Even Atheists." *Salon*, Nov. 21, 2014, www.salon.com/2014/11/21/reza_aslan_sam_harris_and_new_atheists_arent_new_arent_even_atheists (last accessed April 4, 2017).

Atran, Scott. "Beyond Belief: Science, Religion, Reason and Survival." *Edge*, Nov. 29, 2006, www.edge.org/discourse/bb.html#atran (last accessed April 4, 2017).

van Bakel, Rogier. "'The Trouble Is the West'." *Reason*, Oct. 10, 2007, http://reason.com/archives/2007/10/10/the-trouble-is-the-west (last accessed April 4, 2017).

al-Bayhaqi. *Al-Sunan al-kubra*. Edited by M. Ata. 11 vols. Beirut: Dar al-Kutub al-'Ilmiyya, 2008.

BBC (British Broadcasting Corporation). "Al-Qaradawi Full Transcript," July 8, 2004, http://news.bbc.co.uk/2/hi/3875119.stm (last accessed April 4, 2017).

"Islamic State Releases 'al-Baghdadi Message'," May 14, 2015, www.bbc.com/news/world-middle-east-32744070 (last accessed April 4, 2017).

"London Bomber: Text in Full," Sept. 1, 2005, http://news.bbc.co.uk/2/hi/uk_news/4206800.stm (last accessed April 4, 2017).

"Religion and Violence: Dawkins, Ramdani and Fraser," Jan. 13, 2015, www.bbc.co.uk/programmes/p02gv6x6 (last accessed April 4, 2017).

"Video of 7 July Bomber Released," July 6, 2006, http://news.bbc.co.uk/2/hi/uk/5154714.stm (last accessed April 4, 2017).

Bennet, James. "In Israeli Hospital, Bomber Tells of Trying to Kill Israelis," *The New York Times*, June 8, 2002, www.nytimes.com/2002/06/08/international/middleeast/08BOMB.html (last accessed April 4, 2017).

Berg, Herbert. "*The Origins of the Koran: Classic Essays on Islam's Holy Book* by Ibn Warraq." *Bulletin of the School of Oriental and African Studies* 62 (1999): 557–558.

Bergen, Peter L. *The Osama bin Laden I Know*. New York: Free Press, 2006.

"Bill Maher to Muslim Rep. Keith Ellison: The Qur'an Is a 'Hate Filled Holy Book'." *YouTube*, March 12, 2011, www.youtube.com/watch?v=mVTK_XffAvk (last accessed April 4, 2017).

bin Laden, Osama. *Messages to the World: The Statements of Osama Bin Laden*. Edited and introduced by Bruce Lawrence. London: Verso, 2005.

Osama Bin Laden: America's Enemy in His Own Words. Edited by Randall B. Hamud. San Diego: Nadeem Publishing, 2005.

Black, Ian. "Charlie Hebdo Killings Condemned by Arab States – but Hailed Online by Extremists." *The Guardian*, Jan. 7, 2015, www.theguardian.com/world/2015/jan/07/charlie-hebdo-killings-arab-states-jihadi-extremist-sympathisers-isis (last accessed April 18, 2017).

Blankinship, Khalid Yahya. "Parity of Muslim and Western Concepts of Just War." *The Muslim World* 101 (2011): 412–426.

"Sword Verses." In *The Oxford Encyclopedia of the Islamic World*. Oxford Islamic Studies Online, www.oxfordislamicstudies.com/article/opr/t236/e0979 (last accessed April 6, 2017).

Bond, Anthony. "Video: Gruesome Footage Showed a Blood-Stained Michael Adebolajo Shortly after Butchering Lee Rigby." *Mirror Online*, Dec. 19, 2013, www.mirror.co.uk/news/uk-news/lee-rigby-murder-trial-gruesome-2943281 (last accessed April 4, 2017).

Bonner, Michael. *Jihad in Islamic History: Doctrines and Practice*. Princeton, NJ: Princeton University Press, 2006.

de Borchgrave, Arnaud. "Mullah Omar: bin Laden – 'Null and Void'." *United Press International*, Dec. 10, 2001, www.upi.com/Business_News/Security-Industry/2001/12/10/Mullah-Omar-bin-Laden-Null-and-void/70171008031323 (last accessed April 4, 2017).

Brahimi, Alia. *Jihad and Just War in the War on Terror*. New York: Oxford University Press, 2010.

Bridge Initiative Team. "Here Are the (Many) Muslim Condemnations of ISIS You've Been Looking for." *Bridge Initiative*, April 26, 2015, http://bridge.georgetown.edu/here-are-the-many-muslim-condemnations-of-isis-youve-been-looking-for (last accessed April 4, 2017).

Brown, Jonathan A. C. "The Issue of Apostasy in Islam." *Yaqeen*, July 5, 2017, https://yaqeeninstitute.org/en/jonathan-brown/apostasy (last accessed July 12, 2017).

"Jizyah." In *The [Oxford] Encyclopedia of Islam and Law*. Oxford Islamic Studies Online, www.oxfordislamicstudies.com/article/opr/t349/e0127 (last accessed April 4, 2017).

Misquoting Muhammad: The Challenge and Choices of Interpreting the Prophet's Legacy. London: Oneworld Publications, 2014.

Bukay, David. "Peace or Jihad? Abrogation in Islam." *Middle East Quarterly* 14 (Fall 2007), www.meforum.org/1754/peace-or-jihad-abrogation-in-islam#_ftn58 (last accessed April 4, 2017).

Bulliet, Richard W. *Conversion to Islam in the Medieval Period: An Essay in Quantitative History*. Cambridge, MA: Harvard University Press, 1979.

Bunting, Madeleine. "Friendly Fire: Madeleine Bunting Meets Sheikh Yusuf al-Qaradawi in Qatar." *The Guardian*, Oct. 29, 2005, www.theguardian.com/world/2005/oct/29/religion.uk1 (last accessed April 4, 2017).

Bunzel, Cole. "From Paper State to Caliphate: The Ideology of the Islamic State" (Analysis Paper). *The Brookings Project on U.S. Relations with the Islamic World* 19.Washington, DC: Brookings Institution, March 2015.

Burns, John F. "A Nation Challenged: A Fighter's Tale; Bin Laden Stirs Struggle on Meaning of Jihad." *The New York Times*, Jan. 27, 2002, www.nytimes.com/2002/01/27/world/nation-challenged-fighter-s-tale-bin-laden-stirs-struggle-meaning-jihad.html (last accessed April 4, 2017).

"Can Terrorism Be Justified by the Fatwah of Ibn Uthaymeen? – Sh. Dr. Yasir Qadhi." *YouTube*, July 24, 2014, www.youtube.com/watch?v=SmmxEdIowv8 (last accessed April 4, 2017).

Casptack, Andreas. "Deradicalization Programs in Saudi Arabia: A Case Study." Middle East Institute, June 10, 2015, www.mei.edu/content/deradicalization-programs-saudi-arabia-case-study#_ftnref9 (last accessed April 4, 2017).

Chittick, William C. *Imaginal Worlds: Ibn al-'Arabi and the Problem of Religious Diversity*. Albany: State University of New York Press, 1994.

Chomsky, Noam. *9–11*. New York: Seven Stories Press, 2001.

"Christopher Hitchens and Tariq Ramadan Debate: Is Islam a Religion of Peace?" *YouTube*, Feb. 4, 2013, www.youtube.com/watch?v=mMraxhd9Z9Q (last accessed April 4, 2017).

"Christopher Hitchens – Don't Waste My Time with Islam [2010]." *YouTube*, Oct. 10, 2014, www.youtube.com/watch?v=5sEcBzxoMB8 (last accessed April 4, 2017).

Chulov, Martin. "Abu Bakr al-Baghdadi Emerges from Shadows to Rally Islamist Followers." *The Guardian*, July 6, 2014, www.theguardian.com/world/2014/jul/06/abu-bakr-al-baghdadi-isis (last accessed April 4, 2017).

"A Clear Criterion: Muslim Scholars and Intellectuals Condemn Attacks in New York and Washington." *MSANEWS*, Sept. 14, 2001, http://web.archive.org/web/20010920150230/msanews.mynet.net/MSANEWS/200109/20010917.15.html (last accessed April 4, 2017).

CNN (Cable News Network). "CNN Presents: Soldiers of God" (transcript), Sept. 29, 2001, http://transcripts.cnn.com/TRANSCRIPTS/0109/29/cp.00.html (last accessed April 4, 2017).

"Zakaria, Harris Debate Extremism in Islam" (transcript), Nov. 2, 2014, http://cnnpressroom.blogs.cnn.com/2014/11/02/sam-harris-on-gps-islam-has-been-spread-by-the-sword (last accessed April 4, 2017).

Cook, David. "Ibn Warraq's *Virgins? What Virgins? and Other Essays*." *Reason Papers* 34/2 (2012): 234–238.

Understanding Jihad. Berkeley: University of California Press, 2005.

Crone, Patricia. *God's Rule: Government and Islam*. New York: Columbia University Press, 2004.

"'No Compulsion in Religion': Q. 2:256 in Mediaeval and Modern Interpretation." In *Le Shi'isme imamate quarante ans après: Hommage* à *Etan Kohlberg*, edited by M. A. Amir-Moezzi, M. M. Bar-Asher, and S. Hopkins, 131–178. Turnhout, Belgium: Brepols, 2009.

Dabiq. *Jihadology*, July 31, 2016, http://jihadology.net/category/dabiq-magazine (last accessed April 4, 2017).

al-Dardir. *Al-Sharh al-kabir*. Edited by Muhammad 'Allish. 4 vols. Beirut: Dar al-Fikr, n.d.

Dawkins, Richard. *The God Delusion*. New York: Houghton Mifflin Company, 2006.

The Selfish Gene. Oxford: Oxford University Press, 1976.

(@RichardDawkins). *Twitter*, Feb. 28, 2013–Jan. 7, 2015, https://twitter.com/RichardDawkins (last accessed April 4, 2017).

Defense Science Board Task Force. *Report of the Defense Science Board Task Force on Strategic Communication*. Washington, DC: Office of the Under Secretary of Defense, Sept. 2004.

Dennett, Daniel C. *Breaking the Spell: Religion as a Natural Phenomenon*. New York: Viking Penguin, 2006.

"Common-Sense Religion." *The Chronicle of Higher Education*, Jan. 20, 2006, www.chronicle.com.proxy2.cl.msu.edu/article/Common-Sense-Religion/22587 (last accessed April 4, 2017).

Dickson, Rory. "Religion as Phantasmagoria: Islam in *The End of Faith*." In *Religion and the New Atheism: A Critical Appraisal*, edited by Amarnath Amarasingam, 37–54. Leiden: Brill, 2010.

Donner, Fred. "*The Quest for the Historical Muhammad* by Ibn Warraq." *Middle East Studies Association Bulletin* 35 (2001): 75–76.

"The Sources of Islamic Conceptions of War." In *Just War and Jihad: Historical and Theoretical Perspectives on War and Peace in Western and Islamic Traditions*, edited by J. Kelsay and J. T. Johnson, 31–70. New York: Greenwood Press, 1991.

Doornbos, Caitlin. "Transcripts of 911 Calls Reveal Pulse Shooter's Terrorist Motives." *Orlando Sentinel*, Sept. 23, 2016, www.orlandosentinel.com/news/pulse-orlando-nightclub-shooting/os-911-calls-released-orlando-shooting-20170922-story.html (last accessed April 10, 2017).

Dubuis, Anna and Sebastian Mann. "Maajid Nawaz Sent Death Threats by ISIS and Installs Panic Alarm at Home because of Lap Dance CCTV." *Evening Standard*, April 15, 2015, www.standard.co.uk/news/london/maajid-nawaz-sent-isis-death-threats-and-installs-panic-alarm-at-home-because-of-lap-dance-cctv-10177562.html (last accessed April 4, 2017).

Elgot, Jessica, Claire Phipps, and Jonathan Bucks. "Paris Attacks: Day after Atrocity – As It Happened." *The Guardian*, Nov. 14, 2015, www.theguardian.com/world/live/2015/nov/14/paris-terror-attacks-attackers-dead-mass-killing-live-updates#block-56471333e4b0ced428cb289a (last accessed April 11, 2017).

Esposito, John L. *The Future of Islam*. New York: Oxford University Press, 2010.

Esposito, John L. and Ibrahim Kalin (eds.). *The 500 Most Influential Muslims 2009*. Washington, DC: Georgetown University Press, 2009.

Esposito, John L. and Dalia Mogahed. *Who Speaks for Islam? What a Billion Muslims Really Think*. New York: Gallup Press, 2007.

Filiu, Jean-Pierre. *Apocalypse in Islam.* Translated by M. B. DeBevoise. Berkeley: University of California Press, 2011.

Finn, Melissa. *Al-Qaeda and Sacrifice: Martyrdom, War and Politics.* London: Pluto Press, 2012.

"Fiqh of Jihad by Sheikh ibn Uthaymeen." *YouTube,* July 26, 2013, www.youtube.com/watch?v=bPVpv_afBHA (last accessed April 4, 2017).

Firestone, Reuven. *Jihad: The Origins of Holy War in Islam.* New York: Oxford University Press, 1999.

Friedman, Thomas L. "Foreign Affairs; World War III." *The New York Times,* Sept. 13, 2001, www.nytimes.com/2001/09/13/opinion/foreign-affairs-world-war-iii.html (last accessed April 4, 2017).

"If It's a Muslim Problem, It Needs a Muslim Solution." *The New York Times,* July 8, 2005, www.nytimes.com/2005/07/08/opinion/if-its-a-muslim-problem-it-needs-a-muslim-solution.html (last accessed April 4, 2017).

"Spiritual Missile Shield." *The New York Times,* Dec. 16, 2001, www.nytimes.com/2001/12/16/opinion/16FRIE.html (last accessed April 4, 2017).

"www.jihad.com." *The New York Times,* Dec. 15, 2009, www.nytimes.com/2009/12/16/opinion/16friedman.html (last accessed April 4, 2017).

Gallup. "Views of Violence," Sept. 2011, www.gallup.com/poll/157067/views-violence.aspx (last accessed April 4, 2017).

Gerges, Fawaz A. *The Rise and Fall of Al-Qaeda.* New York: Oxford University Press, 2011.

Gil, Moshe. "The Jewish Community." In *The History of Jerusalem: The Early Muslim Period (638–1099),* edited by J. Prawer and H. Ben-Shammai, 163–200. New York: New York University Press, 1996.

Glad, Betty. *An Outsider in the White House: Jimmy Carter, His Advisors, and the Making of American Foreign Policy.* Ithaca, NY: Cornell University Press, 2009.

Goldman, Adam. "FBI Has Found No Evidence That Orlando Shooter Targeted Pulse because It Was a Gay Club." *The Washington Post,* July 16, 2016, www.washingtonpost.com/world/national-security/no-evidence-so-far-to-suggest-orlando-shooter-targeted-club-because-it-was-gay/2016/07/14/a7528674-4907-11e6-acbc-4d4870a079da_story.html (last accessed April 18, 2017).

Gomaa, Ali. *Al-Bayan li-ma yashghalu al-adhhan.* Cairo: Dar al-Muqattam, 2009.

Greenwald, Glenn. "Sam Harris, the New Atheists, and Anti-Muslim Animus." *The Guardian,* April 3, 2013, www.theguardian.com/commentisfree/2013/apr/03/sam-harris-muslim-animus (last accessed April 4, 2017).

Griffel, Frank. "Apostasy." In *Encyclopaedia of Islam, THREE,* edited by K. Fleet, G. Krämer, D. Matringe, J. Nawas, E. Rowson. Leiden: Brill Online (consulted online on Aug. 15, 2016).

Gwynne, Rosalind W. "Usama bin Ladin, the Qur'an and Jihad." *Religion* 36 (2006): 61–90.

Hallaq, Wael. *An Introduction to Islamic Law.* New York: Cambridge University Press, 2009.

Hamid, Tawfik. "Does Moderate Islam Exist?" *Jerusalem Post,* Sept. 14, 2014, www.jpost.com/Experts/Does-moderate-Islam-exist-375316 (last accessed April 4, 2017).

Harris, Sam. "Can Liberalism Be Saved From Itself?" *SamHarris.org*, Oct. 7, 2014, www.samharris.org/blog/item/can-liberalism-be-saved-from-itself (last accessed April 4, 2017).

The End of Faith: Religion, Terror, and the Future of Reason. New York: W. W. Norton, 2005.

"The End of Faith Sessions 1" (*Waking Up* podcast). *SamHarris.org*, April 25, 2016, www.samharris.org/podcast/item/the-end-of-faith-sessions-1 (last accessed May 31, 2017).

"Further Thoughts on the Death of Osama bin Laden." *SamHarris.org*, May 4, 2011, www.samharris.org/blog/item/our-dead-enemy-still-has-friends (last accessed April 4, 2017).

"In Defense of Profiling." *SamHarris.org*, April 28, 2012, www.samharris.org/blog/item/in-defense-of-profiling (last accessed April 4, 2017).

"Lifting the Veil of 'Islamophobia': A Conversation with Ayaan Hirsi Ali." *SamHarris.org*, May 8, 2014, www.samharris.org/blog/item/lifting-the-veil-of-islamophobia (last accessed April 4, 2017).

"My Response to Rep. Keith Ellison." *Huffington Post*, March 15, 2011, www.huffingtonpost.com/sam-harris/honesty-the-muslim-worlds_b_836005.html (last accessed April 4, 2017).

"The Problem with Atheism." *SamHarris.org*, Oct. 2, 2007, www.samharris.org/blog/item/the-problem-with-atheism (last accessed April 4, 2017).

"Response to Controversy." *SamHarris.org*, April 4, 2013, www.samharris.org/blog/item/response-to-controversy (updated June 21, 2014; last accessed April 4, 2017).

"Sleepwalking Toward Armageddon." *SamHarris.org*, Sept. 10, 2014, www.samharris.org/blog/item/sleepwalking-toward-armageddon (last accessed April 4, 2017).

"What Do Jihadists Really Want?" (*Waking Up* podcast). *SamHarris.org*, Aug. 17, 2016, www.samharris.org/podcast/item/what-do-jihadists-really-want (last accessed April 4, 2017).

Harris, Sam and Maajid Nawaz. *Islam and the Future of Tolerance: A Dialogue.* Cambridge, MA: Harvard University Press, 2015.

Hashmi, Sohail H. "9/11 and the Jihad Tradition." In *Terror, Culture, Politics: Rethinking 9/11*, edited by Daniel J. Sherman and Terry Nardin, 149–164. Bloomington: Indiana University Press, 2006.

"Islamic Ethics and Weapons of Mass Destruction: An Argument for Nonproliferation." In *Ethics and Weapons of Mass Destruction: Religious and Secular Perspectives*, edited by Sohail H. Hashmi and Steven P. Lee, 321–352. West Nyack, NY: Cambridge University Press, 2004.

Hassan, Nasra. "An Arsenal of Believers: Talking to the 'Human Bombs'." *The New Yorker*, Nov. 19, 2001, www.bintjbeil.com/articles/en/011119_hassan.html (last accessed April 4, 2017).

"Head of Bosnia's Muslims Urges Bush to Exercise Caution." *BH Press* (Sarajevo). Sept. 16, 2001.

Hedges, Chris. *When Atheism Becomes Religion: America's New Fundamentalists.* New York: Free Press, 2009.

Hitchens, Christopher. *God is not Great: How Religion Poisons Everything.* New York: Twelve, 2007.

"Holy Writ." *The Atlantic,* April 2003, www.theatlantic.com/magazine/archive/2003/04/holy-writ/302701 (last accessed April 4, 2017).

Hubbard, Ben. "Inside Saudi Arabia's Re-education Prison for Jihadists." *The New York Times,* April 9, 2016, www.nytimes.com/2016/04/10/world/middleeast/inside-saudi-arabias-re-education-prison-for-jihadists.html (last accessed April 4, 2017).

Huntington, Samuel P. *The Clash of Civilizations and the Remaking of World Order.* New York: Simon and Schuster, 1996.

ibn Hajar. *Fath al-bari bi-sharh Sahih al-Imam Abi 'Abdullah Muhammad ibn Isma'il al-Bukhari.* Edited by A. al-Hamd. 13 vols. Riyadh, 2001.

ibn Kathir. *Al-Sira al-nabawiyya.* Edited by M. Abdul Wahid. 4 vols. Beirut: Dar al-Ma'rifa, 1976.

ibn Rajab. *Fath al-bari: sharh Sahih al-Bukhari.* Edited by M. Abdul Maqsud et al. 10 vols. Medina, Saudi Arabia: Maktabat al-Ghuraba' al-Athariyya, 1996.

Jami' al-'ulum wa-l-hikam fi sharh khamsin hadithan min jawami' al-kalim. Edited by M. Abu al-Nur. 3 vols. Cairo: Dar al-Salam, 2004.

Ibn Warraq. *Why I Am Not a Muslim.* Amherst, NY: Prometheus Books, 1995.

Ibrahim, Raymond (ed. and trans.). *The Al Qaeda Reader.* New York: Doubleday, 2007.

"An Analysis of Al-Qa'ida's Worldview: Reciprocal Treatment or Religious Obligation?" *Middle East Review of International Affairs,* Dec. 6, 2008, www.rubincenter.org/2008/12/ibrahim-asp-2008-12-06 (last accessed April 4, 2017).

"How Taqiyya Alters Islam's Rules of War: Defeating Jihadist Terrorism." *Middle East Quarterly* 17 (Winter 2010), www.meforum.org/2538/taqiyya-islam-rules-of-war (last accessed April 4, 2017).

"Islam's Doctrines of Deception." *Middle East Forum,* Oct. 2008, www.meforum.org/2095/islams-doctrines-of-deception (last accessed April 4, 2017).

"Ten Ways Islam and the Mafia Are Similar." *RaymondIbrahim.com,* Dec. 7, 2014, http://raymondibrahim.com/2014/12/07/ten-ways-the-mafia-and-islam-are-similar (last accessed April 4, 2017).

"The Two Faces of Al Qaeda." *The Chronicle of Higher Education,* Sept. 12, 2007, www.chronicle.com/article/The-Two-Faces-of-Al-Qaeda/122042 (last accessed April 4, 2017).

Inspire. Jihadology, Nov. 12, 2016, http://jihadology.net/category/inspire-magazine (last accessed April 16, 2017).

"Intentional Killing of Non Combatants Is Not Permitted." *The Final Revelation,* Aug. 23, 2014, http://the-finalrevelation.blogspot.com/2014/08/intentional-killing-of-non-combatants.html (last accessed April 4, 2017).

"Islamic State Leader Abu Bakr al-Baghdadi Encourages Emigration, Worldwide Action." SITE Intelligence Group, July 1, 2014, https://news.siteintelgroup.com/Jihadist-News/islamic-state-leader-abu-bakr-al-baghdadi-encourages-emigration-worldwide-action.html (last accessed April 4, 2017).

Jackson, Sherman A. "Jihad and the Modern World." *Journal of Islamic Law and Culture* 7 (2002): 1–26.

"July 7 Bombings Were Last Successful al-Qaeda Attack Osama bin Laden Played a Role in, US Claims." *The Telegraph*, July 13, 2011, www.telegraph.co.uk/ news/uknews/terrorism-in-the-uk/8633919/July-7–bombings-were-last-successful-al-Qaeda-attack-Osama-bin-Laden-played-a-role-in-US-claims .html (last accessed April 4, 2017).

al-Kasani. *Bada'i' al-sana'i'*. Edited by A. Mu'awwad and A. Abdul Mawjud. 10 vols. Beirut: Dar al-Kutub al-'Ilmiyya, 2002.

Kelsay, John. *Arguing the Just War in Islam*. Cambridge, MA: Harvard University Press, 2007.

 Islam and War: The Gulf War and Beyond. Louisville, KY: Westminster/John Knox Press, 1993.

Kepel, Gilles. *Terror in France: The Rise of Jihad in the West*. Princeton, NJ: Princeton University Press, 2017.

Khalil, Mohammad Hassan. *Islam and the Fate of Others: The Salvation Question*. New York: Oxford University Press, 2012.

 "War or Peace in Israel? The Bin-Baz Qaradawi Debate." *Journal of Islamic Law and Culture* 13 (2011): 133–139.

Khan, Shaykh Abdool Rahman. "Islam Condemns Extremism." ICNA, Nov. 27, 2014, www.icna.org/islam-condemns-extremism (last accessed April 4, 2017).

Khatab, Sayed. *Understanding Islamic Fundamentalism: The Theological and Ideological Basis of al-Qa'ida's Political Tactics*. New York: American University in Cairo Press, 2011.

Kister, M. J. "The Massacre of the Banu Qurayza: A Re-Examination of a Tradition." *Jerusalem Studies in Arabic and Islam* 8 (1986): 61–96.

Kurzman, Charles (ed.). "Islamic Statements Against Terrorism," March 15, 2012, http://kurzman.unc.edu/islamic-statements-against-terrorism (last accessed April 4, 2017).

 The Missing Martyrs. New York: Oxford University Press, 2011.

"Last Words of a Terrorist." *The Guardian*, Sept. 30, 2001, www.theguardian .com/world/2001/sep/30/terrorism.september113 (last accessed April 4, 2017).

LeDrew, Stephen. *The Evolution of Atheism: The Politics of a Modern Movement*. New York: Oxford University Press, 2016.

Lewis, Bernard. *The Crisis of Islam: Holy War and Unholy Terror*. New York: Modern Library, 2003.

 What Went Wrong? Western Impact and Middle Eastern Response. New York: Oxford University Press, 2002.

Lewis, Bernard and Buntzie Ellis Churchill. *Islam: The Religion and the People*. Upper Saddle River, NJ: Wharton School Publishing, 2009.

MacDonald, Myra. "Al Qaeda Leader Urges Restraint in First 'Guidelines for Jihad'." *Reuters*, Sept. 16, 2013, www.reuters.com/article/us-security-qaeda-idUSBRE98F0I920130916 (last accessed April 11, 2017).

Maher, Shiraz. *Salafi-Jihadism: The History of an Idea*. New York: Oxford University Press, 2016.

Mashal, Mujib. "Taliban 'Offered bin Laden Trial before 9/11'." *Al Jazeera*, Sept. 11, 2011, www.aljazeera.com/news/asia/2011/09/2011911533416663.html (last accessed April 4, 2017).

McCants, William. *The ISIS Apocalypse: The History, Strategy, and Doomsday Vision of the Islamic State*. New York: St. Martin's Press, 2016.

McCants, William and Mohammad Fadel. "Experts Weigh In (Part 4): How Does ISIS Approach Islamic Scripture?" *Brookings*, May 7, 2015, www.brookings .edu/blog/markaz/2015/05/07/experts-weigh-in-part-4-how-does-isis-approach-islamic-scripture (last accessed April 4, 2017).

McCants, William and Sohaira Siddiqui. "Experts Weigh In (Part 2): How Does ISIS Approach Islamic Scripture?" *Brookings*, March 26, 2015, www .brookings.edu/blog/markaz/2015/03/26/experts-weigh-in-part-2-how-does-isis-approach-islamic-scripture (last accessed April 4, 2017).

McDowall, Angus. "Saudi Arabia's Grand Mufti Denounces Islamic State Group as Un-Islamic." *Reuters*, Aug. 25, 2014, http://blogs.reuters.com/faithworld/ 2014/08/25/saudi-arabias-grand-mufti-denounces-islamic-state-group-as-un-islamic (last accessed April 4, 2017).

Mirza, Younus Y. "'The Slave Girl Gives Birth to Her Master': Female Slavery from the Mamluk Era (1250-1517) to the Islamic State (2014-)." *Journal of the American Academy of Religion* (Feb. 2017), https://academic.oup.com/ jaar/article-abstract/doi/10.1093/jaarel/lfxoo1/3079491/The-Slave-Girl-Gives-Birth-to-Her-Master-Female? (last accessed May 31, 2017).

al-Mujtama' 1133. [Kuwait]: Jan. 10, 1995 (Sha'ban 9, 1415 AH).

al-Mujtama' 1140. [Kuwait]: Feb. 28, 1995 (Ramadan 29, 1415 AH).

al-Mujtama' 1141. [Kuwait]: March 14, 1995 (Shawwal 13, 1415 AH).

"Muslim Statements Condemning Terrorism: Overview. Beliefs. Quotes from Sacred Texts. Statements by ISNA." *ReligiousTolerance.org*, July 30, 2005, www.religioustolerance.org/islfatwa1.htm (updated March 22, 2010; last accessed April 4, 2017).

al-Muslimun 516. Jeddah: Dec. 24, 1994 (Rajab 21, 1415 AH).

Nafi, Basheer M. "Fatwa and War: On the Allegiance of the American Muslim Soldiers in the Aftermath of September 11." *Islamic Law and Society* 11 (2004): 78–116.

Nasr, Seyyed Hossein (ed.). *The Study Quran: A New Translation and Commentary*. New York: HarperCollins, 2015.

al-Nawawi. *Sharh Sahih Muslim*. Edited by K. al-Mays. 18 vols. Beirut: Dar al-Qalam, 1987.

"New Atheism." In *A Dictionary of Atheism*, edited by Lois Lee and Stephen Bullivant. New York: Oxford University Press, 2016.

Nyberg, Per. "Explosions in Stockholm Believed to Be Failed Terrorist Attack." *CNN*, Dec. 12, 2010, http://edition.cnn.com/2010/WORLD/europe/12/11/ sweden .explosion/index.html?hpt=T1 (last accessed May 30, 2017).

al-Oadah, Salman. "A Ramadan Letter to Osama bin Laden." *IslamToday*, Sept. 18, 2007, http://en.islamtoday.net/artshow-417–3012.htm (last accessed April 4, 2017).

"Open Letter to Al-Baghdadi." Sept. 19, 2014, www.lettertobaghdadi.com (last accessed April 4, 2017).

Pape, Robert A. "The Strategic Logic of Suicide Terrorism." *American Political Science Review* 97 (2003): 343–361.

Paz, Reuven. "The Saudi Fatwa Against Suicide Terrorism." *The Washington Institute*, May 2, 2001, www.washingtoninstitute.org/policy-analysis/view/the-saudi-fatwa-against-suicide-terrorism (last accessed April 4, 2017).

Peters, F. E. (ed.). *A Reader on Classical Islam*. Princeton, NJ: Princeton University Press, 1994.

Peters, Rudolph (ed.). *Jihad in Classical and Modern Islam*. Updated and Expanded Edition. Princeton, NJ: Markus Wiener Publishers, 2008.

Pew Research Center. "Concerns about Islamic Extremism on the Rise in Middle East," July 1, 2014, www.pewglobal.org/2014/07/01/concerns-about-islamic-extremism-on-the-rise-in-middle-east (last accessed April 4, 2017).

"What the World Thinks in 2002," Dec. 4, 2002, www.people-press.org/2002/12/04/what-the-world-thinks-in-2002 (last accessed July 23, 2017).

"The World's Muslims: Religion, Politics and Society," April 30, 2013, www.pewforum.org/2013/04/30/the-worlds-muslims-religion-politics-society-overview (last accessed April 4, 2017).

"The World's Muslims: Unity and Diversity," Aug. 9, 2012, www.pewforum.org/files/2012/08/the-worlds-muslims-full-report.pdf (last accessed July 10, 2017).

Pingree, Geoff. "Spanish Muslims Decry Al Qaeda." *Christian Science Monitor*, March 14, 2005, www.csmonitor.com/2005/0314/p06s01-woeu.html (last accessed April 4, 2017).

Poushter, Jacob. "In Nations with Significant Muslim Populations, Much Disdain for ISIS." *Pew Research Center*, Nov. 17, 2015, www.pewresearch.org/fact-tank/2015/11/17/in-nations-with-significant-muslim-populations-much-disdain-for-isis (last accessed April 4, 2017).

Qadhi, Yasir. "The Path of Allah or the Pathos of Allah?: Revisiting Classical and Medieval Sunni Approaches to the Salvation of Others." In *Between Heaven and Hell: Islam, Salvation, and the Fate of Others*, edited by Mohammad Hassan Khalil, 109–121. New York: Oxford University Press, 2013.

al-Qaradawi, Yusuf. *Fatawa mu'asira*. 3 vols. Beirut: al-Maktab al-Islami, 2003.

Fiqh al-jihad. 2 vols. Cairo: Maktabat Wahba, 2009.

al-Qarafi. *Al-Dhakhira*. Edited by Muhammad Bukhubza. 14 vols. Beirut: Dar al-Gharb al-Islami, 1994.

Kitab al-ihkam fi tamyiz al-fatawa 'an al-ahkam wa-tasarrufat al-qadi wa-l-imam. Edited by A. Abu Ghudda. Aleppo: Maktabat al-Matbu'at al-Islamiyya, 1967.

al-Quds al-'Arabi 13/3838. London: Sept. 14, 2001.

al-Qurtubi. *al-Jami' li-ahkam al-Qur'an*. Edited by A. al-Turki. 24 vols. Beirut: Mu'assasat al-Risala, 2006.

Qutb, Sayyid. *In the Shade of the Qur'an (Fi Zilal al-Qur'an)*. Translated and edited by A. Salahi and A. Shamis. 18 vols. Leicester, UK: Islamic Foundation, 2001.

Social Justice in Islam by Sayyid Qutb. Translated by John B. Hardie. Translation revised and introduction by Hamid Algar. Oneonta, NY: Islamic Publications International, 2000.

Rabasa, A., S. Pettyjohn, J. Ghez, and C. Boucek. *Deradicalizing Islamist Extremists*. Santa Monica, CA: RAND, 2010.

al-Razi. *Tafsir al-Fakhr al-Razi*. 32 vols. Beirut: Dar al-Fikr, 1981.

"Real Time with Bill Maher: Ben Affleck, Sam Harris and Bill Maher Debate Radical Islam (HBO)." *YouTube*, Oct. 6, 2014, www.youtube.com/watch?v=vln9D81eO6o (last accessed April 4, 2017).

Reiter, Yitzhak. *War, Peace and International Relations in Islam: Muslim Scholars on Peace Accords with Israel*. Eastbourne: Sussex Academic Press, 2011.

Reuter, Christoph. "The Terror Strategist: Secret Files Reveal the Structure of Islamic State." *Spiegel Online International (Der Spiegel)*, April 18, 2015, www.spiegel.de/international/world/islamic-state-files-show-structure-of-islamist-terror-group-a-1029274.html (last accessed April 4, 2017).

Rizvi, Ali A. *The Atheist Muslim: A Journey from Religion to Reason*. New York: St. Martin's Press, 2016.

Rosenberg, Matthew. "In Osama bin Laden Library: Illuminati and Bob Woodward." *The New York Times*, May 20, 2015, www.nytimes.com/2015/05/21/world/asia/bin-laden-bookshelf-list-released-by-us-intelligence-agency.html (last accessed April 4, 2017).

Rosenblatt, Nate. "Inside the ISIS Enlistment Files: All Jihad Is Local." *Defense One*, July 20, 2016, www.defenseone.com/ideas/2016/07/all-jihad-local/130046 (last accessed April 4, 2017).

Roy, Olivier. *Jihad and Death: The Global Appeal of Islamic State*. Translated by Cynthia Schoch. London: Hurst, 2017.

"Who Are the New Jihadis?" *The Guardian*, April 13, 2017, www.theguardian.com/news/2017/apr/13/who-are-the-new-jihadis (last accessed June 8, 2017).

Rumiyah. *Jihadology*, June 7, 2017, http://jihadology.net/category/rome-magazine (last accessed June 14, 2017).

Ruse, Michael. "Why I Think the New Atheists Are a Bloody Disaster." *BioLogos*, Aug. 14, 2009, http://biologos.org/blogs/archive/why-i-think-the-new-atheists-are-a-bloody-disaster (last accessed April 4, 2017).

Saad, Lydia. "Palestinians and Israelis Favor Nonviolent Solutions." *Gallup*, Jan. 8, 2008, www.gallup.com/poll/103618/palestinians-israelis-favor-nonviolent-solutions.aspx (last accessed April 4, 2017).

Sacks, Jonathan. "The Future of Religion Is at Stake Today, as Much as the Future of the West." *The Office of Rabbi Sacks*, Feb. 8, 2001, www.rabbisacks.org/the-future-of-religion-is-at-stake-today-as-much-as-the-future-of-the-west-published-in-the-times (last accessed April 4, 2017).

"Sam Harris: Islam Is Not a Religion of Peace." *YouTube*, Nov. 10, 2010, www.youtube.com/watch?v=LfKLV6rmLxE (posted on Dec. 30, 2010; last accessed April 4, 2017).

Samuel-Azran, Tal. *Al-Jazeera and US War Coverage*. New York: Peter Lang, 2010.

"Saudi Mufti: Suicide Bombers Are 'Criminals'." *Gulf News*, Dec. 12, 2013, http://gulfnews.com/news/gulf/saudi-arabia/saudi-mufti-suicide-bombers-are-criminals-1.1266324 (last accessed July 4, 2017).

Scheinin, Richard. "Expert Says Islam Prohibits Violence Against Innocents." *San Jose Mercury News*, Sept. 15, 2001, http://web.archive.org/web/20010920073355/www.mercurycenter.com/local/center/islo916.htm (last accessed April 4, 2017).

Scheuer, Michael. *Osama Bin Laden*. New York: Oxford University Press, 2011.

Through Our Enemies' Eyes: Osama Bin Laden, Radical Islam, and the Future of America. Revised Edition. Dulles, VA: Potomac Books, 2006.

Segal, David. "Atheist Evangelist: In His Bully Pulpit, Sam Harris Devoutly Believes that Religion Is the Root of All Evil." *The Washington Post*, Oct. 26, 2006, www.washingtonpost.com/wp-dyn/content/article/2006/10/25/AR2006102501998_pf.html (last accessed April 4, 2017).

Shaikh, Amad. "Muslim Scholars on Charlie Hebdo." *MuslimMatters.org*, Jan. 12, 2015, http://muslimmatters.org/2015/01/12/muslim-scholars-on-charlie-hebdo (last accessed April 18, 2017).

"Sheikh Yusuf Al-Qaradawi Condemns Attacks Against Civilians: Forbidden in Islam." *Islam Online Archive*, Sept. 13, 2001, http://archive.islamonline.net/?p=17698 (last accessed April 4, 2017).

Sookhdeo, Patrick. "The Myth of Moderate Islam." *Spectator*, July 30, 2005, www.spectator.co.uk/features/13968/the-myth-of-moderate-islam (last accessed April 4, 2017).

Understanding Islamist Terrorism. McLean, VA: Isaac Publishing, 2009.

Sperry, Paul. "Gitmo Prisoner Reveals that Saudi 'Terrorist Rehab' Center Is a Scam." *New York Post*, Nov. 28, 2016, http://nypost.com/2016/11/28/gitmo-prisoner-reveals-that-saudi-terrorist-rehab-center-is-a-scam (last accessed April 4, 2017).

Stavrou, David. "The Debate over Swedish Troops in Afghanistan." *The Local*, Dec. 15, 2010, www.thelocal.se/20101215/30858 (last accessed July 17, 2017).

Steinberg, Jacques. "Experts Say bin Laden Is Distorting Islamic Law." *The New York Times*, Oct. 8, 2001, www.nytimes.com/2001/10/08/national/experts-say-bin-laden-is-distorting-islamic-law.html (last accessed April 4, 2017).

Stenger, Victor J. *The New Atheism: Taking a Stand for Science and Reason*. Amherst, NY: Prometheus Books, 2009.

Stern, Jessica. "Mind over Martyr: How to Deradicalize Islamic Extremists." *Foreign Affairs*, Jan./Feb. 2010, www.foreignaffairs.com/articles/saudi-arabia/2009-12-21/mind-over-martyr (last accessed April 4, 2017).

Stern, Jessica and J. M. Berger. *ISIS: The State of Terror*. New York: HarperCollins, 2015.

Suleiman, Omar, Nazir Khan, and Justin Parrott. "The Myth of an Antisemitic Genocide in Muslim Scripture." *Yaqeen*, March 28, 2017, https://yaqeen institute.org/en/nazir-khan/the-myth-of-an-antisemitic-genocide-in-muslim-scripture (last accessed Aug. 28, 2017).

Syed, Mairaj. "Jihad in Classical Islamic Legal and Moral Thought." In *Just War in Religion and Politics*, edited by Jacob Neusner, Bruce D. Chilton, and R. E. Tully, 135–162. Lanham, MD: University Press of America, 2013.

al-Tabari. *Kitab al-jihad wa-kitab al-jizya wa-ahkam al-muharibin min kitab Ikhtilaf al-fuqaha'*. Edited by J. Schacht. Leiden: Brill, 1933.

Tafsir al-Tabari: Jami' al-bayan 'an ta'wil ay al-Qur'an. Edited by A. al-Turki. 25 vols. Cairo: Dar Hajar, 2001.

Tahir-ul-Qadri, Muhammad. *Fatwa on Terrorism and Suicide Bombings*. London: Minhaj-ul-Qur'an International, 2010.

"Taliban Condemn Attacks in United States." *People's Daily*, Sept. 12, 2001, http://en.people.cn/english/200109/12/eng20010912_79947.html (last accessed April 4, 2017).

Tayler, Jeffrey. "Free Speech and Islam – In Defense of Ayaan Hirsi Ali." *Quillette*, June 17, 2016, http://quillette.com/2016/06/17/free-speech-and-islam-in-defense-of-ayaan-hirsi-ali (last accessed April 4, 2017).

Tharoor, Ishaan. "It Turns Out Many ISIS Recruits Don't Know Much About Islam." *The Washington Post*, Aug. 17, 2016, www.washingtonpost.com/news/worldviews/wp/2016/08/17/it-turns-out-many-isis-recruits-dont-know-much-about-islam/?utm_term=.84528b6962a2 (last accessed April 4, 2017).

"Unclassified: The Detainee Session for ISN 682 Opened at 0944, 23 June 2016." Periodic Review Secretariat (U.S. Department of Defense), Sept. 15, 2016, www.prs.mil/Portals/60/Documents/ISN682/20160623_U_ISN682_TRANSCRIPT_OF_DETAINEE_SESSION_PUBLIC.PDF (last accessed Jan. 4, 2017; not available as of April 18, 2017).

"Unclassified: Guantanamo Detainee Profile." Periodic Review Secretariat (U.S. Department of Defense), Jan. 14, 2016, www.prs.mil/Portals/60/Documents/ISN682/20160114_U_ISN_682_GOVERNMENTS_UNCLASSIFIED_SUMMARY_PUBLIC.pdf (last accessed April 4, 2017).

al-Waqidi. *The Kitab al-Maghazi of al-Waqidi*. Edited by Marsden Jones. 3 vols. London: Oxford University Press, 1966.

Warrick, Joby and Souad Mekhennet. "ISIS Quietly Braces Itself for the Collapse of the 'Caliphate'." *The Independent*, July 13, 2016, www.independent.co.uk/news/world/middle-east/isis-islamic-state-caliphate-terrorism-daesh-territory-decline-a7134166.html (last accessed April 5, 2017).

Wasserstein, David J. "Conversion and the *ahl al-dhimma*." In *The New Cambridge History of Islam*, Volume 4: *Islamic Cultures and Societies to the End of the Eighteenth Century*, edited by Robert Irwin, 184–208. Cambridge: Cambridge University Press, 2010.

Whitaker, Brian and Ewen MacAskill. "Bin Laden Talks of Truce but Threatens US with New Attacks." *The Guardian*, Jan. 19, 2006, www.theguardian.com/world/2006/jan/20/alqaida.usa (last accessed April 4, 2017).

Wiktorowicz, Quintan. "A Genealogy of Radical Islam." *Studies in Conflict & Terrorism* 28 (2005): 75–97.

Williams, Pete, Tracy Connor, Eric Ortiz, and Stephanie Gosk. "Gunman Omar Mateen Described as Belligerent, Racist, and 'Toxic'," June 13, 2016, www.nbcnews.com/storyline/orlando-nightclub-massacre/terror-hate-what-motivated-orlando-nightclub-shooter-n590496 (last accessed July 20, 2017).

Williams, Thomas Chatterton. "Maajid Nawaz's Radical Ambition." *The New York Times Magazine*, March 28, 2017, www.nytimes.com/2017/03/28/magazine/can-a-former-islamist-make-it-cool-to-be-moderate.html (last accessed April 4, 2017).

Wolf, Gary. "The Church of the Non-Believers." *Wired*, Nov. 1, 2006, www.wired.com/2006/11/atheism (last accessed July 22, 2017).

Wood, Graeme. *The Way of the Strangers: Encounters with the Islamic State*. New York: Random House, 2017.

"What ISIS Really Wants." *The Atlantic*, March 2015, www.theatlantic.com/features/archive/2015/02/what-isis-really-wants/384980 (last accessed April 4, 2017).

Wright. Lawrence. *The Looming Tower: Al-Qaeda and the Road to 9/11*. New York: Alfred A. Knopf, 2006.

Zaman, Muhammad Qasim. *Modern Islamic Thought in a Radical Age: Religious Authority and Internal Criticism*. New York: Cambridge University Press, 2012.

al-Zayyat, Montasser. *The Road to Al-Qaeda: The Story of bin Laden's Right-Hand Man*. Translated by Ahmed Fekry. Edited by Sara Nimis. London; Sterling, VA: Pluto Press, 2004.

"Zbigniew Brzezinski to the Mujahideen: 'Your Cause Is Right and God Is on Your Side!'" *YouTube*, Sept. 4, 2014, www.youtube.com/watch?v=A9RCFZnWGEo (last accessed April 4, 2017).

al-Zuhayli, Wahba. *Athar al-harb fi al-fiqh al-Islami: Dirasa muqarana*. Damascus: Dar al-Fikr, 1981.

Index

Index